THE MANAGER'S TALE

*To Ellie and Flo, my beloved daughters.
To Cathy, for everything.*

The Manager's Tale
Stories of Managerial Identity

PATRICK REEDY
University of Nottingham, UK

ASHGATE

© Patrick Reedy 2009

All rights reserved. No part of this publication may be reproduced, stored in a retrieval system or transmitted in any form or by any means, electronic, mechanical, photocopying, recording or otherwise without the prior permission of the publisher.

Patrick Reedy has asserted his right under the Copyright, Designs and Patents Act, 1988, to be identified as the author of this work.

Published by
Ashgate Publishing Limited
Wey Court East
Union Road
Farnham
Surrey, GU9 7PT
England

Ashgate Publishing Company
Suite 420
101 Cherry Street
Burlington
VT 05401-4405
USA

www.ashgate.com

British Library Cataloguing in Publication Data
Reedy, Patrick
    The manager's tale: stories of managerial identity
    1. Executive ability 2. Executives 3. Leadership
    I. Title
    658.4'09

Library of Congress Cataloging-in-Publication Data
Reedy, Patrick.
    The manager's tale : stories of managerial identity / by Patrick Reedy.
        p. cm.
    Includes bibliographical references and index.
    ISBN 978-0-7546-4664-8
    1. Executives. 2. Identity (Psychology) 3. Management--Psychological aspects. I. Title.

    HD38.2.R44 2008
    658.4001'9--dc22
                                                                    2008033486

ISBN 978 0 7546 4664 8
eISBN 978 0 7546 8993 5

Printed and bound in Great Britain by
MPG Books Ltd, Bodmin, Cornwall.

Contents

Preface   *vii*

1   Once Upon A Time   1
    Telling Stories   4
    Making Sense of Stories and Story-Tellers   8
    The Narrators   10
    How the Book is Organised   13

2   The Managers' Tales   15
    The Researcher   15
    The National Health Service (NHS) Manager   21
    The United Nations Security Manager   30
    The Mental Health Charity Manager   37
    The Engineer   45
    The Information Systems Consultant   51
    The Squadron Leader   58
    The Human Resources Manager   63
    The Insurance Account Manager   70
    The Airport Security Training Manager   77

3   Understanding Identity   85
    Humanist and Poststructuralist Models of Identity   86
    The Self of Humanism   90
    The Shattered Cogito   92
    Death and Identity   96
    Beyond the Limits   100

4   Narrative Identity and the Existentialist Quest   103
    Heidegger   105
    Jean-Paul Sartre   109
    Ricoeur   114
    Narrative Identity and Identity Narratives   119

5	**My Generation: Life-Stories as Historical Narratives**	**123**
	My Generation	126
	The Twilight of Management Identity	138
6	**Telling Tales**	**141**
	Management Folk Tales	144
	Performing Narrative	160
7	**And They All Lived Happily Ever After?**	**167**
	The Story So Far	167
	Who is Speaking?	169
	Who is Listening?	177
	Just Institutions	179

Bibliography	*183*
Index	*191*

Preface

I began to write this book about the way in which all our lives unfold as stories, both told and enacted, at a time when I expected the future narrative of my own story to be fairly settled and predictable. I was, of course, completely wrong and my life has undergone some cataclysmic changes in the past few years, some appalling, some wonderful, some merely time-consuming and stressful. These experiences have forcibly impressed on me the point made at several points in the book that our lives may both change radically and yet still be incorporated into a narrative that is recognisably our own singular unique life. This life will only be given its final narrative form when it is over by which point it ceases to be one's own story.

The main effect of these changes on the writing of the book was to delay its completion considerably and I would like to thank Ashgate for their forbearance in giving me the time to finish it. I would also like to thank Professor Martin Parker for his help, advice, criticism, suggestions and friendship all of which were essential to the completion of this text.

Patrick Reedy, 2008

Chapter 1
Once Upon A Time

The mystery of how we come to be who we are, as individuals; as members of families, communities, nations and other groupings, is a subject of endless fascination and speculation to human beings. To paraphrase Heidegger (1926/1962), we are the only being for whom its own existence is an issue for it. The vast historical repository of stories from which human societies are constituted, and which we draw on to explain ourselves to ourselves, reflects this fascination. All of these stories ultimately address questions such as who we are and what our relationship is to the world we inhabit, as well as to the others we share it with.

This book was written from just such a desire to understand how I came to be who I am and how this was related to how others understand themselves. The primary method by which I have tried to accomplish this has been to listen to the accounts others have given of their lives as well as reflecting on my own life story. This book, however, also deals with a more specific phenomenon, that of the rise of the managerial career, a subject that is intimately linked to my purpose because such careers have become an increasingly important aspect of how many of us define ourselves and seek to achieve their life projects. The global constituency of business school postgraduate courses preparing students for just such careers indicates that they are now a far from parochial concern of developed Western societies. The increasing pervasiveness of management language and ideas throughout all social institutions similarly points to the significance of management in how we think about ourselves. Thus the stories considered in this book are all stories of how becoming a manager, of pursuing a career as a manager, has been central to the way in which the individuals involved have sought to construct a life worth living. The implications and nature of the pervasiveness of the managerial career are then a key theme of this book.

In this introductory chapter, therefore, my task is to explain why the use of narrative in the form of life stories can contribute something worthwhile to an understanding of our own existence and so provide some answers to the related question of how and why being a manager has become so significant for so many in making a life for themselves. Rather than just theorising about stories, however, I wish the stories themselves to be at the heart of the book so that 'the authors of the utterance are put on stage' as Ricoeur (1992, 48) puts it. In other words, that the book stands as a testimony to their experiences, their strivings, hopes, suffering, disappointments or triumphs; in other words of how they made a life for themselves.

It might seem an obvious point that lives should be understood through stories, through biographical/autobiographical narratives, after all what it is to be a human being and live a life is almost always represented through different sorts of stories. The books, films, plays, television programmes, and songs with which we fill a good deal of our lives consist of just such stories (Czarniawska 1998; Boje 2001). On meeting new people, even in relatively casual ways, we almost always feel that some account of ourselves and backgrounds is required. Throughout human history (itself rendered as a story) people have told stories, have through them founded the cultures, religions, movements, empires and myths by which the world and their place in it were formulated. Science itself is seemingly not free of this dependence on stories from grand narratives such as evolution – the ascent of humankind from the primeval soup, to the numerous accounts of discovery and progress, and the accompanying triumphs and, sometimes, tragedies.

Despite the centrality of stories to an understanding of how human beings understand themselves, accounts by managers of their own lives are strangely lacking in the vast body of books and papers that deal with what it is to be a manager. The idea that identity is primarily a narrative achievement, an enacted story, is well known but even in those books that take story-telling and narrative in organisations as their main subject matter there is a tendency to present the accounts of managers as quotes or vignettes, snippets to illustrate the author's arguments.

Why should longer, more complete accounts have a particular value though? The rest of this opening chapter will attempt to answer this question, expanding on why I believe that stories in general and autobiography/biography in particular can contribute to understanding how a managerial identity has become central to many life projects. In the next few pages therefore I will explain the approach I have taken, trace the use of stories in related sociological enquiries and discuss some of the issues that have arisen in the course of my research. Before I engage directly with these matters, it seems appropriate to begin with a story, one that explains to the reader how this book came to be written, enabling them to better understand from my own story what my intentions are for this book and how my background and purposes have shaped the accounts of others given in subsequent chapters.

I work as an academic in a large business school which is part of an English red brick university. I came late to my career as an academic, being forty when I began it, having escaped from ten increasingly difficult years as a manager and teacher in a number of further education colleges, the equivalent of the community colleges in the United States. The means of escape from a job I found so irksome was paradoxically a part-time Master of Business Administration (MBA) course, paradoxical because most students pursue such qualifications as a route to a managerial career not as a means of exiting one. In the case of the course I followed many of my teachers were highly sceptical of the claims made by mainstream management theory about what being a manager was meant to entail. I thus became aware of the existence of a whole body of writing that supported such scepticism. This discovery was something of a watershed for me as it accorded closely with my own unhappy experiences as a head of department at the college I worked at during a period when the axioms of managerialism became the official ideology within the sector. My enjoyment and success as a mature student encouraged me to think that I might find myself a home in academia, a place or community where I could be myself with similar others rather than continuing to work in a job where I found myself increasingly unhappy. After a dispiriting period of unsuccessful job applications to universities, I finally found myself an opening that seemed to make just such a new identity and career a possibility.

As I started my new life as a university lecturer I quickly realised that transforming myself was going to be a more difficult endeavour than I had anticipated. I soon realised that the title *Mr* in front of my name in the university phone book was more of a badge of shame than a polite form of address in the rather elite university in which fortune had somehow deposited me. My transformation was incomplete, I would have to acquire the title of *Dr* by 'doing a PhD' but what could I do? I did what I suspect many others would have done in the same circumstances; I started with what was familiar from my own experience. Many years as a teacher and my attraction to critical writing about management gave me a starting point. If my Masters degree had been a turning point in my life then would the same be true for others? I duly began what I had intended as an evaluation of the transformative potential of such educational projects. In this way my own identity project as putative academic and the narrative of its pursuit became bound up with the stories of a number of my students.

This interconnection became more and more apparent to me as I began to have conversations with my students about why they had come on the course and what they were hoping to achieve. Thus my understanding of how our lives were connected was framed by stories and so the idea of storytelling as in itself a significant aspect of my research began to take shape. Initially this was as a way of theorising the ongoing construction of identity by individuals and also as a fruitful methodological approach. Eventually this interest took over the entire project. I quickly realised that critical approaches to teaching managers had only a very limited effect on them. They had their own reasons for coming on the course and these overrode any aims I had to persuade them of my way of thinking about management, I have given an account of this dawning realisation elsewhere (Reedy 2003). Instead I began to become increasingly intrigued with the life projects that brought my students on the course. I became caught up in the plot of their lives, wanting to know what would happen next, fascinated by the different ways in which individuals used the same discursive elements to build narratives that were both similar to each other and unmistakably unique.

As I began to collect their stories I found that I could not separate them from my own. Most of my students were around the same age as me, and all could be said to be members of the post-war baby boomer generation. This collection of stories is thus one portrayal of a shared experience and understanding of what it has meant to grow up in the later decades of the twentieth century in the United Kingdom. It foregrounds the way in which managerialism and managerial work have become a significant part of our lives, despite none of us starting out with any aspirations to be a manager 'when we grew up'. I found myself constantly reminded of my own childhood and the political, economic, and societal events that have made us both the same and different from each other.

To summarise this preamble, my original intention to critically evaluate the transformative claims of critical pedagogy in the lecture room was substantially modified, both by the growing conviction that these claims were unlikely to have much light shed upon them by what I was doing, but also because I was ambushed by something that seemed much more interesting, an attempt to present and then theorise the identity narratives of managers. I began to explore beyond the confines implied by the phrase 'managerial identity' in order to get a sense of a wider life than that which occurs at work. For the problem with asking people only about their experiences as managers is that this is what they will tell you about. For some of my interviewees, this wider perspective revealed that a managerial identity seemed to have a weaker hold on their overall conception of themselves than some other work in this area might suggest. Rather, becoming a manager had entailed fairly conscious trade-offs between the demands of their career and the ability to pursue what, for them, were more important aspirations. This is not to say that they entirely rejected the idea that being a manager could in itself be a desirable aspect of themselves and I explore later both the allure of the management career and its discontents.

Telling Stories

So much for the story of the evolution of the research but what have I actually done as a result of these changing aspirations? I hope that it is already clear that the backbone of the book is the idea of narrative, particularly life history. I thus present a number of life histories designed to reflect the experiences of people who are managers at the start of the twenty-first century and who have all completed a critically orientated masters in management, and all of whom I have taught. These narratives are intended to be more than merely 'data'. Although not as adverse to some who work with autobiographical narratives to their theoretical analysis (see Bochner 2001, for example) I also wished them to stand as accounts of the lives of managers in their own right, as stories that might interest, inform, amuse, move or provoke their readers. Despite this wish I also wanted to adequately theorise such narratives, in a way recognisable as academic research. It is to a large extent unavoidable that these stories are thematised and generally dissected as a result. I have attempted though to preserve their integrity as stories, no matter how contrived and edited such accounts must be by my authorship. This wish was stimulated by a feeling of obligation to the people who had taken part, many of whom had become friends during the course of the research. I felt that I had a duty to them to present their stories as accurately as I could, according to my understanding of what they wished to communicate about themselves, to do justice to their struggles, hopes and suffering. It was only as my theoretical work developed that this desire was reinforced by the work of Ricoeur (1985; 1992), who became an important influence on the development of my analysis, confirming me in my intuition of how a certain ethics of representation should guide me.

I would argue that preserving the stories in a way that is faithful to their original narrated form has enabled me to better understand how identity is worked upon and modified. One can trace in these extended accounts how contradictions, tensions, constraints and opportunities emerge and are sometimes resolved through the process of making sense of one's life in the accounts one gives of it. Thus individuals construct a coherent sense of self from the seeming chaos of 'ordinary' lives. As the empirical work progressed, it also became clear to me that such an approach underlined the complexity and heterogeneity of individual responses to the shared social context of their lives. Retaining these narratives in the form of individual stories provided an important safeguard against seeing such managers as a univocal group all responding in similar ways. Wishing to treat the stories in this fashion inevitably meant gravitating towards the idea of my interview transcripts being a form of life history.

Life histories are usually more the province of biographers and historians than social scientists but there is a strong tradition of their use in sociology also. Radical intellectual movements have seen life histories as a way of unearthing marginalised voices. For example feminist epistemology has made a strong case for their use in sociological research as a way of re-discovering the silenced voices of women and countering the dominance of patriarchal interpretations of the world (Cotterill and Letherby 1993; Griffiths 1995). A similar impulse appears to lie behind the classic ethnographies of working life by writers such as Beynon (1975) in the 1970s and, more directly, by edited collections of working life histories such as *Work 2* (Fraser 1969). A relatively forgotten but striking example of the use of life stories, not just to chronicle individual voices but also to paint a rich portrait of a place and time, is Ronald Blythe's *Akenfield* (1972). Through the stories of a cross-section of villagers, Blythe builds up a vivid picture of social change in a Suffolk village from the beginning of the twentieth century to the mid-1960s.

Perhaps better known is the work of the *Chicago School*, most notably represented by Studs Terkel (1970), who again attempts to build up a rich picture of working life for those whose voices are rarely directly heard, as opposed to their indirect and abstracted representation by others. According to Denzin and Lincoln, the Chicago School:

> with its emphasis on the life story and the 'slice-of-life' approach to ethnographic materials, sought to develop an interpretative methodology that maintained the centrality of the narrated history approach ... This led to the production of texts that gave the researcher-as-author the power to represent the subject's story. Written under the mantle of straightforward sentiment-free social realism, these texts used the language of ordinary people (2000, 13).

Such life history research is much rarer as a way of studying manager's lives within contemporary organisation studies, though there is a rich stream of narrative studies which shares some of the same impulse to understand the experiences of individuals as recounted by themselves (Czarniawska 1998). Such work, however, tends not to look at accounts of whole lives, rather it takes 'story-telling' as its basic unit of analysis. Typically this literature looks at the stories that organisational members give of particular events or of organisational episodes (see Watson 1994; Czarniawska 1997; Czarniawska 1998; Knights and Willmott 1999; Gabriel 2000; Boje 2001; Wajcman and Martin 2002; Cunliffe; Luhman and Boje 2004; Humphreys 2004, for some noteworthy examples). What I think is lost from these approaches is the literary and empathetic quality that goes with an extended account of a whole life as it has been lived and that is a characteristic of the best sort of biography. Such writing can place the singularity of an individual life within a wider historical context, both shedding light upon the other. On the other hand the story-telling literature shows a much greater awareness than the 'naturalistic' Chicago School material of the ethical and philosophical problems associated with an author-crafted account being presented as someone's life in their 'own words'.

An alternative approach, mostly to be found in the US, although operating on a broader level of social science research than just organisational studies is what is sometimes known as 'autoethnography' much of which can be found in the journal *Qualitative Inquiry* (see Bochner 2001; Spry 2001; Ellis 2007, for examples). Although the emphasis here is firmly back on the stories themselves for reasons I have some sympathy with, many of the theoretical strengths of the story-telling tradition are lost, including a desirable wariness as regards the sometimes subtle forms of domination reproduced in narratives. My wish for this book has been to try to have my cake and eat it, to combine a rigorous theoretical approach to narrative and identity with well told stories of individual lives taking place within a social and historical context.

One important aspect of this aspiration is to acknowledge that it is not possible to simply present life stories as representing people as if they spoke directly to the reader. Like all authors of such stories, my selection of voices is premised upon the 'political' motivation that they deserve to be heard. One also cannot escape the problem that, to a large extent, the processes of selection, editing, and framing of the narratives is opaque to the final reader. In addition, it is easy to assume that life stories are straightforwardly referential of an external reality rather than an account constructed cooperatively between discussants in a particular social context (Stanley 1992). Nevertheless, I believe that foregrounding the stories themselves can still make an important contribution to the understanding of identity. In too many accounts supposedly based on storytelling the stories themselves are demoted to a fragmented and supporting role, subordinated by the author's wish to assert their own identity over others. I have placed my narratives at the heart of this book and before their analysis in order to avoid this demotion of the stories as stories.

It might seem odd to position a generally elite group within society, managers, alongside the marginalised and silenced that often form the subjects of the life histories I have mentioned. It would be ludicrous to suggest that they are in the same position as casual agricultural labourers in 1930s Suffolk. I would maintain, however, that managers' voices are not often heard, and that they are more often spoken for than heard speaking. The seemingly never ending deluge of management texts, consultancy products, and research papers that constitute what being a manager is meant to be like, are overwhelmingly normative and prescriptive, constituting an endless uninterruptible shout, drowning out the experiences of those who are trying to manage to be managers.

To summarise my discussion thus far, my principle aim in this book is to understand how pursuing management careers has become bound up with the aspirations and hopes of a particular generation of individuals, a generation which includes myself. In order to do this I have tried to develop a rigorous theoretical approach to the underlying processes of narrative identity construction whilst trying to retain the richness and distinctiveness of stories as accounts by living, hoping and suffering individuals, following in the ethical and methodological tradition of Ricoeur about which more below. Such an attempt is not, of course, disinterested. Most obviously the publication of this text as a book is part of my own career as academic and will, I hope, enhance my standing with my peers. Less obviously I would define myself as broadly 'against management' (Parker 2002), as believing that the spread of management thinking and the discourse of the enterprising self, with its elevation of individualistic competitive success to a supreme good, is one of the contributors to the social and political problems that have arisen in late capitalism. Perhaps these predispositions encouraged me to expect managers to tell me 'misery stories', accounts of oppression and alienation, and, in some cases, they can be read in this way.

In most cases, however, the stories seemed to point to a more complex reality that went some way to explaining why management careers had proved so attractive. This does not mean that they are entirely happy with their lives or blind to the problems and contradictions of being a manager in modern organisations and much of this book explores the way in which these accounts attempt to make sense of these sometimes complex experiences. One important influence on how managers formulate what being a manager means is provided by the normative ideals of the management development industry and the university business school to which all of the managers featured in this book had looked to in order to pursue their careers.

One theme of more critical writing on management and organisations is that management careers and the framework of management qualifications that support them constitute a struggle for the identity of managers themselves (Currie and Knights 2003; Reedy 2008). If the business school reproduces the dominant ideal of what being a manager constitutes then this will be a major influence on how students construct their own identities as managers. This process of identification is often obscured, however, by the implicit assumptions within mainstream approaches to management that managing is something one 'does' – that is, that it is a set of techniques based on knowledge that can be acquired as part of one's management education and then practiced as part of one's occupation. The essential 'self' simply expands its repertoire of behaviours in order to perform the acts of management more effectively.

My argument in this book is that being a manager is something one 'is', and management education is one of the mechanisms by which one 'becomes' a manager. The accounts given by managers in this book suggested very early on that, when they speak of the aspirations and hopes which brought them onto a management development programme, it is usually in terms of 'being' and 'becoming'. They wished to acquire the right ways of thinking, speaking and behaving in order to be seen as legitimately occupying the identity of 'manager' in the eyes of others. They also wanted to feel authentic in this identity. That they all experienced contradictions and difficulties when actually attempting to perform this identity in their day to day lives was apparent in their accounts of themselves and sometimes took the form of a commonly experienced sense of imposture (Parker 2004).

Making Sense of Stories and Story-Tellers

Having explained the general background to the book, how did I then go about selecting, collecting and editing the narratives that form the heart of this book? I shall begin this section by stressing that throughout I tried to maintain a critical reflexivity as regards claims for my statements to be accepted as knowledge of a certain type and status (Alvesson and Deetz 1999; Alvesson and Skoldberg 2000). I therefore need to draw the reader's attention to what I believe are the inevitably contestable and provisional claims to knowledge made later. To anticipate my discussion of Ricoeur, the understanding of narratives is always arrived at by a dialogic process between authors and readers, 'configuring' and 'refiguring' (Ricoeur 1985). By making the grounding of my own reading explicit, I hope to enable my readers to come to their own judgements regarding its plausibility. A significant aspect of this reflexivity has been to include my own narrative amongst the others so that the inseparability of biography with authorial autobiography (Stanley 1992) is open to the scrutiny of the reader.

As explained above, my starting point has been the centrality of the importance of the experiences of managers. I believe that these experiences are fundamental to understanding how and why the pursuit of management careers has become an important aspect of the life projects and indeed the identities of a generation of individuals. Both the hopes and disillusionment that accompanies such a pursuit are dependant upon a particular social and historical context which I analyse in detail in Chapter 5. I only need to point out in this introductory chapter that many organisations are currently dependant on the extent to which their managers are prepared to commit themselves to their careers and so shifts in the underlying social structures which underwrite such a commitment should be a central concern of both organisation theorists and management practitioners. For those like myself who regard the convergence of such career paths with the maintenance of the current social and political order with alarm, there is a particular interest in understanding both the powerful attraction of such careers but also the precariousness of this attraction and the possibility that this order might be less secure than it sometimes appears. With these considerations in mind, I have treated these accounts as more than self-contained, self-referential texts; rather I have sought to make use of them as stories *about* lives and the world in which they are lived, stressing their significance as indicators of a wider social context.

This does not mean that I have assumed that the narratives are literal representations of an independently existing set of events and experiences as recounted by a stable observing and recording self. Rather I take these accounts to be a developing and sometimes contradictory narrative by which individuals actively construct their sense of identity using the discursive resources available to them at a given historical and cultural location (Giddens 1991; Cunliffe 2001). Therefore the particular readings I will make of these accounts will be critically informed by the theoretical positions established in Chapters 3 and 4. Thus readers must come to their own judgements regarding the plausibility of these stories as representative of wider social formations.

I have attempted to assist the reader to make these interpretative judgements in a number of ways. Firstly, I have included my own narrative amongst the other narratives, including my own purposes and convictions as a teacher of management. This at least assists my reader in making judgements about how I am likely to have gone about my authoring and perhaps to be able to tell different voices apart. Secondly, and constrained by the limitations of word counts and readability, I have included as much of the original words spoken by the narrators as possible. Thirdly, I have attempted to take account of the context in which the words were spoken or written, presenting this context alongside my interpretations, where practical, thus giving my reader a chance to make their own judgements about the plausibility of my interpretations.

Despite these safeguards I could, depending upon my skills as a writer, just as easily write my 'characters' as a piece of fiction, without my reader knowing the difference and would it indeed make any difference? It could be argued that fiction is no less a 'true' account of selves than historical narratives. Is Tolstoy's (1869/1979) Pierre Bezuhov more or less 'true' or 'real' than his Czar Alexander I? This point suggests that, in the end, the reader's only guarantee of faithfulness is to have a measure of confidence in the writer's ethics of representation. My position on this has been derived from Ricoeur's (1985) work on historical narratives, explained in more detail in Chapter 4. Briefly, I have sought to recognise the moral imperative of the debt I owe to others in representing their attempts to give an account of themselves.

The distinction between fiction and history is also not a simple one. Indeed Ricoeur makes a case that the two ought to be combined, albeit in carefully circumscribed ways. He argues that similar strategies of production characterise and are appropriate to both genres. For example, if one wishes to generate pity in the reader proper to the sufferings of those represented then the descriptive techniques associated with fiction may legitimately be deployed in historical writing (Ricoeur 1985; Kearney 1996a). Any genre of writing that makes use of biographical and autobiographical accounts has a close relationship to fictional writing by the time it has been through the processes of selection, editing, and framing with other sections of text, reflecting the author's intention to tell a particular story (Clifford and Marcus 1986; Stanley 1992). The process by which an author decides on this crafting in turn depends upon their assumptions about who the text is for. Thus I must construct my readers in order to know how to construct my characters. This adds a further layer of complexity and uncertainty to the task of making sense of the stories in this book.

If nothing else is clear by now, it should at least be evident that I do not regard the construction and interpretation of narratives as a marginal or straightforward issue. In seeking an understanding of this complexity I have naturally turned to the work of others, particularly in two distinct areas. The first of these is concerned with exploring managerial identity through personal narratives or 'story-telling' (see, for example, Czarniawska 1998; Franzosi 1998; Knights and Willmott 1999; Gabriel 2000; Boje 2001; Watson 2001). This was supplemented by the life history approaches, already mentioned, of Blythe (1972) and Terkel (1970). A preliminary study of this literature suggested that narratives were an engaging way of stimulating reflection on identity and suggested a number of ways of approaching the writing and analysis of managers' narratives. In many cases, though, I was left with an impression that there was more to be done on the theorisation of the link between narrative and identity, leading me eventually to look at what I have termed 'existentialism' in order to address this.

The Narrators

Having discussed some of the epistemological issues in the construction and interpretation of the various narratives that are the core of this book, it remains to explain how I went about collecting the 'raw material' that has been worked up into the stories in the next chapter. Firstly, as I discussed in the opening paragraphs of this introduction, I decided to use the Masters course that I was responsible for as a way of identifying individuals to base the research on. This was partly opportunistic, as it meant that I already had a relationship with my interviewees, which made the sort of conversations that I wished to have with them much easier to instigate.

It might reasonably be argued that by restricting my interviewees to those who came on this course I would only get a very narrow range of people and in some respects this is true. All but one of my interviewees were between the ages of 35 and 45, which is just what one might expect of those seeking to give themselves a mid-career boost with a Masters degree. Another similarity was that almost all were from what might be described as a similar class background, upwardly mobile upper-working or lower-middle-class, making good what they regarded as a missed opportunity for university study when they were younger. Only one of my interviewees had been to university the traditional way, after full time schooling. It was easy for me to empathise with this group of people as they were similar to me in age, social class, and their experience of growing up in the later decades of twentieth century Britain. I had also returned to part-time study in my 30s in an attempt to make changes to my life. I think, on balance, that this partial homogeneity can be considered a strength. The underlying social origins of those occupying middle management positions is not often foregrounded in research and the empirical analysis in Chapters 5 and 6 demonstrates that these origins are of great significance in understanding the particular way in which being a manager is regarded by this group.

Despite the commonalities it soon became clear that there was also a great deal of diversity within the group. Differences of gender, ethnic background, upbringing, and experience appeared to account for significant differences between each of us and, even where our circumstances were very similar, different individuals had often responded in very different ways to them. Accounting for the similarities and differences is one of the major themes that emerges both in the theoretical chapters and in the empirical analysis of Chapters 5 and 6.

Focusing on a small number of interviewees enabled me to build a close relationship with them over a longer period of time than would have been the case with a larger group. I followed the lives, and collected the stories, from a group of ten students drawn from two cohorts in 1998 and 1999, all of whom were interviewed at least twice over this period. The last set of interviews was completed in 2003. Four students were interviewed three times, as I did a set of 'pilot' interviews in the early stages of the research. Thus I was in contact with these managers for a period of around four years. I was fortunate in being able to keep in contact with a group whose lives appeared to be changing significantly during this period but I still 'lost' four students at different stages of the research. Three women had babies and, understandably, simply did not have the time to contribute to the far less important task of helping me with my research and one, an officer in the Royal Air Force (RAF), was sent overseas to serve in the Iraq war. Two of these interviewees left at an early stage in the research and I was able to replace them without serious difficulty. The remaining two left towards the end of my research, when I had already interviewed one of them twice, and so this also did not unduly affect the research. Only eight narratives appear in this book, reflecting the most complete and diverse accounts, however, material from all interviewees has informed the thematic analysis in Chapters 5 and 6. Although such a small group might be thought to lead to problems of 'generalisability', I believe that this is more than compensated for by the advantages of presenting detailed, rich and empathetic accounts of manager's lives based on longer term relationships with them than would be possible with a large number of participants.

Despite some of the similarities between participants already mentioned, I did make a conscious effort to ensure that a reasonable range of different people were represented in the research. Most obviously by balancing the numbers of men and women, even though women were in a minority in the cohorts of students the group were drawn from. It has not been my intention to write about gender *per se* but it is clearly a significant division within the group when considering managerial identity. For my female interviewees, balancing their desires for career progression with expectations of, or desires for, parenthood loomed large in a way it did not for male interviewees. It was also clear that negotiating a secure sense of being a manager, that was affirmed by those around them, was also more problematic for women than for men, an observation that is borne out in many other studies specifically investigating the links between management identity and gender (Wajcman and Martin 2002).

My group also represented a range of occupations that included a senior health trust manager, a chief executive of a medium sized engineering company, a quality manager for an IT company, a business development consultant, a mental health charity regional manager, an RAF squadron leader, a security administrator for the United Nations, an airport security training manager, a human resources manager for a large food processing group, and a corporate account manager for an insurance company. I believe that this group provides a fairly good cross section of what counts as managerial work in contemporary Britain as well as a striking illustration of how management careers have become extraordinarily pervasive. All of my interviewees defined themselves as managers, though some more reluctantly than others. It seems unlikely that those in the public sector, for example, would have thought of themselves in this way 30 years ago (Pollitt 1993; Clark and Newman 1997).

I tried to arrange interviews at places of work. I already knew my interviewees as management students and was familiar with how they presented themselves in the setting of the university. I was, therefore, interested in how they presented themselves at work as I believed that this was more likely to reveal aspects of their managerial identity. I also wanted to de-emphasise the lecturer-student relationship by conducting interviews on 'their' territory rather than mine. I succeeded in doing this in almost all cases for at least one interview, although in the case of the Squadron Leader, John, this proved to be impossible. In other cases, the workplace was their home and so interviews took place in both simultaneously.

In the first full set of interviews, interviewees were asked to tell me their life history via a series of prompts and questions. Each one of these interviews began with me asking 'Tell me about your childhood' partly in an attempt to circumvent the expectations that respondents had of the interviews. I wanted to get beyond a practised managerial persona and encourage interviewees to talk about themselves in a wider context. It was evident that most, if not all, were taken by surprise by this question but interestingly all recovered quickly from this and demonstrated a remarkable facility in the spoken autobiographical narrative form. Interviewees found it natural to talk about their experiences through this chronological self-narrative (all perhaps were familiar with talking through their CVs to prospective employers). These interviews were recorded and transcribed and the accounts given in the next chapter were derived by listening several times to the tapes and reading the transcripts until I was confident that the edited versions of their stories presented in the book were as faithful as possible to original conversations. This process was aided by the field notes I took on each visit to an interviewee recording as much as I could about the context of each interview.

How the Book is Organised

Finally in this introduction, I shall give an account of how the following chapters develop the themes I have begun to discuss. In Chapter 2, I present the narratives that form the empirical basis of my analysis, presenting my own autobiography first for the reasons outlined above. I debated whether I should use the first person for the stories of others, according to the life history tradition. I finally decided that my own artifice as author would be more open to the judgement of my readers if the boundary between the actual words of my interviewees and my linkages between them were made explicit. Inevitably this produces a less 'literary' and engaging text but one that is more compatible with the conventions of presenting academic research.

In Chapter 3, I discuss the various ways in which being a manager is understood within organisation studies. I critically evaluate both those positions which retain the possibility of autonomous agency and authenticity, as well as post-structuralist critiques of these positions, which view identity as a fractured product of competing discourses. Significant limits to these debates are suggested via a reflection on the significance of death. The chapter argues that our own finitude raises profound theoretical and ethical implications for the dominant understandings of managerial identity. In turn, these understandings have implications for the prospects of engagement with managers by academics. Most significantly, the sociology of death lends support to a narrative conception of identity that is further developed in Chapter 4.

Chapter 4 starts from the position developed by the discussion in Chapter 3 that the facticity of death suggests that identity should be regarded as bound up with the temporal trajectory of our lives and so has an essentially biographical character. The work of Heidegger, Sartre and Ricoeur is reviewed in order to suggest a theoretically rigorous underpinning to a narrative conception of identity and to outline the ethical, theoretical and methodological implications of this conception of identity.

Chapter 5 interprets the narratives presented in Chapter 2 in the light of the theoretical position established by Chapters 3 and 4. It utilises the first of three distinct but complementary aspects of narrative to make cumulative sense of the life histories and to interrogate the concept of managerial identity. The first of these interpretative modes stresses the 'history' aspect of the stories, treating the narratives as illustrative of a collective generational experience having its roots in the specific political, social and economic circumstances of the late twentieth century. In Chapter 6, I employ the second mode of analysis which foregrounds the generic narrative elements drawn upon by the narrators in order to reveal the discursive features selected from the cultural repository of such features. The work of Propp (1968) on folklore is used to provide an interpretative framework for this second mode. Finally, the narratives are treated as story-telling performances and so the third mode uses a framework suggested by the work of Holstein and Gubrium (2000) designed to reveal the various strategies used by storytellers to present their identities to their listeners.

Chapter 7 seeks to draw the various strands of the book together, returning to the initial aims stated in this introduction. The potential of a narrative conception of identity for management research is discussed, particularly by evaluating the outcome of its deployment in Chapters 5 and 6. The implications of this theoretical conception and the understanding of managerial identity it produces for more critical approaches to management theory are also evaluated. In the next chapter, though, I begin with my own story.

Chapter 2
The Managers' Tales

The Researcher

I was born in 1959, on the eve of the sixties, a last echo of the baby boomer generation. I grew up in the north London suburb of Barnet and I have three brothers. I am son number three. I suppose my parents could be described as being upper-working to lower middle-class. My mother's parents came from an impoverished background in inner north London. My grandfather once told me of how he had lied (as many did) about his age in order to get into the army at fifteen during the First World War and had found life more comfortable in the trenches than at home because at least he had a bed to himself. My maternal grandparents were determined to 'better' themselves. My grandmother did not go out to work but my grandfather worked at a number of jobs after the war; as a steward on passenger liners, as a warehouseman on the London docks and finally talking his way into a job 'on the print' in the days when the print workers' unions ruled the printing shops. My grandfather eventually became 'Father of the Chapel' in his union. So my mother grew up in a politically active family dominated by my grandfather, part of what used to be called the 'working-class aristocracy'.

My father's family I know much less about, partly because he rarely talked about them to us and partly because they lived sixty miles away and so we saw them only occasionally. My father is half-Irish but we did not visit our relations in Ireland until I was in my teens and other than my name this ethnic background cannot be said to have had any noticeable influence on us. Even my father's Catholicism was dropped early on in favour of his new secular faith, communism, both my father and his older brother were committed members of the British Communist Party from the 1940s. My father worked as an accounts clerk and later chief group accountant, in the heart of the City of London, for a large insurance company. In those days being a management accountant did not entail either the professional status or salary which we assume now, and so there was never much money to spare when we were growing up. My father must have had to keep very quiet about his communism in the Square Mile and perhaps this partly accounts for his profound reticence when it comes to talking about himself.

My mother suffered from an ear disease in her infancy which left her partially deaf and had a significant effect on her. She struggled to hear radio and later television, as well as group conversations, and so took refuge in books. Like most other working-class girls in the 1940s, she left school at fourteen with no qualifications and began to train as a dressmaker; however, she hated this and found herself a much more enjoyable job as one of the growing army of office workers in the City. Like most of her peers her working life was put on hold when she married my father. Despite the sheer hard work of bringing us up and her sometimes precarious health, my mother's restless intellect needed a challenge. There were no part-time courses to speak of in those days and so, over a fourteen year period, she studied for four 'A' levels and then an honours degree in history from London University, entirely by correspondence course.

My parents' shared hope for a swift workers' revolution after the war gradually gave way to disillusionment. My mother returned to her childhood love of the Church of England. My father clung on to his political faith for a few years longer, but as with everything else, eventually followed my mother's determined lead. As a result, I too became a regular church attendee and a member of both the church choir and youth group as did all of my brothers to a greater or lesser extent.

I thus grew up in what became a middle-class suburban family but one with a serious political and intellectual atmosphere. I was surrounded by my mother's books and so, almost inevitably, I too became a bookworm, browsing freely amongst the family book store. Left wing views, however, were seemingly absorbed from the atmosphere, as my parents rarely talked about politics directly to us. I can remember being a little shocked at the existence of opposing opinions at secondary school, our own views seemed simple and universal common sense. As I grew older, I found myself swimming against the tide of my middle-class peers almost without realising it.

I did not enjoy my school days either at primary or secondary school. Perhaps inevitably, given my family background, there was always a strong sense of rebellion against authority and being told what to do, something I still don't like very much! I was a bright and articulate child who chose to channel these abilities into arguing with my teachers and avoiding doing what I was expected to do and this made for a great deal of conflict. This was not of an overt disciplinary kind but rather a background war of non-cooperation and refusal. I still managed to get to the local grammar school, because my voracious unofficial reading had led to my English being reasonably advanced for my age.

I hated my all-boys grammar school with a particular vengeance: I was scruffy and uncooperative, I never did my homework and the usual punishments for not doing so did nothing to change my behaviour. I do not think that this was a conscious rebellion; I just could not manage somehow to fit in or to overcome my reluctance to waste my home time on dull school work, however much unpleasantness it would have saved me to have done so. The inevitable result was that I came bottom of the class in every subject for the first four years of school. In the end simple self-preservation won out and my awkward streak was channelled into a determination to prove the dire predictions of many of my teachers wrong. I did just enough work to pass my 'O' levels and then left school at the earliest opportunity, aged 16.

I then went to the local further education college to top up my 'O' levels with maths and science, neither of which I had undertaken at school, being totally unable to motivate myself in these subjects. For the first time I enjoyed being in an educational environment. We were treated like adults (mostly), given a good deal of freedom about attendance and I had chosen what to study, I had vague ambitions of eventually going to medical school, however, it was at this point that my father made one of his intermittent interventions in my upbringing.

My father came from a more middle-class background than my mother and had stayed on at school until 16 and taken his 'matriculation' as the school leaving exam was then called. He had then gone to work for an insurance company in the days of paternalistic financial institutions. He had a break from this work while he served in the RAF during the Second World War but returned to the same firm after this, where he stayed for the next 40 years or so until his retirement. For my father, this was the desirable model for our working lives also. He wanted us to leave school and get a good secure job in a bank or insurance company, which is just what my eldest brother did, though it turned out to be much less secure than hoped for.

It never crossed my parents' minds that people of our social class could send their children to university. My eldest brother had not passed the eleven plus and so had been sent to a secondary modern school where the emphasis was on vocational education not academic achievement. By the time my next eldest brother left school, in the early 1970s, it was a different matter. He did his 'A' levels at the local college, rather than at school, and then went on to university, with the support of my mother and the reluctant acquiescence of my father. When my turn came my father's influence appeared to prevail and I was encouraged to look for a job. I duly worked for two years in insurance companies.

My first job was a disaster, I felt like I was back at school being given endless dull but detailed tasks requiring a numerical precision I was incapable of and there never seemed to be anyone approachable enough to ask for help. I was sacked for making too many mistakes and general uselessness after about three months. I then spent three months 'on the dole' which I quite enjoyed until I got bored of it and began to feel the pressure of the expectations of my parents and others that I really ought to do something with my life. I then got a job in the City as a marine insurance clerk, following in my father's footsteps. This was better; I liked the people I worked with, going out to lunch with them each day usually followed by a trip to the pub.

The company seemed to run entirely under the steam of its own bureaucratic rules. There was a hierarchy but management seemed to happen invisibly. One's superior showed you what to do when you arrived and usually checked and initialled your completed work but after that you just got on with it. The work was easy, undemanding and rarely changed and so the sort of pro-active interventionist entrepreneurial management more familiar to us now simply did not exist.

The lack of overt authority left me feeling quite content in many ways with this job and it was nice to have a bit of money in my pocket (annual salary £2,000) but even a benign bureaucracy has a down side and in this case it was the sheer soul-destroying boredom that built up over a period of weeks and months. As my 18th birthday slipped away in 1977, I realised that I would have to get out. The only solution was to return to college and then go straight on to university. In this way I could have five years of relative freedom as a student and could thus avoid having to face the unpleasant and boring business of earning my living for what, at eighteen, seemed like an eternity.

When I returned to college I found studying very different from my school days. My time at work had changed me more than I thought. To spend four or five hours a day at college and another couple of hours a day in private study (when feeling diligent) seemed a permanent holiday compared to office drudgery, for the first time I began to do well and was regarded as one of the brighter prospects by my teachers. I got decent enough 'A' level grades to go to university and study geography, again with no particularly clear strategy other than it was my strongest 'A' level subject and so was a convenient ticket to a continuation of my student life.

Being very politically aware, even though distracted by my first enjoyments of the various pleasures of adulthood, I was acutely conscious that things seemed to be going seriously wrong from my point of view. The Callaghan government ran into the sands and the first election in which I voted brought Margaret Thatcher into power. The progressive sixties and early seventies were giving way to something quite different.

Hull University was, in most respects, a continuation of my college student life but with the added bonus of not being at home. The other difference was that it quickly became evident that studying geography was a mistake. By the end of the first term I had completely lost interest in it. I read, as usual, voraciously, but not in my subject. Other than this disappointment my student days wore on in a mostly happy alcohol induced haze but I always had a clock ticking in the back of my mind; the moment when I should have to decide what to do with my life. In the meantime I met my future first wife. By my third year we were pretty serious about each other and decided to move to London and live together. I would need to find a job, the trouble was doing what?

In desperation I applied for a long shot, a job in financial journalism in London. What possessed me to apply for it, I have no idea but, to my great surprise, I survived two interviews and was finally offered the job. I was both pleased and appalled. The problem of earning my living was solved and my parents and girlfriend's parents were pleased with me. It was a bit of a 'flash' job that I could show off about to my as yet un-placed friends. On the other hand, I had no idea whether I would like it or whether I could do it and worst of all my dread of the boredom and oppressiveness of employment was as strong as ever, I simply did not want to go out to work

The next few months saw me finding a flat to rent in Stoke Newington and so moving out irrevocably from my childhood home. My girlfriend moved in and so began my adult life: living in my own flat, being part of a couple and going to work everyday. My job though quickly turned into the nightmare I feared: I liked the writing part of journalism but my boss was a hard-nosed manager of the old school and an incredible bully. I felt trapped by the expectations of family and friends in a job that confirmed all my fears about the world of work. I became more and more depressed until one day, after about four months, I woke up and realised that I couldn't face going any more and so I never did. I was free but unemployed and it took me another eight months to find a job, this time working for Harrods in the wine department, which again was un-taxing and bearable but quickly became once more very boring, I could not see myself working behind the counter there for the rest of my life.

Casual encounters leading to lucky breaks seem to be a theme of many of the stories in this book and so it was in my own story. I got chatting to a college lecturer at a party who suggested that teaching in a further education (FE) college was an option for me. I realised that this could be a lifeline, a straw to clutch at. I had loved my days as an FE student, and being a lecturer was the next best thing to being a student. I got a place at a teacher training institute, leaving Harrods after a year to become a full time student again. When I began my teaching practice at Hackney College, I realised that I was not at all a bad teacher and that I enjoyed it. There was a lot of autonomy in how the job was done which I valued enormously. For the first time I could envisage a job that I might like doing for more than a few months, find interesting, and that I felt good at. At the end of the year I walked into a job teaching economics as a result of another casual encounter, this time with a teacher in a pub, and have been a professional educator of one sort or another for the rest of my working life. I had finally found my vocation and no matter how bad some of my jobs in education have been, my love of teaching, and the pleasure of knowing I do it well, has always been enormously comforting and satisfying.

My first teaching job, as with so many others, started to go downhill following a re-structuring by the local education authority. We also could not afford the spiralling cost of housing in London and so started to look at jobs in the north, where house prices were more reasonable. Eventually I got an FE lectureship in IT and my wife transferred to an accountancy firm in Manchester, I was to be to be the first member of my family to settle outside of 'the south'.

Oldham, what seemed to me to be a run-down mill town, was very different from our life in London but I enjoyed my job for the first year. I was second in charge of the computing department. Everything seemed to be going well until I managed to fall out with the new vice principal, although I'm still not quite sure how this happened. When my boss was forced to leave under a cloud, I found myself passed over for promotion and feeling increasingly vulnerable. I had only been at Oldham for a couple of years but I started looking for new jobs once more. I had developed a degree of career ambition that made such promotion important to me. During this time my wife and I also decided to start a family and when a senior lectureship came up at Hull College, I applied, as much as anything else because we thought it would be handy to be near my wife's family when our first child was born.

So, as I turned 30, we moved to Hull as my first daughter was born. I was a senior lecturer in computing at Hull which I hated almost from the first day I started work, although later I found camaraderie, friendship and solidarity there as well. The college seemed a cold, impersonal and unfriendly place after Oldham, and the students dour and uncommunicative. Management was autocratic and relationships between senior managers and lecturers frequently mutually hostile. Within twelve months all senior lecturers were moved onto new conditions of service and I lost my treasured long summer break.

I seemed to be well regarded by the college management, however, and after two years I was transferred into the business studies department to be Head of School of IT and Computing. I was now a 'proper' manager, with staff to manage, budgets to monitor, targets to meet and plans to present and implement. For the first year or so I enjoyed this immensely. I led a small, idiosyncratic, but generally committed and effective team of staff and got great plaudits for managing to turn around what had been seen as a problem department. However, FE was coming under increasing pressure from a right-wing government who were simultaneously cutting funding and introducing marketisation into the sector. I found myself under great stress in the classic middle manager's trap, caught between the demands of both subordinates and superiors, with little control over either.

My FE career ambitions were still not dead, however, and I began applying for assistant principal jobs and was picking up interviews, as by now my CV was quite strong. The experience of going for the interviews was salutary; the colleges I visited seemed even worse than the one I was at. Senior managers were invariably expected to be 'macho arse-kickers' and at their desks seventy hours a week, when they were not at meetings mindlessly spouting the latest education strategic management gobbledegook. I oscillated between the desire to do well at the interview and get a 'better' job and the dread of actually having to do the job if I accepted. After one interview where I had come a very close second I decided I had to make a definite decision about what I wanted to do. It seemed at the time and in retrospect to be one of the few moments when I really deliberately changed direction in my life rather than drifting into things. I can remember driving back from Northamptonshire having not got the job and feeling nothing but relief, suddenly sure that I could not stay in FE any longer.

Changing jobs now though was no longer so simple as it had been when I could just walk out of one job and wait for another to appear. I had a well-established career in further education, responsibilities for two children and was moving all too swiftly into middle age. What I would really like to do, I decided, was to be in higher education. I had always thought of myself as having a good intellect and had always pursued my intellectual interests over the years through my reading. The problem was that I was not very well qualified, only having a first degree. The first step then, I reasoned, would be to get a Masters degree and the logical choice of this was a Masters in Business Administration (MBA) which would enable me to make use of my experience as a manager. I signed up for a two year part-time MBA programme at the local university.

For a couple of years after my MBA, my escape plan seemed to have failed. I had got some part-time university teaching but I was an expensive proposition for straight lectureships at cash-strapped new universities but I didn't have the research credentials for more traditional ones. Then I got another lucky break.

I had applied at York for a hybrid administration and teaching post in a small management centre. Over the summer I got a call. Was I still interested in a job? After Hull, York seemed incredibly free. I had a fraction of the workload and almost none of the stress. All this was very welcome but in other respects my position was precarious. I had wanted an academic contract but my lack of a track record in research made this impossible and I had had to compromise by accepting an academic related administration contract albeit with vague promises of a transfer if I proved myself as a researcher. The next step then was to turn myself into a 'proper' academic and so I signed up for a PhD, which is how this book came to be written, an off-shoot of my doctoral research.

Postscript

The above story takes the reader to the point when the other life histories in this book were collected: around four years ago. In Chapter 4, I write about how Heidegger observes that living narratives are never complete until our deaths, that no life is a whole life until then. This is certainly true of my life, since completing my PhD I have (arguably) managed to establish myself as an academic, changed jobs twice, divorced, moved house, settled down with a new partner and remarried, taken up scuba diving and am now staring my fifth decade in the face. Despite these sometimes profound changes I was not tempted to re-write my story in any substantial way, none of these major life events seem to have changed who I feel I am or to have shattered too much the sense of continuity with the past, indeed a feeling of knowing who I was and where I came from enabled me to weather the sometimes severe storms of the past few years. It is the future that seems much more unpredictable and uncertain than it did to the PhD student setting out hopefully on a new second career. The past in this sense seems to have been more durable, less amenable to reinterpretation than some of the theoretical approaches in Chapter 3 might assume. It is the future rather than the past that seems to be the place where they do things differently, and all around us our stories are still changing in ways that are incalculable and unfathomable, beyond theory and analysis, understandable only as lived experience.

The National Health Service (NHS) Manager

Janet was a member of the first *Masters in Management* group run at York starting in 1999. I first interviewed her in 2002 and then again a year later. Both interviews took place at the quality and organisational development division of a large teaching hospital. At the time Janet was a divisional manager for quality and organisational development, which included managing projects to improve the efficiency of processes in clinical departments and to manage a wide range of management training. In other words, Janet is a part of the new managerial apparatus of the modern NHS, despite her professional background as a nurse. At the time of the interviews, this was a relatively new job for her, taken up initially as a promotion to an acting post. As with all the main interviews, I began by asking her about her childhood.

> I am the youngest of five children. I was born in Middlesbrough, and I was brought up as a Catholic. I didn't have a very happy childhood, being the youngest of five; I felt I was constantly teased by my older brother and sisters. They all thought that I was spoilt by my parents and then my father died when I was twelve, which caused me to be extremely unhappy for a few years. My mother really never got over it.

Janet explained that her upbringing was a reasonably prosperous working-class one until her father's death, which meant changes such as moving to a smaller house, Janet's mother going out to work, and the battered but useful family car being sold.

> He [Janet's father] was an administration clerk in the old power station. He was a very intelligent man but I think he never really got to move on. My mother never worked, but we still managed to move to a bigger house. We lived in a two bedroomed terraced house and then we moved to a three storey terraced house when I was about seven. This had quite a big mortgage with it so, when my father died, although he had some life insurance, my mother had to go to work for the first time and we had to sell the house and move.

> We were working-class. I can remember at school, you would compare yourself to children in your class that always seemed to have new shoes or the latest fashion. We didn't get that. That was a luxury. Being the youngest, I always thought of myself as 'Second Hand Rose' as I got the shoes and the clothes that got handed down from the others.

> We had a car. It was always breaking down, but most of the time we managed to have a car. When my father became ill, he was ill for about two years before he died, we didn't have a car because he was the only one who drove.

Janet talked about her older siblings who were already 'grown up' by the time her father died. They mostly took the traditional route to upward social mobility for bright working-class children, by becoming teachers.

> Both my brothers are head teachers plus their wives are teachers. My eldest sister is a teacher. The sister before me, she doesn't have a career, she remained as a mother but her husband earns mega-bucks so she doesn't need to work full time.

Much of Janet's story recounted how she struggled, as the youngest in a big family, to establish herself and to overcome the resentment of older siblings about perceived favouritism. She talked of feeling 'abandoned' by her siblings after her father's death in a way that reminded me strongly of traditional stories, Cinderella in particular.

> They didn't let me come home when my father died and that was a big split to me. I felt that continued throughout the years and it was only as we got older, and I became not perceived as the baby anymore, but as an adult that could argue with them on the same terms, that we started to talk to about these things.

> They all felt that I was extremely spoilt by my father, and then, when he died, there was this separateness. She [her mother] doted a lot more on my brothers and spent a lot of time with them. It was really weird that they all moved away. I was the one left. I felt responsible for staying with her.

> My mother was a convert and so she was more of a Catholic than an ordinary one, the converts are the worst. Now they were very very strict with my older brothers and sisters. I felt that they were just as strict with me but I think when my father got older, he relaxed a bit. So I probably did get more of his attention than the others and perhaps they resented that, I don't know.

> I suppose the only other thing [about her childhood] happened when I was fifteen. We had been brought up as Catholics and after my father died that continued. I used to go to church and I used to stand there and think, 'What are we doing standing here doing these rituals? Madness! Crazy! Well! I don't actually believe in all this, I am going to stop.' Once I had that confidence, I used to just question everything and I think, again, that my father brought us up to do that.

Both religion and political activism were important influences on Janet's early years, and it seems that it was Janet's mother who was the leading influence here, although Janet is adamant that her father was a much greater presence in her childhood. The family's Catholicism was rooted in her father's Irish descent, although Janet showed little sense of being 'different' in this way. Rather, she grew up in a close-knit Catholic working-class community. Again she made a sharp distinction between her own experience and that of her older siblings and developed further a central theme of her story, the importance of her intellect to her sense of who she is.

> I got hassled over it [giving up Catholicism] but I felt it was difficult for them to defend why I should continue. I had many arguments with them and couldn't understand how, if they are intellectually able, they can justify this strange spiritual practice. It wouldn't be so bad if they were spiritually attached, for want of a better expression, but they are not. A lot of it, I think, has been out of

> respect for my dead father and my mother, to maintain a pretence, I suppose. We were all brought up in Catholic schools and very much in a Catholic community. My mother was the president and the secretary of the local and national Union of Catholic Mothers. She was very heavily into a lot of the community aspects of that, so we didn't know any different; it was just part of our upbringing.
>
> He [her father] died when I was twelve and my mother died last year. I think that while he was alive, he had a big impact; he was a very strong presence on us all. We all have a very very strong sense of what we believe is right and wrong, and hate any injustice of any kind, and that certainly came from my father.

Janet's school days provided one of the more positive aspects of her childhood and she looked back on them for confirmation of her sense of herself as intellectually capable, as an individual who was different from those around her. She started at her Roman Catholic secondary school in 1969.

> Well in the old system at junior school you used to get your own reports and they used to mark you 'A', 'B's and 'C's, in all your different subjects, I always used to get 'A's. In secondary school you used to get a prize at the end of each academic year. I got the 'best girl'. The children always teased me about it, best girl 1969 and 1970. I got an atlas one year, a book of poetry the next.

Another theme emerged at this point in the story, Janet's determination to do what she wished with her life, even at the cost of family relationships, career and academic progress. She turned down the chance to do her 'O' levels at the more prestigious grammar school, despite her mother's unhappiness with her decision, and continued her education in the secondary modern school that most of her friends were at. Janet justified this decision by recourse to her developing political sensibilities.

> I didn't want to go to the grammar school as I thought it was snobby and, even at that time, felt that this separation of things was totally out of order. I couldn't see the advantage. I argued that I would get as good an education where I was. After my father died, my friends were a security, because it was stable and it was consistent and I didn't really want to leave at all. I mean Catholic grammar schools were notorious, run by nuns and priests, and were fairly unpopular places to be. My two brothers had gone to the grammar school, to the boys' grammar school and the horror stories ... So I suppose, if you had any sense, you wouldn't particularly volunteer for that kind of two years. So I stayed there.

Janet got nine 'O' levels and then went on to study 'A' levels at the local sixth form college. However, rather than following the expected trajectory of 'A' levels and then teacher training or even university, Janet decided to abandon her course at the end of an unhappy first year.

> I only stayed for a year, it was the first time the school had opened the sixth form to girls and I think it was total chaos. I managed the study, that wasn't the problem, but the teachers just didn't care. I didn't go to any of the classes and nobody bothered to find out where I was. I had a long long discussion with my mother over the summer and I just ... at that time of my life, just didn't feel that I could go back.

Janet only persuaded her mother to agree to her leaving school on the condition that she got a job and so, desperate to escape, she jumped at the first thing that came to hand, a chemical technician's job that her boyfriend suggested to her. Although she quite enjoyed being 'one of the lads' in a male dominated occupation, Janet's came to regret this decision.

> I was going out with a guy who worked at British Steel and who said 'Oh, there is a chemical technician's trainee job. You train for two years and then you get this job'. I thought 'That sounds alright, anything to shut my mother up', so I started doing that and I stuck that for about three months and it was just soul destroying.

> I remember going to college on an evening, as you did training as well. I sat there thinking 'This is worse than doing geography, what use is this going to be to me in my life?' So I stuck that for three months. I thought 'There must be something better to do than this.'

> It was very male dominated in the workshops at British Steel. They used to just swear all the time. It was good in the respect that they didn't discriminate against you because you were female. They just treated you as one of the lads and I preferred that.

Janet decided that she could not continue with her apprenticeship and started looking for voluntary work as an escape route, a choice she attributed to her Catholic sense of service. Again, her mother would only let her do voluntary work if she had a job to go back to and so, again to placate her, Janet signed up for a deferred nursing training place.

> I wanted to leave. It just didn't serve any purpose, it is a useful job but it just didn't do anything for me. My mother was panicking, as I had given up college to go into this job. Perhaps it was a delayed reaction to my father dying but I wanted to do something useful, so I said that I wanted to do some voluntary work. I found a voluntary organisation down in London that would take me but my mother wouldn't let me go until I had something to come back to, so I went to the Job Centre. They said 'nursing', and I said 'I don't want to do nursing', but they said 'This is psychiatric nursing' and I thought 'Oh! I like the sound of that.' I didn't intend to do it anyway because I was only applying.

Once outside of her childhood home and community, Janet suddenly became aware that others considered her as Irish and made jokes about her assumed ethnicity, something she did not recall with any discomfort, in fact she looked back on this first taste of adult independence with obvious pleasure.

> It was working for a Catholic organisation. I drank Guinness in London, and as 'the Irish girl' you got jokes about being in the IRA. I met some wonderful people, it was great. It was a half way house, so there were priests and people coming over from Ireland, looking for work, they used to stop here. They paid your keep and gave you a bit of pocket money and it was great. That lasted for eight months.

After her eight months of voluntary work Janet returned home and, as nothing better turned up, took up the nursing training she never seriously intended to do when she applied. Again she stressed the role of service and familial duty as a factor in her decision-making.

> I knew that I had to earn a living and somewhere at the back of my mind I was worried that I might have to support my mother as she got older, everybody else had left home. I became a 'staff nurse' in psychiatry, just a basic qualified, you did three years training.

Despite the way she drifted into nursing, once Janet was qualified she began to develop a serious interest in her profession, studying for additional qualifications and looking for a specialism that would satisfy her need for intellectual challenge. This career story is interrupted by her getting married, something she almost presented as an unexpected happening rather than a choice on her part, an aspect of her past that caught up with her and led her down a blind alley.

> I qualified as a staff nurse and got a job on acute admissions and did that for about a year and then thought 'This is boring! I want to do something else'. I thought 'I will do my general nurse training, just to widen my repertoire'. I got interested in neuro-surgery, somebody had mentioned to me that patients having operations on their brains and spinal columns often have psychotic or psychiatric symptoms afterwards, and I thought 'That is a good combination'. So I did that, then I met my husband and got married and it all changed.

Janet attributed her abandonment of her new found career ambitions to her Catholic upbringing. She distanced her current self from this episode in her life, describing it as a 'blip'.

> The institution of marriage was very important to me. We didn't get married in a Catholic church but I felt a duty, or responsibility. I had been brought up to

understand how important marriage was. That meant that if I was going to have a career I was putting it on hold, I think I had a blip.

Janet's abandonment of work and career to dedicate herself to her marriage did not last long, her career ambitions proved stronger than her upbringing, and she soon decided to return to full-time work when she was asked to undertake what she saw as being her first managerial role. However, another event interrupted her upward progress, she had another child, again presented as something happening *to* her, in fact described as a 'fall'.

> I think that the reason it didn't last long is that it happened quite quickly. I was just taken up with the emotional feeling that somebody loved me and wanted to marry me and all that sort of thing, that only lasted about three months, after that I thought 'What am I going to do? I want to do something else'.

> After I had been back a while they asked me, if I would be acting manager on the psycho-geriatric ward, which I did for a year. I had got a senior staff nurse's post and had started to think 'I could manage this ward easily'. Then in 1985, I fell pregnant and I hadn't intended to, I had decided that we weren't having any children.

Although having children was unintended and meant going back to part-time work, Janet was delighted to become a mother but things then started going seriously wrong with her marriage, which propelled her back into full time work. Despite the difficulties she continued to pursue her career.

> It was the best accident that ever happened to me, he was a little miracle. I had two miracles but didn't expect to have them. I was part time from 85 to about 89. I would have stayed part time but my personal circumstances meant that I had to go back full time, because my husband, my ex-husband unfortunately, was an alcoholic. Things were going downhill rapidly and I ended up having to come off nights to look after the children, as it wasn't safe for him to look after them. So again, I couldn't do anything with my career, and then I ended up being a single mother. I was glad just to have enough salary to bring the kids up but even then, when I was on my own, I went back to university and got my diploma in nursing.

As Janet continued to pursue her ambitions she increasingly thought of herself as a manager and was keen to distance herself from the potential professional identity of a nurse. The values mentioned earlier, of service and of being motivated by a strong sense of social justice, are re-introduced as important to her sense of what sort of a manager she is.

> I think I have always thought of myself as a manager, I never really thought of myself as a nurse. I have a strong motivation due to my socialist upbringing, a sense of justice and injustice. My mother was a member of the Labour Party, very staunch, and I suppose we were brought up with socialist principles, I work for the National Health Service and I work for patients. I know that sounds melodramatic but it is true and that is why it doesn't matter where I work. Whatever I do has to be to improve the care for the patients, if I do it in a clinical professional sense, as a nurse, that is good. If I do it in a managerial sense, it is still the same thing.

Janet demonstrated her commitment to being a 'good' (i.e. ethical) manager with a story of an incident on the ward. The reward for her principled stand is a new career opportunity.

> I was the ward manager and I had an incident and I didn't want to stay there. A patient died and I strongly felt that it was gross misconduct on the part of this nurse. We had the disciplinary but, because of the lack of evidence, they didn't dismiss her. She came back on supervised practise and I said 'That is fine but not on my ward!' That decision was overturned so I said 'I am going' and at that point I was prepared to become unemployed. I went to talk to the director of nursing who said 'Oh no! We can't lose you. I'll see if I can find you an opportunity'.
>
> There was a secondment opportunity in clinical education, so I went into that. A requirement for that was a teaching certificate, so I did that at Durham, part time and really enjoyed that. I did that for a year and then they offered me a permanent post, doing clinical education.
>
> We joined what was then our staff development department that used to do basic management development training. We managed to get a training contract for the community trust and we had a lot of income and got quite a good reputation. It was quite a landmark in those days that a nurse had gone into management development training but by then I had lot of experience. To be honest, it was probably one of my happier times.

This move into management development started Janet on the route to acquiring management qualifications and eventually her Masters degree.

> I did management development training for about three years and it went really well. I was always thinking 'Oh! I don't have a management qualification'. Then the staff development department went into the Personnel Department so my job didn't exist anymore and I had to take a job as a personnel and training adviser, which I hated.

Eventually a promotion came up in 'quality and organisational development' but with an expectation that the post-holder should be a graduate. Janet got the post on the basis of her experience but then felt that the time had come to do a degree.

> That level of post required a degree, so I asked my manager if I could do a degree and she said 'yes', but not a first degree. She felt I was past that and that was how I came to York. I had a look around different universities and I thought 'I like the look of that, it looks different. It looks like really getting underneath what management is about and that would really interest me'.

Janet was next promoted to divisional manager when her boss was seconded. She presented this as an accident, a lucky break, the result of a joke.

> The divisional manager was looking for somebody and I used to mentor him for his leadership development. He happened to say one day, when we were doing a feedback session, 'You know, I am thinking about going on a secondment' and I just jokingly said 'I'll do this for you while you are away. It'll be good to have 'divisional manager' on my CV' and that is how it happened really.

Janet went on to talk about the significance of studying her Masters on her understanding of what it meant to be a manager, particularly the validation that more critical work on management gave to her own misgivings about some of the management theory and practice she had previously come across.

> The Masters gave me a security to think that these thoughts that I have been having, were not only acceptable, but there was a world of literature out there that actually challenged it. It makes it more difficult on the other hand because I am left even more uncertain than I was. It gives me the freedom not to get bogged down, so that I can believe that, actually, you don't have to take management at face value.

Towards the end of her story, Janet reflected on where she is now and whether it was what she wanted to be doing, she was ambivalent about the idea of completely dedicating herself to her job and future career and she tries on an alternative identity of a teacher as providing a possible escape from demands that are becoming burdensome and from a sense of having lost part of herself that valued service to others as an important aspect of her work. Janet also reflects on her age, that she was now moving into a stage of life when she wanted to slow down and look at alternatives to managerial work.

> I am a young senior manager, in the sense that I have only been doing it a year, and if I compare myself with some of the other divisional managers, they have been doing it about ten years and I find some of their actions and behaviour inappropriate. The longer you spend in the role, though, the more difficult it is

to maintain your principles. You ask yourself why you keep doing it. Most of them say 'Because the salary is good'. They might spend 100-odd hours here in a week but they will make sure that they get expensive holidays and nice cars. I haven't got to that stage yet and I will get out before I do.

The only thing that will stop me going into teaching is if I don't get my degree. I am 45 now and I do not want to be at this level of stress, because the energy and the time that you put in, really, it doesn't go anywhere. You have to learn to value yourself and what you can give without burning yourself out. I suppose if I can't be useful here I could be useful somewhere else. The feedback I have had is that I am a good teacher and I would love to do that, I would be good at it.

The United Nations Security Manager

When I met him, Ethan was a big, muscular, man in his late thirties with a shaved head: certainly not the typical middle manager studying for a Masters degree and indeed his work background is not what might be traditionally thought of as managerial. Somewhat at odds with his appearance I always found him softly spoken, polite and thoughtful, though very single-minded and self-contained. He came onto the Masters course on which I taught in 2001. He had left his full time job in order to do the course and when I interviewed him he was eking out a living working as a sales assistant in a petrol-filling station. Consequently it was impossible to interview Ethan at work and so both interviews with him were undertaken in a spare office at the university.

Ethan grew up in what he described as 'small-town America', though this was small-town industrial America. He told me that the nearest large town to him was where the opening scenes of the film 'The Deer Hunter' were shot and this filmic reference seemed to set the tone for the rest of his life story, as usual I began by asking him to tell me about his childhood.

> I grew up in a small town with five brothers and three sisters, so it was a very large family, a traditional family. It was quite nice to have a large family but there is almost a generation between me and the last four children. Our childhood was very active, in the States we have a large sports programme incorporated with our schools, then there was after-school activity and there was also work.

> I come from Ohio in the Mid-West. Have you ever seen the movie 'The Deer Hunter'? It was filmed there. It is a steel mill town, a coal mining and steel mill type of area. Most of the immigrants would have come there, Polish, Hungarian, of that nature.

Ethan himself was from immigrant stock and most of his family worked in heavy industry, although his father also worked for spells in the police and in the construction industry. His mother stayed at home to take care of his large family.

> Poland is where my family came from. They went to the steel mill and coal mining areas of America and that is how my family settled here. My father was in the construction trade and then there was a downturn, there was hardly any work, just like the steel mills and the coal mines of that time. He moved to the Sheriff's department and he was there for about eight years and I think they downscaled there also, about fourteen years ago. He went back to the construction industry and is paralysed now, he was roofing and he backed up off a roof and fell and broke his spine and so now he is an invalid.

Towards the end of his schooling it became clear to Ethan that his options were few and not terribly attractive.

> Well as I said, the industry wasn't doing very well, so before I finished high school I knew I would go into the military because we couldn't really afford college. There weren't many options left, so I decided to do four years in the military. Besides I was interested in travelling, seeing some of the world or at least more of the United States.

Ethan therefore left school and joined the US Marines. He laughed as he told me of how he was tricked into entering the Marines and his subsequent shock at entering this very tough macho world.

> I wanted to take a trade that insured that I got something out of the military so I first went to take the test with the air force, not with the marines. I passed the test at a high enough level to be a jet engine mechanic but the only difficulty was that it was a two-year wait for the next opening and I didn't want to wait that long. When I was talking to the air force recruiter, the marine recruiter was at the next desk and said, 'Well come on in, we will have you next week'. I actually fell for that, being so young.

So Ethan became an infantry soldier in the Marines for four years. During his training he was selected for special presidential security duties and this lucky break set him on his future career path.

> I spent four years and made it to corporal. I got chosen, for some odd reason, for presidential duty, which was a very good break in my career. I had to spend a lot of time seeing a psychiatrist and having interviews, all the while going to the military training boot camp. This was to make it to Camp David, to provide security. It is only one in every 5,000 that get that opportunity.

Ethan found his new role much more varied and interesting, however, there are few opportunities for promotion and so he returns to the infantry after two and a half years before considering his future outside of the army.

> Infantry is just so repetitive, 'Attack this! Attack that!' It is great exercise when you are young but there was nothing new to it, there was no scope to it whatsoever, whereas, at Camp David, the work was very interesting. The problem was you only had one sergeant and three corporals. So you could spend as long as you wanted up there, but until the one above you died or left, it became a huge bottleneck of promotions. I did leave a little bit early to go back to the infantry, to make sure that I wasn't missing anything but I also wanted to get out.

When Ethan returned to the infantry he found that he had to struggle to fit in again.

> I went back to the infantry and this time it was a little bit different. I did reach corporal at Camp David but I'm not so familiar with an infantry team any more. I was at a huge military base where the atmosphere was completely different and everything was 'on form', it was like a prison camp. When I met my squad I ended up in a fight. Their first question was 'Why should we listen to you?' and then it ended up in a pushing, shoving match, and then proper fighting.

After this unpromising start, Ethan won his squad over and things improved, although he increasingly thought of leaving the military.

> After the initial meeting with the squad and the ruckus, it worked out very well. We became a very effective squad actually. We went out on quite a lot of manoeuvres, out to California, and I think in that last year we had a good time and we became very close and very good friends.

> As I said, I wanted to travel and, to tell you the truth, in the military I never left the US. California was the farthest we'd go. Everything was so controlled, so after four weeks you are doing very repetitive stuff. It becomes very boring.

Once Ethan's initial four-year contract was up, he combined his desire for travel with his security and secret service training, becoming part of the security detail in the US embassy in Moscow during the closing stages of the Cold War.

> I applied to the State Department, through a company doing some contracting for them. They were doing security for Moscow and some of the other embassies. So I applied for that and did get it, and spent a year, almost three years, travelling every six months or eight months between Finland and Moscow. It was a wonderful change to see these places. I enjoyed both countries and got to travel to Sweden as well.

After three years, Ethan decided to go back to America and a friend suggested that he could work for the United Nations, again in a security role.

> Then a friend calls me who was working with me on this project and says 'Do you want a job at the United Nations? So I said 'Yes fine!' I wanted to see New York. So I went to New York for a three year period, again in the security division at the lowest rank, just to get in. Soon after, I was working at the house of the Secretary General and his family. It is a different duty altogether as what you end up doing is working weekends, working nights and you are the only one there with the Secretary General's wife, his family, his friends or whatever else is going on. They would turn to you and ask you questions like, 'There is a problem in Angola. Find the person who is responsible for the chief officer for Angola because we have got to discuss the evacuation plan and get the political protocol.' So it became a very interesting job.

Although Ethan found the work fascinating, after three years his desire to travel got the better of him and he changed job once more. By now he had married and was living with his wife in New York. Being British, she returned to England when he took his next post for the UN, in Bosnia.

> I met my wife in Finland, she is British, and she came to New York with me. It was a mutual decision to leave New York; I took a mission to Bosnia when the war went off there and so she went back to England. This was during the height of the war in 1993.

Ethan went on to talk about his work in Bosnia, where he began to form a view of management as collective self-government.

> Yugoslavia was completely different, it was a war zone. It was in complete anarchy. No rules, no traffic lights, no police, nothing. I had quite a few responsibilities, the first being to travel and make preparations for the protection of the senior UN representative. When we had to move from one sector to another, I would go out and contact the troops to tell them that we were going there. If we had to go and meet the Serbian leaders, then I would have to contact them, to check that we would have safe passage to the meeting. So the job whilst I was there became very very active again and very interesting. We were very self-governing there. You could do all you wanted or as little as you wanted.

Ethan constructs a nascent managerial identity out of these experiences but in very 'non-managerial' circumstances. Once he gained experience in Bosnia, he began to provide leadership and training to newer staff.

> I began to have management responsibility because I was there for so long. Most people spent six months there, I spent a year and a half there so, when the

> new rotation would come in, I would train them on the job. Maybe it wasn't management, maybe it was more training. The UN doesn't staff missions to start with, you did everything at first but after eighteen months we were building units with separate responsibilities.

This managerial work was contrasted with the horror and violence of its context, in a war zone.

> In Bosnia they were still firing and they were still bombing. Buildings were still being shattered and I had been fired on. Friends had been shot and had had to be evacuated out. My friend, when he landed on the strip, he hung up his jacket on the plane and they shot a bullet through his jacket, so things like that start making you think and wear plenty of body armour. You just get on with it, you bypass that portion of it and you just get on with the job.

When the Bosnian War Crimes Tribunal at The Hague was set up, Ethan's combination of military, security and diplomatic experience led to him being asked to work in the security and protocol section of the court. When his superior's contract was not renewed he unexpectedly found himself running security operations.

> They were starting up a new war crimes tribunal, there were no court rooms, no judges yet, no prisoners yet. I was hired in the security section and I spent six years there setting up a security operation. My chief would sit there on his soap box and preach the rules and regulations, not to the staff, but to the staff above him, the people who we were working for. I think that they became tired of it because when it came to his second contract it just never got renewed. One day I just got called in and they said 'You've got the job'. So, after I had taken the job, my first point to them was 'Hire someone else very quickly' because I wasn't getting paid for it, it was too big a jump in level. I was chief for almost a year and a half, then a deputy chief for a year and a half, so I ended up doing the job for quite some time.

The discrepancy between his qualifications and his new found seniority persuaded Ethan to pursue a Masters degree without which he could not gain further promotion, even though the idea of management is often frowned upon in the UN.

> I could not enter the professional level without a qualification. I'd spent five years doing the job but not getting paid for it. I hit the ceiling on my grade and they were saying to me 'Yes, you can do all of this work but you will never actually have the job or the payment'.

> I never had a management language background and it isn't really used in the UN. It is taboo! You're not managers you're...I don't know what you are but you are anything but managers. You don't say the word 'manager'. So it was an

introduction to the language, most of my management experience is militaristic, by command.

Ethan's annoyance at being expected to work above his grade was exacerbated by being the only one to be willing to lead war crime scene investigations in Kosovo.

> The crime scenes were fresh and we had to be there. Nobody wanted to go although they had the rank, and it was their job to go, they procrastinated for months then the chief of finance said 'Well, Ethan could go', and I said 'Actually, I will consider it.' I came back the next day and said 'Yes, I will go'. I ended up in Kosovo because nobody who was supposedly qualified would do it.

Ethan was at pains to claim a managerial identity in explaining his approach to work, even in Kosovo.

> The good part of management is participative, it is collective. When you go somewhere like Kosovo, you have to find out what people want to do. You've got to have tasks, of course. There are things that have to be done, but why not find out who likes to do what? It may just fall into a natural order of things. I was the manager for Kosovo, whether they called me the manager or the head of mission or the chief administrative officer. I saw it as organising, you would say.

We went on to discuss his plans for the future both in terms of career and private life.

> I may look at the private sector. It has become more interesting to me through the Masters. I am working part time at a petrol station now too, which I think is phenomenally interesting; a return to the shop floor. I am not going to make a career out of a petrol station, but it helps me with the corporate material. I keep going back to the UN though, that is really interesting work, particularly the missions. Public service seems to offer these things more than a private industry.

> We don't plan on having children, so it enables us to be more flexible on moving. It is more the interest of doing different things and still finding them interesting. Maybe I would hate myself 25 years down the same job; I wouldn't want to do that. I think my wife wants to stay in England. One of the reasons we have come back is that her mother is old and getting ill, she has not been able to spend time with her and it is only fair that she does now. I wouldn't change the travel at all and I wouldn't change the experiences with the military. When I look back at experiences I don't think I would ever want to change them or have any need. There is always a thing I would like to do more, but not to change anything that you have already done.

When I next interviewed Ethan in 2003 he explained what had happened to him over the past year.

> In the past year I continued working part time in the petrol station. I completed the Masters course, and then I took a temporary job here in York. In the first week in September I started taking interviews back with the United Nations, then they flew me to The Hague to meet a panel in November and then I got offered a job. My job is in the security and safety division, it covers the courts; it covers the officers in Macedonia and in the field in Kosovo. It is the Yugoslav war crimes tribunal, so it still deals mainly with Kosovo.

Ethan's Masters degree enabled him to gain the promotion he wanted and he seemed to see working in security as a long-term career.

> It is a good promotion. It is more than twice what I was getting before for a job I am very familiar with; it is a full relocation package and quite a high grade now.

> Working for the UN is very meaningful work, and working for the war crimes tribunal I always felt was meaningful work. There is also a moral aspect of it: the justice process is part of healing the feelings of the people that had the atrocities committed against them.

> I am going to stay in the security and safety environment which is actually becoming a huge industry these days but switch to the corporate sector from the public service. I really enjoy living and working in the UK and I will miss the UK. We will be back, given an opportunity, we will be back. I love the coast, we would eventually like living on the coast if we could. We have had quite a good lifestyle and home here and we would like to continue with that, my wife and I.

Ethan had never referred to his native Ohio as home, or expressed a desire to return there and so I ask him whether he wanted to go back and what links he still had with his family.

> I have been away from there for quite some time and home is more about where my wife and I would like to be. I don't have a great deal of contact with my family, I am afraid to say; maybe the email is a lot to blame for that. We are in touch every day but not a great deal, no.

Perhaps not surprisingly, Ethan's vision of a happy life after his experiences in Kosovo was simply one of peace and repose.

> I like the country or the coast more, nature and sea: a quieter lifestyle is the desire, with a nice house, with my wife, spending more time together, doing things together. I found in the UN that a lot of times it was a sixteen hour day,

which is very long, and you can't help but be thinking of these things when you're home. What you have to do the next day, what you did. So you find a lot of that occupies your time at home too. Eventually my wife and I are just going to garden, go to plays or things like that. I just think it is calming, it's pleasant to be near the sea, I have always felt that. People say they want a house and a farm in the country, or some people like living in the city, where everything is happening. I have always liked the sea.

The Mental Health Charity Manager

Mary is a mental health charity regional manager. She became a Masters student in 2000 and I first interviewed her in 2002 at the university, as Mary had not wanted to be interviewed at her workplace. My second interview with Mary took place at her new workplace, which represented a big promotion for her, in the regional headquarters of a mental health charity in a large terraced Victorian house. Her background has some similarities with that of Janet, including going to the same school, but the story she constructed out of these shared experiences was quite different. She began by telling me about her childhood.

> I was born in Middlesbrough and brought up there with a sister, four years younger than myself. I lived in the same house for all of my childhood until I was about to go to university at 18. It was very much a typical working-class childhood I guess, Dad was a steel worker; Mum stayed at home and looked after the two of us. School was across the road, very local. The big change was at the age of 11 when I passed the '11 plus' and went to grammar school in another town. So it was generally a happy childhood, no major incidents. I don't live far from there now, I am only six miles away and we still visit the same sports centre, so I have been away and come back again but I do have quite a strong attachment to the area I guess.

As Mary identified herself so quickly and emphatically as working-class I asked her why this was so important to her.

> I suppose it is the work ethic, I'm of the generation of working-class grammar school girls and I was the first of my family to go to university. My parents hadn't gone beyond the age of 15 at school. Everyday Mum would be supporting me 'Did you have any tests today?', 'Work hard!' and all that kind of thing. So I guess that it is the 'work hard and you will succeed' ethic.

> They owned their own house, which was fairly unusual and they had a mortgage, whereas a lot of my friends lived on the council estate across the road. I don't think of them being particularly aspirational really, Dad never aspired for a management job or anything of that sort. He did what he did and he worked hard

and he earned good money for the time and my mother was very much a stay at home housewife.

Mary's father and mother had strong political convictions, although these swung from left to right as her father grew older.

> My dad was very political but he went from reading the Morning Star in the seventies, to being a Maggie Thatcher supporter in the eighties, he used to have quite left wing views. My mother had always had Labour views, she would never vote Tory. I would never vote Tory but I am not sure if I would vote Labour again at the moment.

Mary's parents were ambitious for her and wanted her to have a university education and Mary was happy to conform to this and strive to meet their expectations.

> They wanted me to do what I did really: to get a degree, to go to university and to get a good job. So from that point of view I think I did what was expected of me, I think that it was expected because I was the eldest as well. My dad was a steel worker, but an intelligent guy, he never had the opportunity to go to university but I think he would have liked to have had that opportunity. Like other parents he lived through his children, I suppose. I think I would have done it anyway, I think I would have found work in a factory absolutely soul destroying.

Mary sailed through her 'O' levels and then went on to do her 'A' levels at a sixth form college. It was the same Catholic college that Janet dropped out of after one year.

> I went to a Catholic junior school, and then a convent grammar school, nuns and all that stuff. It wasn't hideous really, it was alright. A couple of the nuns were a bit over the top with the hellfire and brimstone stuff. The biggest difficulty was that I was in the generation that went through the change to comprehensive schooling, so the lovely little 600-girl convent grammar school that I went to at the age of 11 closed when I was in the fourth year, the year before GCSEs, and we all went into a huge great enormous 1,800 pupil comprehensive. I can remember having a geography lesson in a woodwork room and these skinheads came in and just started lobbing bits of wood at us and you know we just weren't used to that sort of thing and neither were our teachers.

Mary's childhood was described as uneventfully happy though she goes to the other end of the country to study for her degree at Bath. Her choice of subject largely determined by what she enjoyed at 'A' level rather than any clear idea about a future career.

> I did 'home economics' at university, which is hardly a hugely academic subject. Bath struck me as being a nice place to be, the bit that I was in was right in the town and the hall of residence was in a Georgian terrace. It was a very attractive place, very nice.

At her second interview, Mary expressed embarrassment amounting to shame at the nature of her first degree.

> I feel very embarrassed about it, I call it 'economics', I don't like to admit to the home economics bit as they say 'Oh cooking!' I keep in touch with three or four of the women that were on that course and none of us admit to it, we all call it economics or social science or something.

Mary found university plain sailing but her first job interrupted her smooth progression from one life stage to the next. She took a post as a housing officer, largely just because it is the first thing that comes up, in inner London. She was also attracted by the prospect of an independent life away from her parents. This casual adoption of a job then determined her working life in the future.

> In the final year you had to choose a specialism, there was a housing accommodation option which is the one I went for and which landed me in the sort of housing/social work role that I have been in ever since. So, after university, I got a job in London as a housing officer. I didn't want to go and live at home, back with my parents, but I wasn't too bothered about area really, so I just applied for whatever was around and ended up in London.

> It was horrible, absolutely horrible! I worked on two estates; I managed a 300-property patch, doing all the housing management stuff, rent collecting, collecting arrears and repairs, tenant disputes and all of that. Looking back, some of the stuff I did then I just wouldn't do now. I went around knocking on doors, collecting rents and things. I would be very wary of doing that sort of thing now.

Mary stuck this out for two years and then moved back north to another job in housing, partly to be with her partner.

> I got a job as an administrative officer, much more office based, and no contact with tenants, which was lovely. It was much more administrative, paperwork and dealing with applications from housing associations, so a lot less stressful and I wanted to get out of London as well, I'd had enough.

> I enjoyed it whilst I was there and I did all the going to the theatre and having a nice time, but my husband, then partner, was 200 miles away in Leeds. We have followed each other round the country a bit, so that was the other reason for moving out of London.

This job lasted for four years during which Mary got married and bought a house in a nearby town. After a while Mary got bored with administrative work and started to look for a new job.

> At that stage I decided that I didn't like being an administrator, I didn't just want to sit behind a desk and shuffle papers all day, I found that quite tedious. Because I was dealing with the housing associations I knew what they did and that was the next career move, to get out to a housing association and do a bit more practical work but that meant another move so we moved to Darlington next. The plan was that we wanted to move back nearer to where our families were, principally because we wanted to have a family and we thought it would be nice to be near the grandparents.

Mary's new job was exactly what she hoped for, practical housing management.

> I was a development manager with the housing association, so my role was planning new development activity and obtaining the funding for it through the Housing Corporation, then dealing with all the practical stuff: briefing architects, engaging contractors, and so on. I had a team of three people that worked with me.

> It was the first time I had managed people. It was OK, they were a very good team of people who knew what they were at, so it was pretty good for a first experience. I was a little bit anxious about managing the Clerk of Works, as he was a guy quite a lot older than me. He had been in the building trade since he was sixteen and knew everything and I was a bit concerned at how he would feel about this young lass coming in and telling him what to do but he was OK. He accepted his role and my role were different. I relied on him giving me advice about the technical side.

After overcoming these initial difficulties and anxieties, Mary enjoyed her first managerial job but, as with other narratives, what started off well deteriorated, leaving her unhappy in the organisation, which she eventually left. Mary also became a mother which enabled her to take maternity leave whilst deciding whether to go back.

> There were problems with the organisation, I went off on maternity leave, and as I went there was an enquiry into the association's activities. The organisation had set up a couple of sister companies and there was money being moved around from one to another which was strictly against the rules and it was discovered

that this had happened. The Corporation came in and did the enquiry, people were dismissed, and the chief executive was dismissed. I was off on maternity leave when all this was going on, there was a job for me to go back to but I was very unsure about what it was or whether I would have the same job and the same conditions, so it was all a bit difficult.

As a result of these worries Mary did not go back to her old job, however, she did return to work as soon as possible, in pursuit of her career ambitions.

All my life I have always worked up the ladder. It is a measure of success, yes, and interesting as well, although I have branched off and done slightly different things instead of sticking to one career really.

I was off for six months and during that time I decided that I would look for another job. I found one working as a development manager for another housing association, a specialist association working with people with learning disabilities that was as a regional development manager. Again I had a small team of three people and my brief was to start the organisation going in the north of England. I enjoyed that; that was quite a challenging role; I didn't have a manager sitting on my shoulder telling me what to do.

This time Mary stayed in her job for six years but again, eventually, things started going downhill or 'falling to bits' to use Mary's phrase though it was during this time that Mary started to think of herself as a middle manager.

I did that for six years, my longest ever job, it was only a small organisation and I was employee number eight when I joined, I would say I was middle management, I guess. But that all fell to bits as well, there was a restructuring and it meant that my regional base and my colleague's regional base combined into one new one which would have meant moving. By then we had two children and it would have meant moving schools and all that kind of thing, so I decided that I would accept their offer of redundancy and look for another job, which I did.

Then I got a job with another housing association with the wonderful title of 'business procurement manager'. We were a big national general housing association. My role was working from the Middlesbrough office but with a brief for the whole of the north east. Again it was this business development role, looking for new business, not just new accommodation, but other sorts of business that the organisation could get involved in.

Mary's language started to shift at this point and the way she described her job made it sound much more business oriented than previously, the emphasis was now travelling around her region and trying to bring 'business' in.

> It was regional, so it was alright, it was rare that I had an overnight stay. It was a bit of a frustrating job though because it was a very large bureaucratic structure, I would bring new business in and it would take them six months to make a decision about whether they were going to go ahead with it, by which time the opportunity had gone.

Mary continued to enjoy her work but found the relative lack of freedom over how she did her job in this large organisation increasingly irksome and after two years she began to look for another job.

> I would come along with what I thought was a perfectly good piece of business and do reports for the finance director and it would take them a couple of months or more to come back and say 'no'. It was a really good group of people to work with, but the job itself was very frustrating.

Mary's next job was with a mental health charity and this marked a significant increase in managerial responsibility and workload and this is reflected in the more managerial language Mary used to describe herself.

> Next was a move to a charity and this is where people management started in a big way, I was working with a team of seven managers below me who were responsible for managing various projects, £40,000 projects with big staff teams.

> It was also a result of wanting to move up the ladder, to attain a higher status, more money and all the rest of it, you inevitably end up managing people because it is a people business.

As Mary moved into this more managerial work, she also started to study for management qualifications, finding that this had become an expectation for senior managers in the public sector.

> I started on the Diploma and then continued onto the Masters, when I was trying to get another job I kept getting thrown back at me, 'Have you got a management qualification?' 'No, well we think you need a management qualification for this job and that job'. It was always an issue, so that is why I started on the Diploma

> I didn't have anything to show that I knew anything about management even though I did. I think that I went onto the Masters because it was there and the thought of being able to get a Masters degree in 12 months was very attractive because I had always thought that it would be a long process. I suppose it goes back to my dad really, pushing me along saying 'You can do that, you can do that'.

Whatever Mary's initial reasons for coming on the Masters she became interested in it for its own sake and found self-affirmation in her ability to succeed at something that was more challenging than expected. She took pride in successfully combining a career with running a home, being a mother and achieving an academic qualification.

> The whole thing was much more academic than I had anticipated, it was a lot less practically based, but I did enjoy that, I did enjoy that, it was good. I did it for career reasons but I also did it for myself as well, just for interest, something that I could say; 'I have done this, I have achieved this, despite having two kids, a home and a full time job and all the rest of the stuff'. Sometimes women do have genuine problems in managerial situations but I think you have to get on with it really and don't be a bleeding heart, fight your corner.

At the second interview Mary expanded on her idea of herself as someone who got on with things, however, she also reflected on whether this was also a failing, an inability to feel appropriate emotions, in the light of her mother's death.

> I do get on with things, I don't whinge and moan and I get very frustrated with people that do. Maybe I am a bit blunt with people sometimes; you have to be so careful as they will take a grievance out against you because you have been nasty to them.

> My mum died in January, quite suddenly, and I surprised myself, I am not over it by any means, I miss her a hell of a lot, but I have surprised myself at how well I coped with it really, again it is just the 'get on with it' factor. I wonder why I am not feeling worse than I do, I am a bit too accepting of it, I know people who, in that situation, would have been in bits for weeks and weeks.

Mary hoped that her current senior post marked the final stage of a working life spent changing jobs every few years, particularly as her new job is commutable and so enables her to avoid another house move. Mary though did worry about coping with the pressures of this demanding new job and balancing the needs of work and her children.

> Well I only want to work for another ten years, so hopefully this is it now, I ought to stick at something for a while, as I do move around a lot. If this job had come up in the North West, I would never have even considered it. So although my career has been important, so is my family and I would never uproot them and move them all for the sake of me earning a bit more money and having a higher status job.

> I guess the issue here is going to be the 'burn out factor.' Yes, because the person that I took over from here had worked here for a long time. He just got to the

> stage where he wanted to do something different and had had enough of the stress, and he went to be a postman.
>
> With my new job, I try not to let it take over and I try and work sensibly. I put my different hat on when I walk through the door at home, I am not a regional manager anymore, I'm Mum. I get at least some days off at each school holiday and, you know, other than emergencies, no one contacts me.

I commented on our second meeting about how much more like a business manager Mary seemed to be.

> I don't think that because we are a charity that we should be run on any other lines than a business that's trying to make its way in the world and trying to make a profit: It is competitive. The difference really, I think, is that although we have all these business phrases and we work as a business unit, and are given financial targets and all the rest of it, the bottom line is that we are providing quality services for the people that live in our houses.
>
> I have got a lot of belief in what I do and my entire career has been spent in various bits of the voluntary sector with charitable aims and objectives, if you like, but done in a businesslike framework. I am in a relatively privileged position; I have had a reasonably good education. I have been able to earn a decent salary and have a nice house and all of that and, it sounds very trite, but it is a bit about putting something back really and trying to support other people who are less privileged than me, particularly people who are disabled. They don't have a voice.

Mary explained that her wish to retire in ten years was linked to her husband's young retirement age as a firefighter and she speculated, rather vaguely, about what a non-managerial future might look like, as well as life after the children have left the parental home.

> My husband retires at 55 and the thought of me working full time when he is not doing anything doesn't seem very attractive. Realistically I might end up doing something part time or something voluntary. By then the kids will hopefully be ensconced in jobs or at university, I have often fancied the idea of running a restaurant but I would need a bit of money to do that I think.

By the time of the second interview the restaurant idea seemed to have been forgotten in favour of some travelling and a quiet retirement. We also talked about her regrets.

> I'd like to do a bit of travelling, see a bit of the world, because I haven't seen that much of it. I like walking in the hills and I don't get enough time to do it.

> I suppose the only bit of regret is that when the kids were very little I was working full-time and I don't think that they have suffered by it, I think they are well rounded people but that is maybe a bit of a regret. I could have gone off in a different direction career wise, teaching was always a possibility I suppose, if you were a grammar school girl you were either a teacher or a nurse, so teaching was always an option but I couldn't see myself with a class full of kids.

We also speculated on whether she had become middle-class.

> I still don't class myself as middle-class, what does it mean? I don't read the *Daily Mail*; I don't live in Middle England. There was an article in the *Observer* about Centre Parcs, saying that it was a middle-class Butlins. The article was saying that the pile of *Daily Mails* in the shop just proved the category of people that they are aiming at, but I like Centre Parcs, it keeps the kids entertained.

The Engineer

Richard was the oldest of my story-tellers, in his mid-fifties when I last interviewed him. He held the most senior position of all my interviewees and was the only one to own and run his own business. My first interview with Richard took place at his engineering works in February 2002. He proudly showed me around the various workshops explaining what each of them was for. He also explained that his plans to sell out his share of the business to his partner had run into serious difficulty. A large contract in Pakistan had collapsed after the September 11 attacks leading to a dramatic fall in the share price of the company and he was obviously very concerned about this, and indeed looked very careworn. By the time of my second interview a little over a year later, Richard had successfully overcome these difficulties and disengaged (mostly) from his old company and so I interviewed him at his house in a small village in the West Yorkshire countryside.

> My childhood was unusual; my father was a conscientious objector and became interested in childcare after working in the East End of London during the Blitz, where he met my mum. My father was the son of a coal miner from South Yorkshire and my mother comes from a long line of clerics and minor landowners. I was brought up in a residential maladjusted children's home in Leicestershire which was a very radical venture by my parents. It was a very large house on a small estate and my parents were described as 'Warden' and 'Matron'. We lived as a single community, as this was part of my father's philosophy, so I went to the local primary school which had less than a hundred pupils and I was very very happy there. It was like having lots and lots of brothers and sisters and the most enormous playground to play in.

This unusual childhood changed when Richard was sent to boarding school.

> I was put forward for a scholarship, passed, and went to a Quaker school, a boarding school. Going to a Quaker public school was an enormous shock to my system after coming from this very warm environment and I was immensely homesick for the entirety of the seven years that I was there. I felt that it was a punishment and I could not see any reason why I should have gone to such a place. The only good thing that I got out of school was that I was able to develop my sporting skills. On the down side I found myself bullied, I was physically very small until I was seventeen years old. My education declined and declined until, during my 'A' levels, I upped sticks and left, much to the horror of my parents, who had been scratching and scraping to find the money, I also left home within days. I didn't feel angry towards my parents in any respect, I felt angry towards the snobbishness of the school.

Richard then found a job as an agricultural labourer and his physical confidence was restored as the work developed his strength. He also realises that he is a talented sportsman.

> I went to work in agriculture: I worked for eighteen months in Rutland and then I moved across to the other side of Leicestershire, I was doing general farm work. During this time a big change took place in me physically because I went from being under eight stone to nearly 13 stone and being quite a big bloke. That in itself gave me the self-confidence that I had lacked and allowed me to return back to sport again, and my returning to sport was very important to my self-confidence that I had lost in the preceding three years.

> I found that I got on with people and that I hadn't got two heads, all the things that people who are bullied have nightmares about, bit by bit they disappeared, but the chip on my shoulder is still there, 35 years later and it was a very chastening experience.

Although his work in farming began as a short-term way of making a living, it started to interest Richard as a possible long-term career. He decided to go to agricultural college where he discovered his vocation as engineer and inventor.

> I decided that agriculture was where I wished to make my career, land was not particularly expensive and I have always been fond of the land. I have a natural ability with animals and machinery, I enjoyed it, I enjoyed the fresh air and getting to meet the people.

> I applied for agricultural college and to my surprise I was accepted at all the places that I applied to, so I did an 'Ordinary National Diploma' in agriculture. I thought that I might be interested in doing teaching, so I took the 'Higher Diploma' as well. I was a mature student, 21 years-old, I had to fund myself and I realised that I needed to have a skill, I found that, amongst other things, I

> had good skills with welding. Welding paid for my education and I used to weld quite complicated structures, stainless steel milk tankers, petrol tankers, which again you have to know what you are doing to weld them.

Despite his intention to work in agriculture, Richard headed into the oil industry after college, seemingly as a result of a chance encounter.

> A friend was working in the oil industry and was struggling to put paint on the inside of drill pipes. He came to me and said 'Surely, you can think of a way of doing this?' Well I did do. I made a huge thing, like a lathe, that was the opposite of the way that everyone else had been trying to do it. I became works engineer for his firm and did quite a lot of innovative work.
>
> Next, I was head-hunted by an American firm who were looking to establish themselves. We undertook contracts on dangerous structures throughout the world. There was a big trade in taking crude oil from the Gulf back to Le Havre and Rotterdam. The ships were so big, and the money that they made was so immense, that they were looking for ways of doing corrosion protection of the ballast tanks whilst they were at sea. I was appointed as the person to investigate this. I spent part of my life at a desk, part of my life negotiating, and part of my life in a pair of overalls and priming boots, hanging off a crutch harness doing inspections in tanks at sea.

Richard sowed some stereotypical young man's 'wild oats', travelling the world, working on ships and containers, with a 'girl in every port', all the time building his expertise in engineering in extreme conditions. Eventually the attractions of this life paled, not least because he was nearly killed in an accident. He decided to opt for a more settled existence, using his engineering expertise to found his own company.

> This job gave me almost an instantaneous reputation within the marine paints business, which was very fortuitous but I did used to get fed up with being overseas all the time, I had met Angela by this time. I ought to say that when it came to girlfriends I used to try for Olympic records but when I met Angela it was very no nonsense. I realised that probably it was about time to settle down, I had two falls in the oil tanks in the space of three weeks, the second one very serious. I decided to start my own business, simply for stability, I had no ambitions other than to have a small engineering business working in the field I understood.

Richard reflected on how his obsession with work developed while on the ships, and how these traits led to him pushing himself and others to their limits. Richard linked this trait to a feeling of guilt arising from his not following his mother's wishes for him.

> I was actually quite pushy. There were two quite incompetent superintendents running work which irritated me, I asked if I could run the job myself, this resulted in me dismissing the two men who were nearly twice my age. One of them tried to kill me with a 36 inch 'Stillson' wrench at one o'clock in the morning. I had to learn to look after myself in lots of ways.
>
> I pushed myself and pushed myself in front of other people, I was always very conscious that my mother wanted me to follow my Uncle Richard, who had gone to Oxford. I do recognise that I was a disappointment to some members of my family and I thought that this was a second chance, a highly unlikely and unusual second chance.

Richard was very emphatic in linking the way he was so 'driven' by his work with childhood experiences of bullying and his feelings of both love and guilt for his parents.

> I must have been big-headed to think that I could actually do it; I think that the main driver was that I have carried a big chip on my shoulder about my treatment at school. My father went to his death without realising that I was unhappy at school. I never felt I could possibly tell him, knowing the privation that he had suffered, going through his life savings for me to go to school. As a result, I am hugely competitive; I can push myself at most things until I'm absolutely shattered and then a bit further. I wanted to prove that I had got the intellectual capacity and breadth of personality, that I could do something.

Richard went on to tell me that he has had to fight against the tendency to become a bully himself in his determination not to be bullied again.

> My wife was complaining about that part of my character but I did not realise it existed. I actually thought that I was a bit bloody 'marshmallow' to some extent. I have only recently had the balls to write down the fact that I was badly bullied at school. I was determined to be physically able to stand up for myself. It goes against my Quaker ethics, but in hindsight, when I was 14 and 15, if I had whacked one of those people good and hard, good and early, none of that would have happened.
>
> When I stopped working shifts Angela said to me 'Look! You are turning into such a piece of shit'. This was because of the way in which one had to manage groups of construction workers. Those guys would sometimes decide they were going to come at you and it was important to learn how to duck and weave or get in there first. To some extent it was a gladiatorial thing; I had to go through that rite of passage. My dad was a conscientious objector and he preached a faith that would not harm a blade of grass, and this perhaps also was a rebuttal of those values.

I asked Richard if and when he started to think of himself as a manager rather than as an engineer.

> Up until only a few years ago, I always used to describe myself as an engineer. I am slightly uneasy with the description 'director', whereas 'engineer' describes that one has a skill and to some extent a director is supposed to describe what your job is, though it doesn't.
>
> I do like to think of myself as a manager and I hope that I have been a good people manager, but I feel about managing the same way that I feel about engineering. I have evolved as a manager from finding myself needing a salesman, needing people to work on the shop floor, needing to have someone to do accounts and part of the issue of the course that I have undertaken is that I have needed to put some flesh upon the bones.

Richard went on to explain that this feeling of not really knowing the 'right way' to manage, or at least wanting others to see him as a credible senior manager, was partly what motivated him to come on the Masters course, although wanting to prove himself to his intellectually successful family was also important.

> I have been irritated that I have not done a degree. I have wanted to change jobs for some years and I realised that telling people I knew how to manage was utterly insufficient for preparation for doing something different and I felt that this was a necessary rubber stamp. I needed to demonstrate that I was not only competent financially but that I was competent academically, and I would see this as part of removing the chip on my shoulder.

Richard also explained that he hoped that the Masters would enable him to escape from the self he had become to become someone different, someone less driven. His sense of himself as a paternalistic and ethical employer had come under enormous strain as he fought for the survival of the company after September 11. He looked forward to a future as a mentor to an upcoming generation.

> I have worked immensely hard and I don't feel the capacity to do 60 plus hours any more, but I can't stop working the 60 plus hours a week. I need to make a change. The way in which I work, and the dilemmas that I am daily faced with, were brought into focus by the September 11 tragedy. That led me to dismiss people that I was very fond of, people who I have known for years. I took stock of myself as a manager and asked myself some very critical questions about whether this really was where I wanted to be for the next seven years of my life. I have often been the person who is the sweeping brush and the shovel and during this rather difficult period I was working a lot of hours and in one week I clocked over 100 hours. I had a quite clear ethical view that the greater number

> had to survive, but I also decided 'To hell with it! This is the last time I am going to do it.'
>
> I have an involvement in education and I am fascinated by the fact that agricultural college found and unlocked a key in me with engineering. I am fascinated in turning that same key with youngsters and I would like to spend the next part of my life doing that where possible.

When I next met Richard, he updated me on events in his life, and particularly on how he had, in the end, extricated himself from his company.

> In September of 2002 I decided to stop prevaricating and try and achieve my long held ambition to sell out of my business and have a career change. That process took me about six months. As a result of being in the business for 27 years there were various loose ends that needed tying up. I am left now with a small shareholding, but no directorships. I wanted to sell out all of my shares, but the bank wouldn't let me because there is another major shareholder and if he metaphorically hit a tree in his car one day they wanted to be able to have the ability to drag me back into to it.

I asked Richard whether this not quite clean break was what he really wanted. Richard's reply quickly turned into an account of how much of himself he felt he was leaving behind at his company and how difficult it was to simply walk away from it. His work was both something he wished to escape and something that he felt too much a part of himself to abandon.

> I did want to make a clean break and if the bank had allowed me to do that then I would have done that without doubt. On my last day I was clearing out my office and our maintenance foreman, who has worked for us for 20 years, kept hanging around me while I was doing this clean out. In the end I said to him, 'Bloody Hell, Aftar! What are you fannying around with, do you just want a coffee with me or something?' and he walked up to me and threw his arms around me and said, 'I will miss you, you are my brother'. I actually, for the first time, just collapsed in tears and realised I was leaving behind a lot of things from an emotional point of view. So there was really quite a juxtaposition between my emotional feelings and what I felt technically was the right thing to do, which was simply to make a break and allow other people to get on with it. I still feel very ambivalent about it.

Richard even went so far as to suggest that in leaving his engineering business he had become an entirely different person.

> I feel a totally different person because most of my activities are now committee or board based and therefore are utterly consensual and I'm usually not the leader

whereas previously, not to put too fine a point on it, I could quite often either finesse or bully my way through getting the decisions I wanted. It is a different lifestyle without a doubt. I describe myself now as a 'business development consultant' and that is the work I am doing.

Richard talked of his regrets at having worked so hard that he missed out on his children when they were younger and we talked of the dangers of his many interests and projects simply taking over from his old job as a source of excessive demands on his time and energy.

> No I shall never ever go back to doing that! I certainly would like to address some of my hobbies with the same sort of vigour as I have addressed work, but I basically decided that I'm going to refuse to do more than 40 hours a week. You know I have been and watched football matches with my son who is 22. I should have been doing that when he was 12 not 22. There has been a lot of denial amongst all this.

We then discussed his plans for the future and the fact that he was now entering what people tend to think of as the final third of one's life, albeit in his case a very active one.

> Depending on what happens to the economy I can live off my shareholding comfortably. My intention is to use the experience that I have gained, not to get back into the frenetic lifestyle that you have clearly recognised and mentioned, but to use that expertise that I have built up to help other people.

> I feel a lot more fragile than I used to. I know that I have aged beyond the usual aging process and I recognise that if I want to be one of those people who is around to see grand kids that I need to stop what I am doing. If I had retired at age 63–64, within a year I would be boxed up, underground, that just seemed stupid, and it also is selfish. I feel as though I have been selfish quite a long time and I don't want to do those things. I want to make motor bikes and go-karts and things for the grand kids and I actually, stupidly, surprisingly, quite look forward to being able to use those type of skills, imparting my enthusiasm for things mechanical onto another generation. I look forward to being able to be a 'wise owl', which is my children's' nickname for me.

The Information Systems Consultant

Alex was in her mid-30s and started her Masters course in 1999. I interviewed her three times in all with the first interview taking place in 2000, the second in 2002 and the last in 2003. When I first interviewed Alex, she was working as a 'support systems manager' for a local authority and I interviewed her at the council's offices. She managed approximately fifteen staff providing secretarial, administrative and postal services to the division.

When I interviewed Alex for the second time it was at her home which was also her workplace as she had now become a 'business consultant'. Our final interview also took place in her home after she had resigned from what had become a disastrous job move to consulting. She was now about to do some temping for her old employer, the council, while she worked out what she was going to do longer term.

> I was born in Catterick, which is an army town, in a crummy little council house. I was mainly brought up by my grandparents, because my mum had to work. My mum did a lot of different jobs when we were young, ranging from dinner lady at our school, working in a shoe shop, to secretarial work. My dad has always been a lorry driver, so he was out on the road a lot, Mum would take us to Grandma's and would leave us there for the day. Then my mum made a decision that Catterick wasn't the place to bring us up. There were no prospects for us there so we relocated to here and I started secondary school. I have got an older sister and a younger brother, two years between each of us, and we moved here when I was about 12 then, in my options year, Mum and Dad separated and got divorced.

Alex's parents struggled to improve their standard of living and provide better opportunities for their children but this struggle contributed to the break-up of their marriage.

> They just grew apart; Mum wanted more out of life but my dad was always on the road. He was trying to give Mum what she wanted, a good life for us and we hardly ever saw him as he was always travelling. I think one of the things that really sent their marriage off the rails was that my dad thought it would be a good idea if my grandparents moved to York with us and so he took the lead in arranging for them to come and live in our house with us and that just created enormous tension.

As a result of the divorce, the family fragmented, leaving Alex with her mother. A move into a smaller flat led to a long journey to school which Alex believed contributed to her poor 'O' level results.

> For all the rest of my years, I have stuck by Mum. My sister went off and lived with her boyfriend and my brother went up to Scotland, where my dad relocated. We had to move to a really crummy little two bedroomed flat and travel to school on our bicycles across town. I didn't do as well as I should have done, but I also didn't get much guidance at school. When I went to the careers advisor he said 'Oh hairdressing!', and I can't stand touching other people's heads, hairdressing or nursing, no thank you!

> I hadn't got a job and my mum was really struggling, money-wise, but I didn't just want to accept any old job. So I said to Mum that if I couldn't find a decent job to start with I would go back to school for a year and do a business course.

After her course, Alex began work in an insurance company as an office junior. She found this work easy and so she soon moved to a more demanding job in administration at the council. While better pay seems to be the primary motivation in pursuing promotion, Alex discovered that she enjoyed the extra responsibility and the status of being a manager, but she also discovered that she needed qualifications in order to be able to move into more senior jobs.

> I needed to earn more money and that was a big motivator, I wasn't going to fall to the same fate as Mum and end up having to struggle the way she was. I wanted to be able to earn enough money to have a house of my own and have that security before thinking of anything else in life. So I just kept focusing on work and I really enjoyed it for many many years.

Alex stayed with her mother until her mid-20s and then managed to buy a house with a friend.

> I lived with Mum until I was about 24, it wasn't difficult at all. Then I bought a house with a friend, because we were both struggling to buy a property on our own. The relationship broke down with her and so I sold my share of the house, so I came back home and supported Mum again. Then, for a while, I was with a boyfriend who already had a house, so I had plenty of space, I didn't need to buy my own place and then when that didn't work out I thought 'I need to do something, I need to get my own place'.

Alex next told me the story of how she became a manager.

> It was when I was in housing and I had set up all the administration arrangements for the tenants' choice scheme and the assistant director asked me if I would apply for the support service manager's job. I took that job on and I had about 13 staff and millions of pounds of budget and I thought 'God, this is great!' I was only about 21 at the time but I thought 'Yes!' It was quite a testing time but I swam, I didn't sink, and so I thought 'Well, I will have some more of this'.

This successful time in her early career and her growing self-confidence did not last as she ended up managing a team of women administrative staff that she felt little affinity with.

> The team itself had gone through a lot of managers and they were just a pain in the bum, most of them, a really miserable bunch. I managed to improve things a bit whilst I was there but I was tired of dealing with bickering women, because it

> was managing a kindergarten, not a team of intelligent staff. They were there to get a bit of pin money and have a gossip and do as little work as possible. I didn't want to be constantly having to crack the whip and support them when they were in tears because their husband had done something wrong or because they were feeling post-natal. They were dreadful, like women drivers! I hate them!

Alex went on to explain why she then pursued management qualifications.

> I was working at a small neighbourhood office, and the job wasn't challenging at all, so I asked if I could do a course and they funded me to do the IAM diploma at the college. I got a distinction, I surprised myself. I suppose I have always had a lack of confidence in this, what's up here. So then it was 'Well, I have done that, I will do the next stage, the Masters'.

Alex completed her Masters and then decided to apply for a part-time post-graduate teaching certificate (PGCE) in order to pave the way for a change of career. She was then presented with a dilemma when a supplier organisation offered her a consultant's job.

> So I had got enrolled on this course and then I got offered this job with lots of money and a car and everything. I had always fancied doing a consultancy job, I felt like 'I have succeeded'; I felt quite a lot of peer pressure as well. Colleagues and friends were saying, 'Now you have got your MSc, all these doors will open up to you and you will have no problem getting a job, it will be great'.

Alex took the consultancy job and turned down the PGCE, rationalising it to herself at the time as a way of widening her experience and so making her more marketable when she did eventually become a lecturer, however, she came to bitterly regret her decision.

> I thought 'I have still got my ultimate goal of wanting to teach but I need to get a bit more experience.' I thought 'Well I will just do this job for a couple of years' but the reality is that doing this job has turned everything in my life completely upside down.

Alex went on to explain how her relationship with her boyfriend had broken up as a result of her new job.

> He didn't want me to take it because it meant I would be away from home a lot, but I said 'I am only going to do it for a couple of years at the most'. I don't want to do a job where you are on the road all the time but I felt it was something that I needed to do.

Alex went on to explain how her regret at her decision began almost immediately.

> I was ready to walk out after the second week, in my first week I went down to be trained. I'd go down every Monday morning and stay through until Friday and then come home Friday night. I was sitting in a little hotel room by myself, not knowing anyone, it was absolutely horrible.
>
> My new boss, I didn't take to her, in my second week I arrived at ten past nine. She said, 'You're late aren't you?' 'Aren't you supposed to have a meeting with this other guy?' She did this in front of everybody and I had been up since 5.30 in the morning, driving down, with the prospect of another week away from home and I was just really choked by that. She has got a really loud booming voice and she has conversations about my colleagues to other people that are overheard.

Following the first three months of initial training, Alex worked mostly from home with only occasional trips to Head Office and so the friction with her boss and other consultants lessened but her frustration and disappointment with what turned out to be unskilled and repetitive work continued to grow.

> They say I am a business consultant but the reality of it is not very glamorous. I am told where I have to go, I have no choice. For example, yesterday I was talking to a company about how they were going to use the system for doing contacts and referrals in social care, and then you map all of that onto a business model document: a lot of it is really tedious. The nice bit is doing the questioning and probing but then you have to sit and work through lists of code tables and what definitions are going to go into all these budgets and that is really tedious.

Alex told of how she had missed the camaraderie of being in an office with colleagues.

> I work at home by myself and it is hard to keep yourself motivated. If I go to a customer site then I am still on my own because I'm not part of their team, I am just a consultant going in. I'm going down to Milton Keynes, but that is only once a month for a team meeting and apart from that, when I am on the road, I am sitting in hotel rooms night after night by myself.

Alex expressed complete despair about her new job, unable to find a positive side to it despite the encouragement of her friends and former colleagues.

> I hate what has happened to me and how it destroyed my relationship with my boyfriend. It has made me really miserable and I feel that I have been pre-menstrual for the last six months but I still think I have got to try it, I have got to give it a chance. My former colleagues say 'Give it a chance, give it three

months', and then 'Give it four months' or now 'Six months' but I just hate doing what I am doing.

Although Alex had reverted to her first plan of taking up teaching she was unsure as to how she was going to escape from her existing job.

> The difficult thing is that I can't give up work entirely because I need to pay the mortgage and so, if I did it part time, I would need to be in some sort of teaching role to be able to enrol on it. It would be very difficult also because of the travel in this job. If I can get another job then I will definitely do it, I have thought about ringing the council. The director of housing is keen to get me back. The money is not as good though and I would be taking a couple of big steps back, but at least I could just work in an office with a good team and have a home life and be able to pursue the course.

We then went on to discuss the future, if Alex could overcome her present problems what kind of work and life would she like to have?

> I was never one of those people who knew what I wanted to be when I grew up, but definitely working with others, working with young people. I had thought that I was going to enjoy a long happy future with my boyfriend. I was looking forward to being able to enjoy lots more holidays, lots more playing and then, in the long term, to have kids. At the moment I don't feel at all maternal, it is not something that I think I want to go through life without experiencing but now that has all gone out the window.

Alex expressed regret and some guilt about her decision to pursue what for her was a prestigious job rather than the teaching career she had originally intended. She appeared to believe that her relationship breakup was her fault for being seduced by the trappings of success.

> I haven't had time for him; I haven't had time for my relationship because I have always been away. I have what, on the surface, looks like a brilliant job and people see me and I look flash and I have got my posh suit on and I am carrying a laptop and I have got my flash car. I go into sites and people think I am really important but the reality is that the job doesn't tax my brain at all, it doesn't challenge me. The outcome has been that I have lost somebody that I really love, so it is a high price. It is a lesson that I would rather not have learnt.

When I met Alex a year later, things had improved a great deal. She had taken the decision to leave her hated consultancy job.

> Work continued to be awful, but all my friends and family wouldn't let me resign. They kept telling me it was a reaction to me and my boyfriend splitting

up so I managed to stick it for six months then, after being on holiday for a couple of weeks in Canada, I just thought 'I am not doing this anymore' and resigned that week, in a fit of frustration and emotion and so on. I just resigned and I had absolutely nothing to go to or anything.

Alex saw having handed her notice in as a turning point, a decisive intervention to bring a disastrous stage of her life to an end.

> You know one of my friends said to me, after I had handed in my resignation, 'I think you have made more progress in two weeks than you have in the last year'. I have learnt that I don't want to do this work. I spent so many years dreaming of being a consultant but now I know that that doesn't suit me which I suppose has got to be seen as a positive, that I know what I don't want to do.

Alex had also managed to find herself a new job or at least a return to an old one.

> I posted my resignation on the Monday and, straightaway, I rang my old director at the council and said 'I am leaving, have you got any work that I could come and do?' He rang back and said 'We want you to come for a minimum of three months doing projects. We have got lots of work that we want you to do. Don't go and sign on with a temping agency.' And so I thought, 'Maybe I am not completely crap after all. Maybe I can do other jobs'.

Although Alex was obviously relieved at having a job to go to, she was also pleased that it was not a return to a permanent nine-to-five, as she still liked the idea of being a self-employed IT contractor.

> The fact that it is only for a few months will give me a chance to think things through. I am looking forward to next week as I am now self employed, so there are lots of other sites I can work for. I am thinking of using this three months to sort out more contracting work. It's about freedom, because I am not bothered about making loads of money. I just want to make enough to keep my house going, have a few holidays a year and keep my car running and stuff, but not have to work a 50 hour week. Who knows what doors are going to open? But this is the best plan that I can ever have, to have a go at things with my company, working for myself, so I think I should grasp it.

We went on to talk about how she would rebuild her social life and about relationships. Alex was still reluctant to get back into a relationship given another recent break-up.

> I could build up my social life again and then I will be happier at home as well but my Prince Charming has not turned up. I have had my fingers burnt again, fairly recently, so no, I can't be doing with men. I would like to share my life

> with somebody; I would like to have my little partner around supporting me and praising me. It would take the strain of having to do everything yourself, and certainly would take the strain off financially, but I am used to it now. I am pretty fine really; I have been on my own all this time and it is very hard to let anyone else in. I think I will probably be on my own for quite a long time yet. But, you know, there is still a part of me that would like to have a family as well.

I asked her about her relationship with her family at this point as, after her account of her childhood, she had not mentioned them again.

> There is only my sister who has done the right thing, got married and had kids; she is an artist, so she just paints at home. My brother, he split up with his wife, he stayed here for a few months, I talk to my dad every single day. He was quite poorly over Christmas, he drives taxis up in Scotland but he hates the job, as you can imagine. Mum? I just go round for tea, once a week; I don't speak to her very often.

We then went on to talk about where Alex would like to be in the future.

> I would like to be working part-time, just a few little jobs here and there but quality work that stimulates me. I would have a nice country house with a nice horse in the field and motorbike in the garage and family around. My dream used to be having that city pad with all the mod cons and the single lifestyle but that isn't what I want anymore. It is too lonely, and I don't like myself, so I don't want to spend a lot of time by myself. I think when I am on my own I just get obsessive about stupid trivialities.

The Squadron Leader

I first interviewed John in 2002 and was struck by the fact that, despite his acquired aversion to all things military, he still had something of the clipped and precise manner that one stereotypically expects of the officer corps. I was due to interview John again, this time at his Royal Air Force (RAF) base in the West Country in 2003 but he was posted to Iraq just before the outbreak of the war and so this narrative is based on a single interview plus supplementary notes alone.

John was born into an air force family and experienced the rootlessness that came with his father being constantly moved from posting to posting.

> We moved around quite a lot. My father was in the air force as well, so I spent the first few years of my life in Germany and then I think we went to Malta for a while, which is where my mother is from, then we settled back in various parts of the UK. It was a fairly unstable upbringing, stable in terms of family support but not in terms of moving around. I don't think we stopped in one location until

> I was about 10 or 11. By then we had had 15 houses, I think it was. But it was a very happy childhood in the sense that I had loving parents and a younger sister, who is three years younger than me. The usual sibling rivalry, but apart from that we were very close, all three of us, and we went to see my mother's family once a year in Malta for the summer. We went to see my father's parents, who were in Hereford, quite regularly.

The constant moving also gave John a very different experience of school from those recounted in other stories where they tended to symbolise the rootedness and localness of childhood.

> School was very odd; I can't really remember much about it. I was a 'late starter', I think is the word, my parents were constantly called in because I was day dreaming. I found solace in art really, just in drawing and reading, I picked up maths late. I went to a lot of military schools, a lot of local schools and I moved around a lot and it was only when we stopped in Hereford again that I did the 'eleven-plus', which I didn't do too well at. Then I realised that by year two I didn't slip back, I was in the top class for everything and my maths was up there and I did my 'O' levels early and came on from there really.

Despite this sense of not belonging in any one place, John's family did settle long enough in Hereford for him to go to a single secondary school until the age of 16 and then to do 'A' levels at a local sixth-form college. John nevertheless ascribed his decision to join the military to a need to belong.

> I felt a bit of a lost soul, which is why I joined the military, because I wanted some identity in one organisation and it offered you a ready made identity and it was important and jolly nice, I wanted to be a pilot and I joined as a pilot.

> It was all very exciting to me, I loved aircraft and I enjoyed the early years moving around. It was only after I got married and had children that I started to think to myself, 'This is not quite my bag', both in terms of military lifestyle and the instability. Increasingly now, with only a few years left to my option point, I think to myself 'Why am I desperately unhappy and what is going on? Why do I feel so unstable? My son is being affected by it, so, what a silly thing to do, why did I do it?'

John recounted how he quickly felt that he did not belong, that he was different from those around him.

> I realised that I was slightly different, I was enjoying the excitement of it but everybody else had aircraft posters on their walls, I had pictures of Kim Wilde and Madonna and read different books to them. They used to take 'the Mickey' out of me; 'Why aren't you interested in air shows?' But it was just my job

wasn't it? I felt that there was something more out there and I needed to be doing it.

John never did become a pilot although he started to train as one; the lustre of it quickly wore off for him.

> I got a sixth form scholarship, which meant that the military paid while I was doing my 'A' levels, and a part of that was a flying scholarship, which meant you could get your pilot's licence. So I did that and discovered that again it wasn't quite my thing. I just couldn't get excited about it: you take off, you fly around and you land, and there is not a lot going on. So I went for 'supply and movements', which includes management and personnel.

John discovered a nascent identity as a manager away from the more operational aspects of the air force and it is from this point on in his working life that John thought of his work as essentially managerial.

> I was enjoying the management; I was enjoying the banter and all the interaction of people working with me and for me. Certainly I was doing OK at it and I couldn't keep to flying as I couldn't be bothered to go through all that.

> My job was the logistics manager; you are responsible for a mini-airport, for all the staff and the various sections within it, especially welfare matters.

John's aim quickly became to be as 'un-military' as possible and still be part of the RAF. For John, wearing a business suit provided an escape from wearing a military uniform.

> I continue to attempt to head for jobs which have the least military impact on my life. The best job I ever did was when I was working at the Ministry of Defence, I went to work in a suit and I talked to civilian companies for most of the day. I am back in uniform now and I am talking to other officers but they are students. The military ethos impacted on me a lot in my last job, where I was responsible for an airbase, whilst I enjoy the excitement of it, I just hate it really. I hate the annual weapons training we all have to do and I hate wearing a uniform.

However, John was quite aware of the contradictions of his position, of being an anti-militaristic military man.

> It is rather false of me, I shouldn't be taking the money but I have four years to my first option point and I don't get a pension or gratuity until I reach that point. I have realised just how much I do not like the whole culture, I have given them 15 years and I figure I don't want to throw away 15 years and not get a pension. I think 'No! The buggers owe me the pension and gratuity for the 15 years. I'll

force the issue and stay for four more years and try and stay away from the more military aspects and just see my time out.' Which is a bit off really, I shouldn't, but I figure they have used me enough, why not use them?

John contrasted his military identity with a managerial ideal that he implied can be both ethically correct and enable him to resist the demands of military life.

> Treat people as you would like to be treated yourself, not as senior aircraftsmen. When you are the officer there is a huge dividing line between yourself and your juniors. You can't do it in front of the boss, who obviously would chuck you out for it but I want to make their life as pleasant as possible, giving them stand-downs from time to time. You know, when the weather is a bit nicer, if we don't have much work on, say 'Right off we go!' I enjoyed that part.

John would have left years ago at one of his earlier 'option points' if he had not felt that family responsibilities prevented him.

> I got trapped, I would have left after two years but I got married and had children. She was a Gulf Air stewardess working in Bahrain and I was posted down there. We had our first son pretty quickly. We made a few mistakes financially, bought a house straight away, and I felt trapped. By this time I was with the MOD and I was 28 to 29. Then we moved to Lytham, which is a nice place, and she enjoyed the lifestyle there. Now I am 30 and promoted, and it was 'Ooh! I am promoted. That is a lot more money, it is not worth leaving, let's stay for a few more years.' So here I am, just turned 34, and thinking to myself 'God! I have got four more years.' If I had my time again, I would still have got married but I would have left.

John speculated on what might have been had he not joined up at all but this is tempered with a realisation that life has not been as bad as his retrospective disillusionment might make it seem.

> I would have gone to university, yes! I was looking at things like English lit. or journalism but things have worked out, nice wife, nice kids. The first years of my life were good in the air force; it is only once you have a family you realise. My priorities have changed; I have grown apart from it as much as it has grown apart from me.

Almost all servicemen and women know that at some point they will have to face the transition from military to civilian life and John hoped that getting a degree would give him a good future.

> Pretty early on I started thinking to myself, 'Whoops! If at any stage I want to leave I should have a degree'. I got promoted to this teaching job and thought

> 'OK, now I really do need a degree', I thought I would do an MBA; my main drive was employment outside. A friend of mine was on this airport course, I did that for a while but then I thought 'OK! Let's go onto this MSc that York are doing' and that is how I got onto that.

Although his motivations were primarily about making himself more employable, his studies had changed John in ways he did not initially expect.

> Since I have got onto it I have changed quite a lot. I got onto it to get a ticket, but knowing what I know now; I would have gone onto it for the course itself. It has been food for the mind as it were. Ideally I would like to go into academia, in the management field, get a doctorate later on in time.

John hoped that he had at last found his vocation.

> I have always wanted something; I have never really been content with where I am. Maybe my job in life is to be a good father and a good husband and let's just forget the work environment: that was never meant to be for me but I always felt that I should be doing something that I enjoyed or at least found interesting. I accept that I need employment and money, there are lots of things I would like to do but they don't pay, not enough to support a family. So doing this course has sparked an interest in a field that I hadn't actually explored before.

> That is why I would like to teach and then go into research. As I have gone along, each course has given me tons of questions that I really would like to look into, it just fascinates me, all of this. I have had enough of being a pawn in somebody else's game.

The future that John envisaged for himself was that of a management academic, but one who would be highly critical of a lot of orthodox management theory. He liked the idea of being something of a gadfly to the 'establishment'.

> I would like to be some sort of professor in this field, becoming a bit of a pain in the side of the bloody government and people like that, an ex-military officer who has seen through the rhetoric from the government.

At the end of the interview John returned to the theme of regret and the way in which one's past shapes the future.

> I believe in destiny to an extent. I am what I am because of what I have been through, and would I be here if I hadn't been through this? Maybe not and I might not have met my wife, if I wasn't military, and she is my soul mate as it were, so I am grateful for that. I have had some good times and yes, I am beginning to feel bitter now, quite angry now, but I think I might be if I was in

another job as well. Probably I am doing what I did when I was 18, escaping into something, running away again and escaping to an organisation that I feel I can identify with. Happiness in employment isn't as important to me as happiness in life in general. If I am happy at home and the kids and the wife are happy, that is the most important thing. If I can be happy at work, and I think there might be a chance I can be, then that is brilliant.

The Human Resources Manager

I first interviewed Mona in 2000 and at this time she was a middle manager in a chemical plant just outside of Hull, where she lived. She worked in the human resources management (HRM) section and was responsible for training and development. I next interviewed Mona in 2002 by which time she had moved jobs, though still in HRM, to a food processing plant in Grimsby, where the interview took place.

When Mona arrived for her second interview, I thought that she looked rather different from our first meeting, she seemed more self-assured and happier. She explained that she had met someone new, had a 'whirlwind romance', got married and bought a new house and generally felt a different person. Her new job consisted in setting up a centralised training operation for the group which would replace the local plant training team.

Mona characterised her childhood as idyllic, a happy and carefree experience.

> I think I am like most people, I remember my childhood being full of summers and sun, running around playing, particularly with my sister. I don't have any other brothers or sisters, just one sister. I would describe my childhood as being a happy experience but a great learning experience as well, which I am sure is the point.

Mona grew up in an affluent part of Surrey, a seemingly conventional suburban English upbringing.

> I grew up in Kingston upon Thames in Surrey, my parents had a fairly smallish house but a huge garden. My sister and myself spent a long time out in the garden, tea parties and teddies and all that sort of thing, it was typically middle-class, bordering on affluent. My parents moved when I was seven years old to a very nice house, but it was a very old house which they had to spend a long time doing up.

What sounded, however, like a stereotypically comfortable middle-class upbringing took an unexpected turn when Mona revealed that her parents were immigrants.

> My parents are from Mauritius; my mother emigrated with her family when she was 12. My father came over in the 60s, when there were employment opportunities.
>
> He was 21 when he came over and they met, my father's family and my mother's family were friends, and they met through the normal relationships of the family. My father was living in London and my mother was in Birmingham, my nana is still in Birmingham, where my grandfather died 12 years ago now. My parents have lived just outside of London since they got married.

Her father had been a labourer for his entire working life, despite the nice house in the stockbroker belt. Mona explained how, for her parents, her childhood meant struggle and hard work and how they were determined to establish themselves as middle-class Britons, rather than being a part of a distinct ethnic minority community.

> My father has always been a manual labourer, which was why, when they bought their second house, they had to spend a lot of years doing it up, that is what they have poured all of their money into. My mother is now a receptionist for a marketing company and they both bring in roughly the same amount of money now, but prior to that my father was the breadwinner. Early on in my childhood my mother didn't work, and I think a lot of that was to do with the pride that my father had. He didn't want his wife to work, but eventually common sense prevailed and they wanted to afford things and they couldn't, so my mother went out to work before I started school.

Her parents had therefore tried to bring up their children as British, although Mona still experienced being considered different from other children, not least because of the colour of her skin. This sense of difference was also reinforced by her parents' stories of discrimination.

> I think when I was very young there wasn't any feeling of difference but as I became a teenager and went to secondary school, you start to become more aware of yourself and your place in society. I think that is when I started to become a bit more aware of the issues around colour and ethnicity and acceptance. My mother and father still tell stories of when they came in the 60s and of the police and being refused housing. Although I grew up aware of those things, I never really felt them until later on; we were never brought up as religious or reminded of our background.

Mona reflected on her 'lost' ethnic identity but did not believe that she had missed out on closer links to a mother country.

> I can't speak the language that my parents speak which is actually Pidgin French, I don't speak that, I speak 'school' French. My mother, in particular, didn't want either of us to grow up with any kind of accent; we hid it, so consequently I had BBC English. I never really felt that there was something that I was missing out on. I think sometimes, for other Asian children, or other children from ethnic backgrounds, who have bits of their family missing, still in their mother country, probably it is a bit different.

Even the self-description of 'Asian' is a matter of uncertainty for Mona.

> I don't really know where I fit in, it is very difficult, I have very Western values, I don't wear traditional clothes. On the other hand my skin is not the same colour as a native of the UK. Sometimes I just think 'What am I?', because I don't really know, I would call myself British, I have a British passport. I have been to Mauritius once, but I don't feel a pull to keep returning. I don't feel that I belong there but sometimes I feel that I don't belong here either.

Mona's memories of primary school were very happy ones, although she felt less carefree at secondary school because of the pressures of academic competition. She did well at school, but still failed her eleven-plus and so did not get into a grammar school.

> I loved school, I liked to work and I liked to get on, I always have done. I liked to get involved in everything; I am still like that now in my work life. Secondary school was a bit different; it is a bit more competitive isn't it? I found I was extremely competitive and I was very studious. There was very strict streaming and you would have exams every year and you would move up and down the streams and I was always in the top stream, I never moved out of the top stream. So I guess the competition came from making sure I stayed there and didn't drop down.

It was during her secondary school years that Mona became the target of racist name-calling which Mona believed forced her to learn to stand up for herself and so strengthened her sense of self-worth rather than lessening it, a point reinforced by Mona's contrast of her experience with that of her sister. Mona linked her childhood experiences of standing up for herself with her determination to make her voice heard as a manager.

> I couldn't tell when it was, but a turning point in my life would be when I actually started to stand up to people and not take the cat-calling or the bullying. My sister though, is very different to me, she is not as outgoing. She found it quite a traumatic period of her life, whereas, with me, it has made me into a stronger person. If I really believe in something, I have to voice that. I can't just

> sit back and take a back seat and take all the notes and leave it there. I feel my voice should be heard and my opinions should be heard because it is of value.

Mona's parents placed enormous importance on their children succeeding academically and Mona always assumed that she was on her way to university.

> I always thought, 'Yes, I am going to go to university'. For my parents, education was the most important thing in your life so there was never any doubt in my mind that I would go to university. What I did when I got there, there was plenty of doubt about that, but not actually going there.

Her parents' plans were confounded when Mona left her single sex secondary school and went to a mixed sixth form college.

> I went to sixth form college in Esher to do 'A' levels and I discovered boys. The discipline just wasn't there in the classes, so that was difficult as well. Sadly I didn't do brilliantly in my 'A' levels, I did very well in my GCSE's but I didn't do very well in my 'A' levels, and that was another sort of crunch point for me. I think I wanted to enjoy life more than sit my 'A' levels, I wanted to go to pubs, clubs and all the rest of it.

Spending an extra year re-sitting her 'A' levels did nothing to improve her grades and so Mona had to abandon her plans to go to university by the usual route. Instead Mona decided to study for a higher national diploma (HND), followed by professional examinations in personnel management.

> I did my HND at Manchester University because I wanted to leave home and make a break. A lot of my friends, after finishing university, went back and they lived at home and got jobs in London and then moved out. I didn't want to do that, I was determined that that would be it, it would be a clean break.

Mona decided to pursue a career in personnel management rather than do the extra year of study that would convert her HND into a degree. As a result she found a job and then took the Institute of Personnel and Development (IPD) qualifications part-time.

> I was in Hull at this point and the course at Hull was an accelerated course. Instead of doing it in three years, I could do it in two, so that was quite a big pull for me. My boyfriend at the time was working at British Aerospace in Brough, so I moved in with him and I eventually married him, hence my married name, and then we got divorced.

From this point on, Mona expressed some urgency about 'getting-on' with her career, which she linked both to an awareness of the career disadvantages she faced as a woman and a desire to become established before having children.

> When I left university I had this issue of time, I felt that I had to pack everything in a short time. I think a lot of it had to do with the fact that I am a woman and it is difficult to get on in a career, I know how much society has changed, but there still aren't that many women in senior positions. There is the whole thing about, 'If I get married, I might have kids' and how do you fit that all in? I haven't really got that much time so I felt this rush to get on with my qualifications and get on with my career.

We discussed where her drive to 'get to the top' came from and Mona stressed both a personal desire to succeed but also that she saw herself as a representative of ethnic minority women. This ambition was, however, balanced by the desire to have more free time than her parents had been able to.

> I think that I have got something to prove because I am a woman from an ethnic background and I think I can make it so I need to prove to myself that I can do what I said I can do. I am also trying to think about the end of my life, not the end, the total end, but what I would like to do, I would like to travel, to enjoy retirement. I see my parents work really hard all their lives; my dad has worked all hours of the day. He worked shifts, he has gone on to do other shifts, he has had jobs elsewhere, just to put food on the table and it has not been an easy life for them. I don't want to be like that, I want to have time to enjoy my life.

> I believe that if I got to 40 and I hadn't made it in some kind of senior position, I think that as a woman, that is it, I have had it, I am on the shelf, whereas for a man it is very different.

We went back to discussing her first job in Hull for a food processing and retailing company. It was her first managerial job and so she looked back on it as an achievement but at the same time she experienced overwork and a lack of support from senior managers which caused her to look for work elsewhere.

> The job was a training administrator but they didn't have an administration department, no systems, no procedures, no way of monitoring or recording training in any way, shape or form. So that is where I started, I set everything up and did all the things that go with it and then I moved into training delivery. It got a bit too much, running the department, running the systems, and trying to deliver the right courses. I did ask for some assistance but, you know, the usual thing of funding and the rest of it, so I left and went to my next job.

Mona's next job lasted for three years after which she moved to her current post. It was at this point that she really started to think of herself as a manager.

> I did more of a training manager's job there, I set up and built the training department and looked at the systems, looked at how we measured training. While I was there I got involved in other things, I did graduate recruitment, I did competency interviews, and I reviewed the competencies, loads of stuff. I got a lot more reward out of doing those things than my normal day to day job.

During these first two jobs Mona began to study for more general management qualifications.

> A university wanted to pilot a Masters in management with our company and they were looking for a candidate so I started on a diploma and then I went on to the Masters. I didn't want to do a Masters at the time because I had just finished the IPD and then I finished my City and Guilds training qualification and I really wanted a break.

Despite feeling pressured into her Masters once she began she kept at it even though it had a great impact on her personal life.

> I had already started and I see things through, I think the study at that level did have quite a big impact on my life because in the middle of it I got divorced. I think it changed me as I became very insular and very much focused on my career, what I wanted, what I was going to do. It was all about me and it wasn't about my partner or my family. It was all about me and, you know, basically I don't think a marriage can survive that.

Mona told me how these changes in herself led to her estrangement from her husband.

> I was better paid than my husband and that caused a huge issue. We used to row about stupid things, but when you start analysing what is going on, suddenly we didn't have anything in common anymore and all I was doing was studying. I was away with the company all the time and there was just no time for a relationship. I could have done a lot to prevent it but I think that I wasn't prepared to give up my ultimate goal.

Mona did not see the impact of her study as negative overall though; rather she saw it as enabling a form of personal growth.

> The Masters changes the way that you think about things and the way that you look at things. It is about perspectives and it opens your eyes to you as a person. How you see the world, how you see things and how other people are doing

that as well and what mindsets they are using, what values they have, all those sorts of things. I looked at the person I was with and where I was in my life and decided 'No! I don't want any of that and I now want this instead'. The Masters has taught me some self-analysis and it has taught me some analysis of others. What is going on behind the scenes? What is causing these things to happen?

Mona went on to speculate as to what the future might hold for her. She wanted children but she also wanted to carry on with her career.

> I still see myself being at work but in the next five years I would like to have children. I don't see myself leaving work as a result of having children. I am also hoping to stay at this firm but there are a lot of changes within the HR world happening. Most of my team will be redundant by the end of the year, I would hope that out of these changes I might be able to move, I would like to leave this area as well now.

Mona explained that she had begun to feel the pull to return 'home', which for her was where her parents lived and where she grew up.

> I said earlier that I went to Manchester University to get away from my parents and now I feel this pull towards my parents, so I want to go home in effect. Surrey will always be home and I feel quite detached from this area. I feel that this job is a very short term thing, all my staff are going to be made redundant at the end of the year and I don't feel the connection anymore. I want to go where I feel wanted and loved and that is Surrey.

This family-centred future was made difficult by her commitments to both work and home. Mona debated how much commitment she should feel towards her employers, expressing a disillusionment that contrasted with earlier expressions of enthusiasm for her work and career.

> When I was interviewed for this job it was suggested that I might like to move to Walton as my next move. It is quite close to Kingston where my parents are, so that is absolutely ideal. I think the timing is probably a bit wrong as we moved house last year. In five years time we are hoping to be a bit more stable and I want to be in the south, by hook or by crook. I feel no affinity or loyalty to companies, does that sound really awful? It probably does, but at the end of the day if ever they make me redundant they wouldn't think twice, so why should I feel loyal? Part of that is a bit of a change in me as well. It doesn't feel like a career anymore. I am doing this because I want other things in my life.

The Insurance Account Manager

Elaine became a student on the Masters programme I taught on in 2001 and I first interviewed her in 2002 and then again in 2003. At the time of the first interview she was around 35 years of age and a senior manager in a large insurance company based in West Yorkshire. In interviewed her at her office on both occasions, which was tucked away in a series of archetypal cobbled streets, in a West Yorkshire mill town.

Elaine grew up not far away from where she now lives and works and recounted her early childhood as an Arcadian idyll disrupted by a move to the local town.

> I was one of three children, Jane is two years older and John is two years younger. I am in the middle and I think that has always made me a little bit competitive. My mum didn't work until we were probably into our early teens, so we had quite a settled stable home life. It was quite rural where we lived, we had a lot of friends and we used to spend a lot of time playing in the park. My oldest best friend, Al, I met when she was about ten, we are still really good friends now and she is a big part of my childhood memories. I lived in the same place until I was 16.

> Our house was about a mile and a half out of the village, all surrounded by trees and farms. As a child I suppose I had a sheltered upbringing really, a bit soft, a 'daddy's girl' really. We probably had a bit of an 'Enid Blyton's Famous Five' upbringing.

Her father was an engineer and her mother worked part-time in a bakery. In both cases Elaine described them as 'managers'.

> We were semi-privileged, I would say, my dad had a very good job. Income-wise we lived in the exclusive area of the village, he was an engineer, a production manager and Mum was a part time manageress at a bakery; that sticks in my mind because she used to bring home cakes, buns and pies, nice things.

When Elaine was 16, in 1983, her father moved the family to the nearest large industrial town. Her account struck a less happy note here with her portrait of a domineering, hard-drinking and selfish father.

> I think my mum and dad's relationship is different now. My mum was the archetypal housewife, my dad went out, he worked hard, he came home and the tea was on the table. We ate what my dad liked to eat, he went to the pub at seven; we didn't see much of him. As he spent most of his time in the pub he wanted to run his own pub. My mum said that she really did not want to do it but my dad was always the stronger party in the relationship. So when I was 16 we moved and the area that we moved to was not a very nice area.

The move also disrupted Elaine's education and she abandoned plans to go on to college.

> My parents moved in the January and I did my 'O' levels in the May. In August I was looking at college and thinking 'Right what am I doing next?' and my mum and dad dropped this bombshell that we were moving, and my world turned upside down. So I moved with no plans at all, not knowing what I was going to do.
>
> There was a woman who came into the pub, who worked in a place that made nurses' uniforms and I ended up getting a job there, I did that for two years. It was all the design of the garments, all the pattern making, and we learnt some good things and it probably toughened me up actually. I can't remember ever knowing what I wanted to do, although I knew that I didn't want a manual job and I always thought that I would end up in some sort of office environment.
>
> University was not the family line; it never really came into the discussions. It was never said but I always got the impression: 'you are 16 now; you should stand on your own two feet. We have done our job, we brought you up, we have paid for you, it is now up to you'.

At first Elaine enjoyed having some money in her pocket but, after two years, she started to become restless, wanting more out of life.

> I was 16 and my first wage was £34. Even with giving my mum some board money, I was going out five nights a week and buying clothes. Fantastic! But when I got to 18 I thought 'There is more to life than this'. I saw an advert for a job in an advertising agency, which was part of the local newspaper and I rang them up and got the job. I worked there for about four years.

Her new job moved her out of skilled manual work and into quite a creative form of office work, involving managing commercial clients, paving the way for her career in insurance.

> It was an advertising and publishing agency; we produced the Chamber of Commerce magazine and sold the advertising. You did proof-reading for the magazine but also you had to come up with articles. It was selling to businesses, so that was probably when I started interacting with clients, it started to get me more into a semi-professional relationship with people.

Although Elaine liked her job, her desire for further career advancement and for more interesting work propelled her into looking for something different and so she found a new job working for a large roadside assistance organisation.

> I then saw an advertisement and I went to work in their call centre, that was in 1990. I worked there for 12 years. I started in the call centre and did that for two years and then they introduced team leaders and I got a team leader's role and I did that for two years. Then they did a restructure and I became a business process manager. I didn't have any real people responsibility but I was looking at systems and processes and introducing technology.

It was in this job that Elaine experienced what she described as a highly significant episode in her life, her visit to the US on a management exchange scheme. The visit gave Elaine a new confidence because it made her feel that she was marked out for future promotion.

> At that time the company secretary was a member of Rotary, he encouraged me to apply for a 'group study exchange' which is sponsored by Rotary International. West Yorkshire was doing an exchange with the Rotary district of Chicago, so we went to Chicago for six weeks and it was really good. When we were there we were living the American lifestyle. The idea was to get you to understand a little bit more about them. We did all kinds of things, from going to a plastics factory, where they made goggles or something, to visiting a hog farm.

Elaine put her ambition and desire to gain promotion down to a need for more challenging and interesting work and to the fact that once a job has been learnt she becomes bored and wants to move on. She also speculated that her position as a middle child had influenced her.

> I get quickly bored and frustrated, unless I feel I am contributing something or I am learning something, or doing something new, I am not one of life's plodders. There are certain people who want to just come in, do the job and go home, whereas, if I am just coming in and just doing the same thing every day, then I am bored. I like to get into things, get involved in things and understand what's happening.

> I think, being one of three, I have had a slightly competitive thing. I have always wanted to do better than my brother and sister. When I was about ten they changed the border so that we were in Yorkshire, before they changed the border you would sit the eleven plus and go to Skipton Grammar School and that is what my sister did and my brother did. When they moved the border, we did not have access to a grammar school, so I went to a comprehensive school and there was always an unwritten stigma that I had not gone to the grammar school.

Elaine was acutely aware that she was one of the very few female managers in her firm, however, she stressed that, despite the attitudes of some people, she had succeeded and did not expect her gender to prevent her from reaching even more senior positions in her new firm.

> We went to this results presentation and there were all these people in this room and I thought 'God! There are hardly any women here'. In all of the accounts I deal with there are one or two women at most who I am interacting with. I have had bad experiences but I've found that once people get to know you, they do not treat you any differently. In the early days it was almost like 'Well, is she the secretary? Is she here to take the minutes and make the coffee?' When I came here and the guy interviewed me he said 'You know we are looking for people that have got potential to be board members, and that is how we see you'.

Elaine, however, was ambivalent about becoming a director, torn between her desire for success and her desire for a satisfying life outside of work.

> When he said that, part of me said 'Why are you assuming that is what I want?' You are balanced between your life and your job, the higher you go, the more delicate that balance gets. I suppose it all comes down to quality of life and I don't actually know what comes next.

We then went on to talk about this other side of her life that she wanted to keep in balance with work, firstly talking about her partner, Bill.

> Bill's got a completely different background to me, he is an engineer, just like my dad. Bill works at an engineering company who make things for the chemical industry, so I do not understand fully what he does and he doesn't really understand what I do but that is quite good in a way.

Elaine reflected on whether she wanted to have children and what the impact of being a mother would be on her career plans.

> Well it seems that everybody I know at the moment is pregnant. I am not saying definitely 'no', but I think you will have to pin me on the floor and hit me with a hammer to get me to say 'yes' because I could never conceive of giving up working, I couldn't be a home bird. I like people, I like being somewhere where I am using my brain, stretching my mind, doing things that are different, whereas at home 'baking buns', I don't know.

We next discussed Elaine's pursuit of management qualifications which began when she became a team leader in 1992, partly in an attempt to make up for lost educational opportunities.

> In 1993, there was a European grant where females could go to the Women's Technology Centre in Bradford and do a management course, so I went along and did the course. I was always disappointed that I had never done 'A' levels and never been to university and nobody in my family ever got a degree. I think

that was why I wanted to do it really, I wanted to prove to myself that I could, prove to Mum and Dad that I could.

Completing this qualification encouraged Elaine to go on with her studies and so she eventually came to the university I was teaching at.

I was looking at what I could do to give me access to a degree and that was the reason I selected York because you could do a certificate, and then a diploma but once I started I had to finish.

Elaine spent ten years studying part time before completing the Masters. She told me that she had wanted to get her degree for her own satisfaction as much as for career reasons though her choice of 'management' was clearly linked to a need to feel secure in her new managerial role. She also wanted to be a different sort of manager from some of those she had worked with.

I was doing it for me; there were times when I kept thinking 'God Almighty! Why am I doing this to myself?' but it was a goal that I wanted to achieve. The reason that I picked management was that, when we were appointed as team leaders, it was 'Right! There you go, you've got the badge, off you go'. I recognised that you couldn't just become a team leader like that.

There were a couple of supervisors who were the most horrific people that I had ever come across in my life and there was something about them that disgusted me. I thought 'I never ever want to treat people like they treat people'. In a way I think that was the driving force, as I just wanted to understand a little bit more about how behaviours affect other people and why these people feel it is necessary to treat people like shit just because they have got the title of supervisor or manager. I suppose the other thing was being female, I recognised that there may be areas that I would need to be stronger in really, just to show that I was willing and capable and able.

Elaine also felt that her management qualifications had enabled her to prove herself as a young female manager and to demonstrate her commitment and motivation for more senior positions.

I was young and I was female and I was in a male dominated organisation and I wanted something that would give me the edge in certain circumstances. I was one of the youngest senior managers here ever and people used to say that to me in a complimentary way but in the back of my mind I used to think, 'Well, are they saying "Yes, you are young Elaine"'. I think that doing the degree was to ground myself and widen my knowledge and my scope, to be on a level with others that I was interacting with. There were people in my last job, when I was made a senior manager, who remembered me in the call centre and on the phones. It was almost like an image I was trying to change. I had worked my way through but some people would always think of me as the girl on the phone.

I asked Elaine what she thought it meant to be a 'better' manager.

When I first became a team leader, it was a really scary experience; I probably acted in some ways that mirrored some of the people that I saw, in an authoritarian way. Now, my philosophy is that I don't really see that I am any different to anybody else. I always want to treat people like I would want to be treated myself and I would hate it if people thought, 'Just because she is the bloody manager, she thinks she can do what she wants'.

We rounded off our first interview by talking about Elaine's hopes and plans for the future. Initially she interpreted this question as purely being about what level in the company she would reach.

I think I might still be here. I know that more responsibilities are going to be coming my way. Where it will ultimately lead me, I am not really sure and if I get offered the next step up, I don't really have any qualms about that but until I get to that crossroads, I don't really know.

My ten year plan is to get my mortgage paid off and improve my quality of life, by the time I get to 50; work is not going to be important. That is ultimately where I am going. I don't know what I want to do. Some people want to be the MD but I don't know, I think that as you get a little bit older your game plan changes a little bit and some people will always be so driven but I sometimes wonder if there is just a little bit of something missing in their own life and it is just a distraction. I want to come to work and I want to feel like I am adding value and I am doing something but, at the end of the day, work is a means to an end.

By the time I next interviewed Elaine, she had decided to get married and was thinking of having children, something she had not contemplated a year earlier.

Bill asked me to marry him and I thought 'Yes, why not?' So yes, we get married in September, so that is a big change. A lot of focus on that at the moment: what to plan, what to organise. I think it is more a statement of true commitment and I don't know whether we will have children, but if we do, I don't know why, but I feel that I would want to be married, if I had kids.

I asked Elaine why she had changed her mind about having children.

The only doubt that I have about kids is that I have a nice life; I can just come and go as I please. If we want to go to Australia for three weeks, we go to

> Australia for three weeks, but having said that, I think over the last few years I feel now more ready than I ever have done to compromise my own life. I think that if you decide that you are going to have kids, part of that decision is that you are willing to, not to compromise your freedom, but you have got other priorities in your life. I think it is always one of those things that you say I am going to do next year, and 'the next year' is starting to run out. Saying that you are going to have kids is almost admitting that you have grown up at last.

I asked whether this meant that she had abandoned any of her career ambitions.

> Well this has been part of the discussions with Bill in terms of what life would be like post children and I know from the way I am that I need a lot more in life to keep me busy. I would still want to work, so the deal would be that I would still work and it would probably be that Bill would primarily take on the house husband role.
>
> I always have thought that there's a balance between your life and your job, and now that I've moved nearer to work I feel that I've got a better balance between work and home. I've got less travelling, less commuting, and taking that next step would mean that that balance changes, that there would be a bigger expectation of me work-wise than there is at the moment. If we did have a child, then that would mean that things would have to remain as they are for a while.

We returned to where Elaine saw the longer term future, at 60 say.

> At 60, I wouldn't want to be working; I'd probably like to stop working at around 55, maybe a little bit earlier. By the time I'm 60 I hope still to be healthy, still to be married to Bill, to have a child. They would be probably at university if that's what they wanted. There's a lot more places I want to travel to as well, I'd love to go to Australia, probably for a year, get a camper van, just go and see a different side of life. I've never been to South America; I'd love to go to South America. I've not been to India; I'd like to go to Asia.

We talked about the oddness of ageing, the way in which one tends to think of oneself as much the same person as one did at twenty, even though others see us as 'middle aged'.

> Sometimes I have to actually think about how old I am and I still think I'm in my late 20s. It's funny that you can't imagine being 60 and I can't imagine my dad's 60, I think I'm Peter Pan. There was a Golden Jubilee party in our street and there were all the kids at the big tables and I thought 'Last time this happened, I was on the table eating the jelly, and now I've moved on a generation, I'm now the adult'. In 25 years, I'll be the grandparent and it's that weird feeling that you are moving on a generation, but then I never think I'm getting any older!

Elaine thought that much of life was simply luck, rather than planning, and that the acceptance of this uncertainty is what made life worth living.

> It's what life is all about, uncertainty, isn't it? That's the great mystery of life, isn't it? What's going to happen tomorrow? How long are you going to live for? Life is about uncertainty and I think you could drive yourself bonkers if you got hooked up on 'Well, what's going to happen tomorrow?' I mean how do you know that when you cross the road that you are not going to be hit by a meteor and killed? I think mortality stops you from looking too far ahead.

The Airport Security Training Manager

Rob started his Masters in 1999 and finished in 2001 which was when I first met him. He was a big (broad and tall) affable man in his 40s. At the time he was working in a regional airport in the north of England in the security division. I first interviewed him at the airport in 2002 and then again in 2003.

Rob had fond memories of his childhood, growing up in the Medway and he painted an attractive picture of his membership of an enveloping warm working-class extended family; however, this happy childhood was disrupted by the death of his grandfather.

> Childhood memories are really quite pleasant; my father was sent to the south of England to do his national service, from Edinburgh. Mother was a local girl, who was brought up in the Medway towns. My father worked within the aviation industry where he and my mother met. My brother and I were the only two offspring, I was born in 1960; my brother was born four years later.

> We lived first of all with my grandparents and my aunty, in a very big house in the centre of Chatham. My mother and father couldn't afford a place of their own but the town house in which we lived must have been five storeys, so there was plenty of room for everybody. The community in which we lived was very close, it was a very safe, warm environment. The only thing that really upset that was the death of my grandfather, after this people began to move away, we moved, because we could not live with Gran for ever. We moved to an area known as 'Cabbage Island', it was inhabited mainly by the gipsy population; there were also lots of fields and a variety of different allotments.

Rob firmly defined his family as working-class and part of a working-class community.

> We were working-class, Mum gave up work when I was born and we didn't have an awful lot of money. My dad was a toolmaker, we didn't have a car, and

everything was public transport. We didn't know any different, everybody was in the same sort of situation where we were.

This sense of belonging became more ambivalent when Rob passed his 'eleven plus' and so went to a different school to his friends.

> The local primary school that we attended was very small, there were only five classrooms. I was fortunate enough to pass the 'eleven plus', so I went on to a grammar school, after that I was on my own, everyone else went to the two main local secondary schools. I was not an outcast as such, but I was immediately identified as being different as a result of that, I had some problems that first year, I felt very lonely.

Although Rob felt isolated at first he did eventually settle down and enjoy the grammar school, leading something of a split existence between school and home.

> English became my favourite subject, even though I wasn't very good at it. I also started to make a lot of friends, although nobody lived local to me. Anyway, I really looked forward to going to school on a weekday. At home though, we were all football mad, so I had two very close knit groups of friends, at home and at school.

Despite enjoying school, Rob did not do very well academically and this lack of achievement meant that the possibilities of 'A' levels, opened up by a grammar school place, evaporated as his father insisted that he went out and found a job at 16.

> I didn't perform fantastically well at secondary school, I came away with just four 'O' levels. I wanted to stay on but Father took one look at my academic progress and said 'We think the best thing you can do is to go out and find yourself a job of some description', which is when I became an apprentice at the naval base.

Looking back, Rob did not feel bitter about his parents' insistence on leaving school, as he felt that he could now understand the financial pressures that they must have been under.

> To be perfectly honest, I think probably they were right. It must have been a financial burden; it wasn't like an ordinary comprehensive, where you could basically wear what you wanted. It was blazers here and hockey sticks and proper kit all the way through.

His parents felt that learning a skilled trade was his best option, if a less immediately lucrative one than the unskilled labouring that many of his contemporaries were doing. Again Rob felt that he let himself and his parents down with his poor performance in the entry examination for the naval base.

> The apprenticeship was a struggle to be honest with you, you sat two tests in order to get a start and I didn't do that well. Those who came first in the exam got the choice of job they wanted to do, the ones with the most prospects, electrical or mechanical engineer.

Even though a sense of failure accompanied Rob's start in working life he had remained very proud of the craft skills he acquired.

> I am a fully qualified maritime shipwright; it involved all sorts of things from ventilation trunking to building a 14 foot rowing boat using wood and metals. It was 'jack of all trades and master of none' to some people but there are a lot of things I can do that others can't.

Rob's sense of satisfaction reminded me of Richard's work on-board ship; both showed an obvious pride in their toughness and skill.

> There was one particular task I was given on a nuclear submarine which meant I had to get one of the iron caulkers to burn a hole in the outer casing and then you could get into the bilges. You had to go in with a welder who would weld bars across the hole you had created to make a step ladder. I didn't like that very much, it was dark and it was cold and very claustrophobic.

Rob might have carried on as a shipwright for the rest of his working life but the Government's downsizing of the military meant the possible closure of the Portsmouth and Chatham dockyards and the end of work there for its 11,000 employees.

> I joined in June of 1977 and John Knot closed Chatham and Portsmouth in 1982.[1] So I'd done my two years in the shops, and two years afloat, so that was my apprenticeship finished. I was a fully fledged, fully licensed shipwright for 12 months; we thought it would be one of these very cosseted, very comfortable jobs for life.

There were opportunities for relocating and staying in his trade but Rob decided to stay put and do something else, a lack of adventurousness he regretted.

---

1   In fact this is inaccurate, Chatham did not close until 1984 and the dockyard at Portsmouth remains open.

> To my great regret, when the dockyard was eventually closed, I was given the opportunity to go to New Zealand. I was 21, absolutely no ties other than, you know, the apron strings but I decided that it was not for me, life was too comfortable as it was.

Instead, Rob found a succession of jobs and occupations in the new entrepreneurial casualised economy of the 1980s; starting as a bank clerk.

> Most of my colleagues went into things like secondary double glazing because they were used to working with light plate and wood but I gave up all my tools. I decided to make use of the meagre maths and English 'O' levels that I had and go into something completely different, I joined a bank, on £50 a week.
>
> I was 22 and all my friends that didn't pass their 'eleven plus' were laying bricks or baking bread and earning £200 a week and I was on £50 and I thought 'There must be something better than this, they're out every night of the week'. I had some redundancy money behind me from the dockyard and there was an opportunity to join a couple of mates of mine. They were going into a completely new business venture, which was opening a shop that hired videos. It was boom time, we made an absolute fortune. Unfortunately, the two I was with started to get a bit greedy. It got to the stage where they were falsifying accounts; I said 'I want to cash in my chips. I don't know what I am going to do but I don't want any association with, or any part of, this.' I was 26, with a mortgage, and engaged to be married at this time.

Rob had moved out of his parents' house by this stage and moved in with his fiancée.

> I had set up home with my fiancée, who was a local girl as well. We had a reasonable income between us, so we moved away into the suburbs, into a nice little semi-detached house. I was unemployed for about six weeks until I got a job with my fiancée's uncle, he worked for a specialist alloy company who had just got a large contract with a prestige car manufacturer to make alloy wheels. I worked within that little group for three years, it was fantastic, it wasn't a fortune but it kept our heads above water.

This story seemed to be heading in a fairly predictable direction, implying a steady progress through life, with marriage and possibly promotions to come, but then Rob found himself doing something entirely unexpected.

> I came up here [Manchester] to watch the test match and the Australians beat us. Within three days I met somebody else and within two months I had moved here. So the fiancée and me, we parted company! It was an absolutely massive change; I left family, left friends, straight into the unknown.

Even when we spoke, Rob still couldn't make sense of this sudden change of direction in his life. He was adamant that he was perfectly happy in Kent and his family certainly did not want him to go.

> Everything was going extremely well, we'd just bought a new house; we'd bought a new car, it was leaving absolutely everything behind. When I told my parents that the relationship was finished and that I was moving I might as well as said that I was going to New Zealand. 'Oh! We will never see you again.'

After this unexpected turn, Rob's life once more began to take on a more predictable shape, starting with his settling down with his new wife and finding a job at the airport.

> I was supported by my wife until, one day, she heard on the radio that the airport was recruiting people into security. I applied and I was fortunate enough to get a start. I've just progressed since then, I started off working as a security guard on a temporary basis and there was a prospect of a permanent start after that. As soon as I got a permanent job, I was promoted. Then you could become an acting supervisor and then a supervisor and potentially a security manager.

Rob stressed the obvious pleasure he found in working with teams of men just as he had in the dockyards.

> It was just like being transposed back into the dockyards, where you got the camaraderie of the troops that you worked with, there were nigh on 400 security officers at the time. I always seem to perform better in a group, the dockyard was a group, the football was a group and I was back into it.

Rob did not have any definite career plan but was keen to move up a level or two as opportunities became available, both for the extra money and a chance to use a bit of initiative, eventually applying for a vacancy in training.

> There was a very rigid structure to how you moved up; I sidestepped that because I went from a grade five security officer into training. It took me away from shift patterns, away from the coal face as it were. It enabled you to start making decisions that would affect not only the airport but also to get involved on a national level.

As Rob progressed through these levels he found himself described as a manager, to his amusement.

> My official title, believe it or not is: 'Training Logistics Manager.' My primary role is to organise and arrange all aspects of airfield security training. Most of my day to day activities revolve around what I would interpret as a generic managerial

> function, not only the logistics of arranging training, but also staff development. I am responsible for budget controls and financial projections. I am responsible for the sales and marketing strategy of the department. We are getting back to the shipwright scenario where it was 'jack-of-all-trades and master of none'; my role is very, very diverse.

As a member of the training section, it was natural that Rob began to feel his own lack of qualifications and this was the spur to him beginning to study for management qualifications.

> So from aviation studies and the City and Guilds the next thing was 'What do I do now? How do I progress?' That is where the Airport Operators Diploma came in, I think it was a case of 'OK! What I have learned has given me an overview of the way that things are now. How do I move that on because I am interested in how things are going to happen in the future? If there is a qualification attached to that I can improve what I know and get some sort of acknowledgement'.

In becoming a student again, Rob had to overcome his strong sense of having been a failure at academic qualifications in the past.

> It was a huge step and it is something that I agonised over for a long while and my initial fears and worries came to bite me in the backside because I knew my limitations.

Despite his fears, and the struggles he went on to experience before he passed the Masters course, Rob felt an enormous sense of achievement, and a sense of having righted the wrong of earlier failure.

> I think that if I went back and saw my old headmaster at the grammar school and said to him that I had got a degree, well, probably he never thought that I'd ever cut it. Even at the end of the diploma, there was some doubt as to whether or not I would have the ability to go through and do the MSc. It was a struggle, it really was, now I have proved that I can do it, it was not letting people down that drove me forward.

When I next met Rob, I asked him to update me on what had happened to him in the past year. He was doing the same sort of work but he was now attached to the HRM department as opposed to the security division. There were increasing pressures on staff caused by a more market-driven management approach.

> The work force has been reduced by 30 per cent, terms and conditions have been severely reduced, working practices have changed, the rostering has changed, the senior management has changed beyond all recognition. They are using middle managers, similar to myself, to build bridges as part of what it believes

is a change of corporate culture. I'm not so sure how that's going to pan out, it's very early days.

With new staff coming in on new conditions and longer-serving staff leaving, Rob felt that he was less a part of a team of workmates and more of a manager of staff.

> Eighteen months ago I could put hand on heart and say I knew absolutely everyone that worked for the security division. I knew them well enough to be on first name terms and to know some of their backgrounds. There has been such a change of personnel, that if I know 20 per cent now I would probably be very lucky. I feel that the management style that I have had to adopt is slightly different, because I have to gain the respect of these individuals.

The changes at work were enough to prompt Rob into considering finding a job elsewhere after 14 years at the airport. Rob was torn between his training activities and a possible move into teaching. He was also debating whether he wanted to have a senior management position.

> I suppose it depends on how far up the strategic ladder I want to go. If I'm honest, I wanted to go into training because I thought I had something to offer so I could also go into the teaching profession to try and make a difference. On the other hand, I enjoy the powers that I have, as limited as they may be, because something positive comes out of that. Three or four years ago it would have been 'full blast' and this is where I want to be and this how I'm going to get here and perhaps riding roughshod over people.

The thought of moving himself and his family to a new job did not seem to cause Rob any great concern and he also liked the idea of moving nearer to his parents.

> Reece wouldn't mind, he's not bothered, he's very much like his mum. She does have a job here, but she works for social services, so it isn't anything that she couldn't transfer to anywhere. If they build a new airport on the Thames estuary, ten minutes from Mum's house, maybe if that was to happen!

Rob reflected on how turbulent working life had become over the years. He seemed to think that it was both a bad thing, to be constantly unsettled, but also a good thing in that it forced him to 'develop himself'.

> I think of those early experiences, the dockyard and then the bank and then my own business. I'm very surprised to still be in the same job 15 years on. I think the expectancy for that sort of thing is gone within Britain, there is a culture of instability that I think is here. I could say that the past was traumatic because I didn't want to leave and then things happened and it forces your hand. If you get

too settled, unless you've actually got the wish to develop yourself and move forward, then you lapse into those nice comfortable surroundings.

Despite all the changes and Rob's slow transfiguration into a manager, he still thought of himself as the same person as he had always been.

> I'm as childish now as I was 20, 30, 40 years ago, my sense of humour has remained the same. I would like to think that I've matured, but I still feel that the Rob of 20 years ago is still lurking there, under the surface, just waiting for the ideal opportunity to pop out.

Rob was pleased with how prosperous he had become and saw a good income as a great source of happiness when it was spent on the family.

> I quietly gloat sometimes. We have a couple of fine holidays a year. Carol's got her own car, I've got my own car. I would rather spend my money on that than down the pub every weekend. I think I find it my duty, in a way, to be able to provide but changes in terms and conditions might take away my ability to do that. I'm hoping that, in years to come, my children will reap the benefits of the things that I do. Kids don't appreciate that now, necessarily, but they will do in years to come. They have opportunities that I, as a child, never had; I like to be able to do that for them, and for me.

Chapter 3
Understanding Identity

In the last chapter, I presented a number of biographical narratives including an autobiographical narrative. The purpose of these was to relate the life stories of a number of people who had become managers, including my own trajectory from manager to academic. Although I hope that the stories stand on their own, as a testimony to the experiences of the people I interviewed, I begin the work in this chapter of evaluating the theory that will enable me to explore the broader significance of the narratives in a systematic way.

My starting point for this chapter is that all of my story-tellers were able to construct a narrative in which they were the central character or protagonist, all had a strong sense of a coherent self that may have changed in many ways over time but that nevertheless retained a sense of continuity. Indeed even the ways in which they changed were often seen as a process of development whereby a 'true' self that was always immanent in earlier versions of the individual was able to emerge. Thus all seemed to have a strong sense of life as a progress through a number of stages: childhood, youth, adulthood, maturity and eventually the repose of retirement, though there were only one or two passing references in their accounts to the eventual ending of all our stories – decline and death.

In this chapter, I therefore begin my task of examining this sense of self through a number of conceptions of identity and the debates between these different conceptions. I begin to look at how and why we think of ourselves in certain ways and the implications of these views of ourselves. In particular I contrast two currently influential strands of thought about identity in social theory, those that retain the humanist assumptions of an essentially autonomous self-fashioning individual and those that seek a radical break with the assumptions of humanism and that are often grouped together under the banner of post-structuralism. I seek to critique both views of identity through examination of the stage of life most neglected by my story-tellers and by writers on identity in general, that of dying and death. For much of the time the typical career story follows the conventions of biography (for what else is a *curriculum vitae* but a highly stylised form of biography?) but the two areas where typical career stories diverge most radically from conventional biographies is in their lack of attention both to the antecedents of our self in our parenting and upbringing and the completion of our lives in what, for increasing numbers of us, is a substantial life stage, that of retirement, old age and eventually death. In other words our work identity is often examined in isolation from the wider life and self of which it forms only a part. As Alvesson, Ashcraft and Thomas put it:

> Much of the research that is focused on perceptions and practices in particular organisations neglects what is not immediately visible from the vantage point of participants and researchers – that which remains silent in live interviews or obscured by survey instruments. The broader, historical, cultural, institutional and political influences that inevitably shape local dilemmas thus fade from sight (2008, 11).

This book represents one attempt to redress this neglect.

One way of responding to such neglect is to examine the way in which work is woven into the fabric of a wider life and sense of self, a theme explored through the discussion of existentialism in the following chapter. For death and our awareness of our own finitude is argued to be an essential aspect of how we live our lives according to my reading of Heidegger, Sartre and Ricoeur. At the heart of their approach is an emphasis on temporality, finitude, the quest for authenticity, the intentionality of self-conception and the necessity of an existential project (Craib 1976; Kearney 1994; Ricoeur 1996). All of these suggest that identity itself is a narrative achievement. In addition, following Freud (1915/2005; 1917/2005; 1920/2003) one can argue that any consideration of life as essentially biographical cannot be complete without considering the universal experience of our greatest loss, the loss of ourselves and its prefiguration by all the myriad losses, grief and disappointments which are at least as much part of our life stories as the typical account of the successful career as a steady and continuing upward progress, albeit one marked by occasional setbacks and struggles.

To summarise, in this chapter I begin to work out the theoretical underpinnings of my position on identity and develop further my argument in Chapter 1 that it may fruitfully be considered as a self-fashioning narrative. Thus this chapter and Chapter 4 provide the theoretical foundation for my analysis of the managers' stories according to three aspects of narrativity in Chapters 5 and 6. These are that the stories may be viewed as a generational history; as an archetypal form of story structurally similar to folk stories; and as examples of story-telling performances. In this chapter I shall therefore start with my account of how identity has come to be understood in the social sciences before going on to examine the implications of a consideration of death for these understandings.

Humanist and Poststructuralist Models of Identity

How is the self, the 'I' used by the narrators in this book, understood in social theory? Theories of self-identity have become something of a hot topic within social science including within the sociology of work and organisation (Sarup 1996; Holstein and Gubrium 2000; Brown 2001). Within this work there is extensive use of the familiar collective categories by which individuals identify and define themselves (Cerulo 1997). These include race, gender, class, nationality, occupation, profession, age, political conviction, consumption patterns and so on.

The consensus that emerges from this writing is that these ascribed collective forms of identity, associated with more traditional forms of society, do not determine how we think of ourselves in the way they once did. Rather, our identity is more individualised and consumerist, in keeping with the society we live in. We thus attempt to fashion ourselves through life-style choices (Giddens 1991). In other words, according to this view of modern identity, although we still use such categories to define ourselves, they no longer define us.

To take class as an example, Woodin (2005) describes the changes in identity within a working-class writer's group as its members engage in disputes and negotiation over what constitutes an authentic working-class writer. Lawler (2005), on the other hand, describes how middle-class identity is defined through cultural contrasts with (and distaste for) a coded and implicit definition of working-class culture. What both studies suggest is that such identities are not ready made, rather they are shifting, uncertain and contestable sources of self that individuals must constantly reflexively work at in order to integrate them into their lives. Sexuality and gender have likewise been transformed from ascribed collective categories to a problematic aspect of identity that requires a complex set of negotiations and choices, particularly when combined with other gendered assumptions that accompany work identities (Ward and Winstanley 2005). Castells (2004) argues that not all collective forms of identity are dissolving as individualism triumphs, rather globalisation is leading both to the dissolution of some traditional collective identities *and* the simultaneous revival of others in new guises (such as forms of nationalism based upon fundamentalist religious identifications). Identity theory has therefore become a complex terrain exploring as it does the conjunction between pervasive but sometimes no-longer obvious collective identities, the social pressures on individuals to adopt such identities and the processes by which individuals strive to construct a sense of self by selecting, rejecting or accepting various aspects of the self-definitions on offer.

Another feature that contributes to the complexity associated with identity theory for the newcomer is that numerous terms that seem to mean the same thing are, in fact, deployed to signify various differences in emphasis and understanding within debates on identity. Terms such as 'individual', 'agency', 'subjectivity', 'self', 'authenticity', 'autonomy', 'role', 'person', 'actor', 'personal identity' and so on, are selectively deployed in order to signal particular positions on identity (or do I mean 'subjectivity'?). To try and make such distinctions more obvious, where I use alternative terms below (such as person, individual, self or subject, for example) I try to do so in reference to the particular theoretical position under discussion but inevitably not always consistently. One particular conflation that may be unavoidable is between the terms 'identity' and 'self'. These are often used interchangeably in the literature though the former is sometimes used to denote how others see us, particularly within symbolic interactionism about which more below. Thus identity is an occupation of an external social membership, as opposed to our inward consciousness of ourselves. Our 'self', which is a product of a reflexive act of consciousness, may be made up of several identities which can be more or less regarded by an individual as core aspects of themselves. This meaning of identity, as Craib has noted (1998), is therefore closer to the idea of role than some others This distinction, however, is much less clear in other accounts of self-hood and varies from author to author and so the reader should be cautious in thinking that such terms will always carry a consistent meaning.

In order to distinguish more clearly between these various theoretical distinctions upon which the unstable meanings of identity terminology rest, some means must be found to organise them. In this chapter, I have partly followed Elliot (2001) in organizing my thinking about identity around two dualities. These are 'surface/depth' and 'determinism/autonomy' as these dimensions frequently underlie the major debates in identity theory. In the first of these I refer to a sense that theories of identity seem to have a different view of how deep identity goes and how fixed it is within us. This duality also enables an analysis of the direction of identity formation. Identity may be thought of as working from the inside-out; an essential fixed inner nature manifesting itself through outward performance. Alternatively, identity may be imposed from the outside-in; a variable multiplicity of identities resulting from the play of discourses or social structures, more or less actively consumed by the subject; or by a dialectical interaction between the two. The second of these dualities refers to the debate over agency. To what extent can individuals wilfully intervene in their own identities? Are we really able to select a customised identity made available to us by modernity's array of lifestyle choices (albeit constrained in various ways by our pasts and the institutions through which we live our lives) in the way that Giddens (1991) argues or are such choices more apparent than real? Do they simply provide a façade of freedom behind which we are in fact powerless dupes, unknowingly consuming all-pervasive and inescapable ideologies (Althusser 2000) or being determined by prevalent discursive formations (Foucault 1982)? This issue of choice versus determinism is one that I explore in some detail below as it is central to competing views on how the narrating 'I' comes to be.

These differences are important but there seems to be some consensus between theorists also. There is a shared assumption that identity used to be relatively unproblematic, rooted in stable social structures where everybody had a place and everyone knew what it was. Using Griffiths' (1995) phrase, identity could be 'read off' from the structures of class, occupation, family, ethnicity, nationhood and so on. In other words, individuals did not have to take responsibility for themselves other than dutifully occupying their allotted place, 'the rich man in his castle, the poor man at his gate'. This 'traditional' form of collective identity is contrasted with a more recent reflexive self that has its origins in the Enlightenment, with its concept of the transcendent self-fashioning individual (Holstein and Gubrium 2000). Despite its fundamental critique of such humanist understandings of identity, poststructuralism also assumes that traditional collective models of identity no longer apply. The empirical analysis in Chapters 5 and 6 suggests that both Giddensian and poststructuralist approaches underplay the continuing significance of traditional categories of social structure as they are perpetuated through the mechanism of inter-generational transmission. As the examples cited above suggest, even where forms of attachment, such as to class, have lost much of their original collective power, their ghosts still haunt us, exerting a powerful 'pull' from one generation to the next.

This criticism aside, it seems beyond doubt that the modern self is experienced much more as a project and that subjectivity has been both individualised and emphasised to a historically unprecedented extent. The implication of this is that our identity becomes our own responsibility and, like all responsibilities, generates anxiety and doubt. Chapter 4 explores how existentialism insists that we must face up to the responsibility for our own self projects as well as regarding the resultant anxiety as potentially emancipatory but much of the identity theory discussed in this chapter sees such anxiety as evidence of a central problem: how do we know when we have achieved a 'successful' self, if not by comparison with the ideal models held up to us by the society we live in? It has been argued that such models are increasingly provided for us via a combination of the hyper-reality of consumerism and the mass media in terms of lifestyle choices (Eco 1987; Hancock and Tyler 2004) as well by the way in which we increasingly view ourselves through the lens of the psychological sciences, particularly in their popular forms (Rose 1999). This pull to conformity is undercut by the equal imperative to appear to be different, as a deeply felt aspect of modern selfhood is uniqueness, and it is no coincidence that 'uniqueness' is practically a synonym for the word 'individuality'.

We are, then, in the double bind of simultaneously trying to demonstrate to ourselves and others that we are unique but also desperately trying to be the same as the others we wish to claim an affinity with, in order to bolster a sense of ontological security (Giddens 1991; Cerulo 1997). Some have also argued that this desire leads us to define ourselves according to dominant discourses, and that the discourse of enterprise in capitalist societies has, as a result, become the predominant model of identity in our times (du Gay, Salaman and Rees 1996). For the narrators of the stories in Chapter 2, all of whom are pursuing careers in management, the influence of the entrepreneurial self might be thought to be particularly prevalent. The 300 or so books on enterprise in my own university's library attests to Alvesson and Willmott's (2002) observation that such a discourse is deployed in a deliberate attempt to regulate the identities of managers for organisational ends.

Before moving on to explore some of the implications raised by these initial thoughts concerning identity, I need to draw some further distinctions using my two dualities between what I have already referred to as a humanist position on identity and contrast this with a poststructuralist critique of humanism, a critique that has been very influential in how organisational theory has viewed work and managerial identities (Hassard and Parker 1993). I begin, therefore, with an explanation of the assumptions of humanism and its relation to the Christian world-view it was seeking to escape but that it only partially succeeded in transcending.

The Self of Humanism

One of the themes of this book, developed in detail in Chapter 5, is that the way we view our 'self' is fundamentally historical and that this gives rise to the survival of some surprising influences. Despite the virtual disappearance of religious belief from the everyday lives and thoughts of many of us, the religious conception of the self within Western thought is tenacious; particularly the idea of an antecedent core to the self that accompanies the concept of the soul and so deserves some attention. Within Christianity (and also within some other religious belief systems) the idea of an essential humanity and corresponding foundational identity is relatively unproblematic because our inner nature is stamped with God's image (albeit corrupted by sin). Thus the life project for the pious is the uncovering and purification of our souls through faith and the living of a life in accordance with the teachings of the church. This project was a preparatory one which looked forward to the revelation of one's true nature following the final sacrament of death. The Reformation individualised this life-project by rejecting the mediating role of the church. Instead, an individual relationship between the creator and the devout was developed through prayer, worship and the study of the scriptures in the vernacular (Dickens 1967; Anthony 1977).

The rejection of the supernatural aspects of religious belief by later materialist humanism, however, did not lead to the complete abandonment of how selfhood was viewed. The idea of the soul as the essential, universal and inner nature of mankind was modified rather than completely rejected, as was the idea that life is essentially a progressive development of becoming one's true self. Descartes, for example, retained the idea of the soul (Ricoeur 1992) and, more surprisingly, so did Foucault who writes 'it would be wrong to say that the soul is an illusion or an ideological effect. On the contrary, it exists, it has a reality, it is produced permanently around, on, within the body by the functioning of a power' (cited in the preface of Rose 1999). Thus within the humanist tradition the idea of a universal human nature was retained as was the teleological project of the self. As Rose notes

> It was Christianity that furnished this juridical and political personality with an internal existence in the form of conscience, and a universality, through the relationship posited between each human and their God. The Christian soul unified body and soul, consciousness and act, culminating in the Protestant identification of person, soul, self and consciousness. (1999, 221–22).

The humanistic self likewise must be allowed to express itself in each individual but through the exercise of autonomy and rationality, freed not from sin but from ignorance and superstition. Rather than all arriving at the same destination, the presence of God, the autonomous self is free to define its own desires and objectives, thus the trajectory of the individual is an act of self-creation as we each struggle to fulfil our potential as unique human beings (Kumar 1987; Sarup 1996).

Freed from its subordinate status as created being, Dunne argues that this humanist self, became seen as a 'sovereign' self exemplified in the work of Descartes and Hobbes. 'Descarte's "I" or "ego", which is immediately, transparently and irrefutably present to itself as a pure extensionless consciousness already established in being, without a body and with no acknowledged complicity in language, culture, or community' (1996, 138). This consciousness combines with 'Hobbe's notion of the self as a passionate centre of assertion – though one defined in the midst of, or rather over against, a plurality of other like centres' (1996, 138). The resulting concept is that 'the self is a citadel in which a lucid reason is at the service of a naked will' (1996, 138).

It might be argued that this rather heroic, protean self, able to change according to a self-conscious act of will, is not much in evidence in current work on identity. The shift away from autonomy founded upon reason is discernable in the thought of Marx and Freud, who both, in different ways, argue that there are severe limits to our capacity for rationality and free choice, whether these are caused by hegemonic ideologies leading to false consciousness or through the hidden effects of unconscious drives. Even here though the sovereign self is still retained as both an ideal and as a possibility, to be secured either by a collective transformation of the relations of production or perhaps by the therapist (Dunne 1996; Elliot 2001).

More recent versions of the humanist self have, therefore, heavily modified the extent to which individuals may create themselves. One very influential theory of self formation, that of *symbolic interactionism* is represented in the work of Mead, which exemplifies both the shift to a more intersubjective social self and the retention of the autonomous self. For Mead, the autonomous self is relocated within the social world of others (Elliot 2001). A detailed mechanism of self-formation is suggested that relies on the dialectic between social structure and individual agency mediated by our communication with others. Our understanding of ourselves results from a process of exploration into how others see us and this exploration is conducted through the medium of a socially and historically located language. Thus we insert ourselves into the norms and values of the culture in which we live. Mead, therefore, attempts to steer a middle way between determinism and autonomy via a multi-part self, drawing a distinction between 'me', the self that reflects the internalised attitudes of others, and the 'I' which is a more autonomous self, an independent bundle of needs and desires (Elliot 2001). Thus 'the self, in large part, is that aspect of mind directed toward itself, using the "internal dialogue" of mind to conceive, assess, criticise, praise, and motivate itself' (Weigert and Gecas 2003, 277) and it is this self that manages the process of identity formation, 'identity refers to typifications of self as "Me", of self defined by self or other, and often the focus of conflict, struggle and politics. Selves account for identities, not identities for selves' (Weigert and Gecas 2003, 268). The interaction of these two aspects of the self enables unpredictability and creativity to play a role in self formation and allows for individuality in our response to our social environment though Mead has been criticised as being over-cognitive with little recognition of the role of either the emotions or of embodiment (Knights and Willmott 1999).

This socially located, constrained, but still consciously self-fashioning self lives on in the currently most influential theory of humanistic identity, that of Giddens, who retains the idea of a dialectic between an autonomous, rational self and the constraints and opportunities presented by increasingly globalised social structures. Thus he seeks to identify

> The emergence of new mechanisms of self-identity which are shaped by – yet also shape – the institutions of modernity. The self is not a passive entity, determined by external influences; in forging their self-identities, no matter how local their specific contexts of action, individuals contribute to and directly promote social influences that are global in their consequences and implications (1991, 2).

Giddens explores the processes by which this dialectic between a conscious choosing self interacts with social structure, which he describes as a 'reflexive project of the self':'which consists in the sustaining of coherent, yet continuously revised, biographical narratives' (Giddens 1991, 5) taking place in

> The context of multiple choice as filtered through abstract systems. In modern social life, the notion of lifestyle takes on a particular significance. The more tradition loses its hold, and the more daily life is reconstituted in terms of the dialectical interplay of the local and the global, the more individuals are forced to negotiate lifestyle choices among a variety of options....Reflexively organised life-planning, which normally presumes consideration of risks as filtered through contact with expert knowledge, becomes a central feature of the structuring of self-identity' (1991, 5).

To summarise the account of identity thus far, within the humanist tradition we have the development of an essentially inside-out view of identity. In earlier accounts, our true nature can transcend the restrictions of our circumstances by the conscious effort of our wills. Even in later accounts the coherent unitary self is retained, able to stand outside the social, at least to some extent, in order to reflexively act upon itself, others and social structures. In addition the teleological self is retained from Christianity in the form of a biographical coherence of a developing self project over time. It is to the challenge to this notion of a coherent unitary self posed by poststructuralist theory that I now turn.

The Shattered Cogito[1]

The relatively optimistic vision of the autonomous individual constructing a stable and fulfilled self has been comprehensively challenged in recent times. Ricoeur (1992) traces this challenge to the Cartesian humanist self to the work of Nietzsche,

---

1 Ricoeur (1992, 11).

who sees our sense of an internal self as being as illusory as the idea of external objective fact, rather both self and world are the sum of our interpretations of them.

The loss of confidence in the idea of a self that is inserted into the social and yet remains in some sense autonomous of it has been accompanied by a sense that modernity is in the process of dissolving any possibility of secure selfhood. Many now talk of a crisis of identity, whether it be due to the corrosion of character (Sennett 1998), the narcissistic self (Lasch 1980), or the disciplined normalised subject (Foucault 1977). Such views tend to see the current obsessive pursuit of individuality as self-defeating and self-oppressing (Knights and Willmott 1999). Even more pessimistically modern or postmodern identity can be seen as an ideological snare by which we enslave ourselves to newer and more insidious forms of control (Hancock and Tyler 2004). The most influential of these more pessimistic theoretical frameworks concerning how managerial identity is understood has largely been derived from a particular reading of Foucault, which I will now go on to discuss in more detail. In terms of my inside/outside dualism, this is a position that regards identity as largely an effect of external circumstances acting upon malleable human material with a very limited role for the autonomy of individuals in fashioning their sense of who they are.

Foucault takes issue with every aspect of the humanist model of identity outlined above (Cousins and Hussain 1984), although he moved from a more determinist position in his early work to one that appeared to allow more room for individual agency in his later work (Sarup 1996; Hall 2000; Hodgson 2000). According to Sarup, for example, Foucault 'thinks that the individual is not a pre-given entity which is seized on by the exercise of power; the individual with his or her identity and characteristics is the product of a relation of powers exercised over bodies' (1996, 69). The vocabulary of Foucauldianism emphasises the limited role of agency and consciousness in identity formation. Thus one might write of 'inscription' rather than 'interpretation' and of the 'subject' rather than the self to signal that the 'I' is a production of external influences rather than an active mediating individual: 'The subject is produced "as an effect" through and within discourse, within specific discursive formations, and has no existence, and certainly no transcendental continuity or identity from one subject position to another' (Hall 2000, 23). Thus without an overarching 'I' to integrate experience we can no longer talk of an 'identity' or self but a multiplication of identities that change and clash as the body is subject to different discourses and social practices (Dunne 1996). We are then left with 'only a minimal, weak or thin conception of the human material on which history writes' (Rose 2000, 321).

The idea of 'discourse' is a key one in the Foucauldian conception of identity formation, but is also a rather elusive one. It certainly includes what actually happens to people in the routine everyday settings of their lives otherwise known as 'institutionalised practices', as well as what is spoken, written or communicated through language (Sarup 1996). However, this is rather a broad concept, and prompts Armstrong (2001) to claim that it is impossible to pin down or verify its effects empirically, thus casting its validity as an analytical category into doubt. It also provokes Hodgson into asking 'Is everything discourse?' (2000, 59). His response to this question is an attempt to tie down the concept of discourse by defining it as 'a socially and historically specific system of assumptions, values and beliefs which materially affects social conduct and social structure.' (2000, 59). This definition once more raises the suspicion of circular self-referentiality noted by Armstrong (2001). If the operation of discourse can only be detected by its ability to materially affect social practices then the claim that discourse determines such practices is less striking than its rhetorical deployment might suggest; a problem that all deterministic or functionalist social theories tend to share.

These problems aside, what is being claimed is that identity is not something that goes very deep within us because, to return to Rose's (2000) quote above, there is not much depth to start with. It is assumed that performance and utterance add up to what people are, and that this is highly malleable, the individual is thus reduced to the puppet of discourse. This raises an additional issue to do with the 'autonomy-determinism' duality as it is not so easy philosophically to abandon the category of autonomy from a consideration of human behaviour. Removing it from human beings seems to require that it re-appears as a feature of discourse, as it is discourse which now seems to take on a life of its own and have the ability to make things happen, and discourse seems to develop, if not independently of social and historical circumstance, at least to chronically escape the intentions of any original purpose associated with it.

Following on from the previous point there are a number of further problems, recognised by Foucault himself in his later work (Cousins and Hussain 1984). Firstly, without any theorisation of agency and the individual interpretation of discourse, there is no basis for an explanation of the heterogeneity of individual responses to discourse, including its explicitly articulated repudiation (Hall 2000; Hodgson 2000; McNay 2000). One response to this problem has been to argue that even resistance to, or consciously articulated rejection of, a discourse is further evidence of the operation of the discourse (Sarup 1996; Rose 2000), a position that provokes Armstrong (2001) into arguing that this is a self-referential claim that cannot be either verified or disproved by human experience and so is no more than speculation. In addition, I would argue that the richness and variability of our everyday experiences of human behaviour strongly suggest that human beings respond in a more active and creative way than some of the very deterministic readings of poststructuralist identity theory allow for.

One explanation for such variations is argued to be an effect of the infinite variety of discourses as they struggle for dominance within each individual, although how one could either confirm or disconfirm that this is the case is again a moot point. For some this passive subject pose ethical difficulties; any intervention in the lives of others may be reduced to no more than the assertion of one individual's will against the other, both acting as media for the play of discourse, leading Fraser (1989) to conclude that the poststructuralist view of identity sees human relations as a form of intersubjective violence, a view of competitive identity that Sartre amongst others subscribes to (Sartre 1943/1957; Schroeder 1984; Kearney 1994) Others, however, conclude that it is a liberation to be freed from such ethics, echoing the Nietzschean rejection of the morality of care and responsibility as a 'slave morality' (Benhabib 1992, 194).

Foucault's own response to these issues was to theorise a more active subject in his later work via an analysis of the way in which individuals participate in their own subjugation to discourse through the process of self-reflection (Sarup 1996). In *The Use of Pleasure* (1985), Foucault suggests that this more active self-reflecting subject offers some possibility of emancipation through the aesthetics of self-fashioning. In Eagleton's words 'To live well is to transfigure oneself into a work of art by an intensive process of self-discipline' (1990, cited in Sarup 1996, 91). One should be careful, however, not to interpret this as a near-death recantation of Foucault's previous views as 'the autonomous individual that emerges in Foucault's book is a matter of surface, art, technique or sensation' (Sarup 1996, 91).

This more active self has been the focus for something of a reconsideration of more deterministic readings of Foucault within organisation studies in recent years (see Chan 2000; Chan and Garrick 2002; Starkey and Hatchuel 2002; Barratt 2003; Knights 2004; Linstead 2004, for examples). Barratt (2003) amongst others notes that Foucauldian organization theory has been criticised for determinism and fatalism resulting from an abandonment of agency which in turn provides an inadequate basis for political and ethical praxis and calls for a re-reading of Foucault that places more emphasis on his later writing.

Starkey and Hatchuel likewise bemoan the neglect of Foucault's later work, a key concern of which is 'to show people that they are freer than they feel and than he himself previously thought' (2002, 642). Chan and Garrick argue that more attention should be paid to ethical postmodernism where, far from a passively determined subject, one is presented with 'an embodiment of a free and truth-seeking individual ... the liberal, creatively self-representing individual engages in the present to interrogate assumptions and to seek those practices that offer the possibility of inventing ourselves in what we are becoming.' (2002, 693).

It appears then, that an entirely deterministic and passive view of the self is difficult to maintain but that there may nevertheless be severe constraints on the autonomy of individuals to define themselves. The poststructuralist critique of humanism may be regarded as a corrective impulse to its over-optimism; it requires that much closer attention is paid to how and in what circumstances autonomy might be possible and why it is so often abandoned in favour of conformity. What, in any case, would constitute autonomy or freedom?

Foucault's later move towards a more active subject still leaves such questions to be answered as well as presenting other problems. Hodgson (2000) points out that with the return of even a 'thin' conception of agency that can oversee the process of discourse assimilation and performance; we are back to the self-aware individual who exists outside of the discourses that are meant to produce self-identity in the first place. This problem is further elaborated by Craib (1998) who criticises the poststructuralist insistence on there being only multiple and fractured identities, arguing that the idea of multiple identities still requires an identifiable individual in whom such multiple identities can be said to exist and that it would therefore be more accurate to speak of 'roles' rather than 'identity'. This is another debate built around a different conception of the inside-out dualism. For Craib identity is distinguished from role by the assumption that identity is an internal biographical continuity into which different aspects of identity such as role and performance may struggle and conflict but all refer to the story of a single 'deep' individual within which there is a 'dialectic of unity and diversity' (1998, 5); in other words the way in which we come to be ourselves and that we are aware of this remains, in many ways, mysterious. The idea of individuality, of being unique selves, arising from the development of Western Christianity, appears to have a tenacious grip on how we see ourselves and has survived the most determined attempts to weaken its hold upon us.

To briefly summarise the terms of this debate thus far, I have presented a polarisation between identity conceived of as a coherent unity under the control of a reflexive individual, albeit in constrained circumstances, or as a multiplicity of surface performances produced as a power effect of discourse with very little room for escaping and transcending this external determination. Though, as the reconsideration of Foucauldian theory within organisation studies demonstrates, there may be many intermediate positions which place differing degrees of emphasis on inside/outside, surface/depth and determinism/autonomy dimensions of selfhood. In the next section I shall begin my attempt to transcend such dualities, examining them in the light of how human beings experience themselves, particularly in relation to their own mortality. This provides a bridge between the identity theory presented here and the development of a narrative conception of identity based on the existentialist theory presented in Chapter 4.

Death and Identity

In considering death I make my first move towards presenting identity in biographical terms, as a narrative of self that develops over time. It also acts as a link with Heidegger's notion of authenticity that I discuss in the next chapter. There is, however, a tradition within sociological writing that argues that considering death tells us a great deal about life. Craib, for example, argues that our embodiment is an essential aspect of our experience, and furthermore that 'the real scandal of being embodied, one which arguably is a governing feature of all our lives, is that our embodiment comes to an end. We die, and the sociology of death should be the sociology of our lives' (1998, 10). For Bauman the knowledge of our own mortality is the main driving force behind all cultural institutions and personal endeavours. 'It is because we know that we must die that we are so busy making life. It is because we are aware of our mortality that we preserve the past and create the future' (1992, 7). For Giddens (1991), the pursuit of ontological security within routines, institutions and abstract systems is driven by a wish to avoid reflection on death, and for Willmott (2000), the resulting effacement of death prevents its proper consideration in the understanding of human conduct. Mellor also argues that 'the consideration of death is at the heart of the sociological enterprise' (1993, 4). Seale states that 'an understanding of mortality is fundamental for an adequate theory of social life' (1998, 11). However, despite these highly plausible exhortations to reflect on our mortality, there is little within the literature on identity which does so.

So what is it that makes us so reluctant to explore the significance of death? After all as Bauman notes, 'I will not be there when it will have come, I will not experience it when it comes and I most certainly do not experience it now, before its coming – so why should I worry, and why should I worry now?' (1992, 3). This rational defence against the horror of death has a long tradition. Rees notes that the followers of Epicurus in the fifth century BC had the phrase 'I was not – I have been – I am not – I do not mind' (2001, 19) inscribed on their tombs. Bauman goes on to say that, despite this rational knowledge that death has no sting (for after all our non-existence before our birth is no different) we do still fear death and seek to avoid our awareness of it. This is partly because our reason knows of death but cannot fathom its nature. 'Death is the ultimate defeat of reason, since reason cannot "think" death ... The horror of death is the horror of the void, of the ultimate absence, of "non-being"' (1992, 13). In addition, 'death is the cessation of the very "acting subject", and with it *the end* of all perception' [italics in the original] (1992, 13). Thus death is to be feared because of the loss of self-awareness and reason, our sense of consciousness of the world around us and the loss of agency or the ability to act. All of which are the very issues that are central to the debates on identity outlined above and by implication, at the core of our selves. Looking forward to the next chapter, these also amount to the loss of all that makes us human beings, according to existentialist theory.

That we repress the knowledge of our own mortality is common to both Freudian theory (Freud 1915/2005; Freud 1917/2005; Freud 1920/2003; Carel 2005; Carr and Lapp 2006) and to existentialist theory (Heidegger 1926/1962; Sartre 1943/1957). In addition career based identities can be seen as a highly significant instance of this repression (Lapierre 1989; Sievers 1994). Career based identities represent the modern tendency to see the self as a progressive and private project of development with their implicit promise that we simply go on learning and developing for ever. The maintenance of such typically contemporary identities requires the avoidance of reflection on death and so its sequestration (Giddens 1991).

As a result, dying and declining individuals are hidden away in nursing homes and hospitals and the process is smoothly managed by professionals such as doctors, nurses, priests and undertakers. As with identity itself, death has been taken from the public, communal sphere and privatised as an event that only affects the dying and their immediate circle of family and close friends (Clark 1993; Mellor 1993). Littlewood (1993) has suggested that this goes beyond a distaste for the fact of death and echoes Clark who argues that 'the general attitude of western societies towards death is characterised by fear and shame' (1993, 69). This shame is rooted in a sense of personal failure to exhibit the characteristics of the sufficient, independent and autonomous self. Thus, through this sequestration, we protect ourselves against the awareness of our own mortality which is 'particularly disturbing because it signals a threatened "irreality" of the self-project which modernity encourages individuals to embark upon, an ultimate absence of meaning, the presence of death bringing home to them the existential isolation of the individual in high modernity' (1993, 20). Thus death must be hidden if we are to maintain our ontological security (Mellor 1993; Willmott 2000), as an awareness of it threatens to make our lives seem meaningless and futile. However, there is a paradox here, because this same awareness gives our lives a sense of urgency and purpose as long as our heroic denial of mortality fends off the despair of knowing that death will eventually end all our projects (Bauman 1992; Seale 1998).

Despite our usually successful efforts to ensure that death be concealed, smoothed over, medicalised and routinised, in the end it cannot be avoided as a part of our experience. Eventually almost all of us become part of the inner circle of friends and relatives who lose someone they are close to, and all of us live with the knowledge of our own approaching death. Even here, though, there is a tendency to attempt to avoid its contemplation and its unsettling effects for our self-identities, with close family members being increasingly absent as we approach our deaths leading to 'a tendency for all persons now to die in situations of unparalleled isolation' (Mellor 1993, 21). Thus many sociologists of death draw a distinction between biological death and social death, when 'people no longer seek to communicate with that person nor take that person directly into account in carrying out their own actions' (Mulkay 1993, 55). Social death can both precede biological death and occur after it as the living continue to maintain a relationship with the dead, as if they are still present. What does this assemblage of observations about our response to our own mortality contribute towards our understanding of identity?

Firstly, the knowledge of our approaching non-existence highlights the extraordinary mystery of our current experience as living individuals, the profundity of which is simply not captured by the main currents of the sociological theory of identity (Craib 1976). It raises questions such as 'Why should I be 'me', rather than someone else?', 'How did I come to be here and now rather than somewhere else at some other time?' Although, to echo poststructuralist thinking, our existence seems accidental and arbitrary, a coincidence that this consciousness should occupy this body and that I should know this, it still happens to be a coincidence of extraordinary fatefulness for us as individuals (Bauman 1992). This sense of the profundity of individual existence and the significance of death as its termination, at least in its familiar embodied, in-the-world form, appears to be extremely widespread, getting as close to a universal human experience as seems possible for 'The universal, supra-historical and supra-cultural presence of funeral rites and ritualised commemoration of the dead has been one of the earliest and most striking discoveries of comparative ethnography' (1992, 51). The issues that Bauman raises here are the very ones that provide the jumping off point for Heidegger's (1926/1962) enquiry, discussed in more detail in the next chapter, into the nature of existence, one of whose conclusions is that we should reflect steadfastly on the fact of our own oblivion instead of avoiding it.

Other features of our experience of dying also suggest that the positions on identity discussed earlier do not always manage to capture the variety, richness and significance of embodied experience. They also do not appear to interrogate existence with the theoretical rigour that I believe the philosophy drawn upon in the next chapter does. For example, the aged and dying body appears to be becalmed outside the main currents of modern disciplinary discursive formations. One can distinguish here between an outer and an inner body, the inner body denoting how we perceive ourselves to be, for example, despite much evidence to the contrary, I may feel myself still to be a twenty-year-old. Our outer body is our appearance to others and is formed by their interpretation of us, an interpretation frequently mediated by ascriptions of dominant forms of identity (rapidly declining, middle-aged man, in my case). Thus there is a tension between the production of self via the exterior bodily form and the experience of the self via embodiment (Hallam; Hockey and Howarth 1999). In addition, the link that Giddens (1991) makes, amongst others, between identity and the physical cultivation of the body breaks down at the approach of death, as both the high level of reflexive agency and the ability of our bodies to respond to such cultivation declines. Poststructuralist accounts which link the body and identity as both interrelated products of discourse are inadequate in the face of death, because 'they give little space to the grounded, sensual experience of inhabiting a body. This limitation becomes particularly evident when bodies which are old and frail are the focus' (Hallam; Hockey and Howarth 1999, 7). This is not to suggest that poststructuralism fails to recognise material limits but it does suggest that some modification to the notion of the autonomy and power of discourse is required.

Secondly, the futility of building our identities around consumption, appearance, status and stable, predictable, institutionalised routines is unavoidable when one confronts death. This has two related effects; it reframes identity projects as being grounded in ethics rather than simply in the pursuit of pleasure or security because it stimulates our assessment of ourselves in terms of the good or evil that we accomplish and will one day leave behind. How do we decide what we would like to be, as managers, educators, sons, daughters, parents, friends and citizens? It may be that such decisions are partly based on how we would like to be remembered. In other words the fact of our deaths again pulls us back to the fashioning of ourselves as an existential quest, the ethical dimensions of which are a central concern of Ricoeur, as I discuss in Chapter 6. The second effect is a potentially emancipatory one: death reminds us that lives spent in the cultivation of our outer bodies and the avoidance of bodily decay and damage are ultimately doomed, they are simply rearguard actions in our long retreat towards a final defeat. This being so, a consideration of death may free us from the allure of many characteristic discourses of a consumerist postmodernity, including that of the career, and thus suggest one way in which disciplinary norms may be resisted, indeed the enduring phrase 'you can't take it with you' is used in conversation precisely to remind others of the futility of acquisitiveness (Mellor 1993; Willmott 2000).

Finally, many have been prompted by a reflection on death to reconsider the highly individualised model of identity formation apparent in poststructuralism and move towards a more intersubjective view. For one of the characteristics of life that enables us to know that we are not dead, and that life is worth carrying on with, is our engagement with others. 'The uppermost value which makes my life worth living; the very sense of being alive: life is communicating with others, being with others, acting for others and being addressed, wanted, lifted into importance by the need of others and by the bid they make for my attention and sympathy' (Bauman 1992, 37).

The re-framing of identity as a life project undertaken in the face of the fact of death has led some sociologists to look to thinkers such as Ricoeur, rather than to Foucault, for an alternative theory of identity as actively constructed through the telling and re-telling of biography, both drawing upon and re-interpreting the discursive formations which provide linguistic resources and constraints (Hallam; Hockey and Howarth 1999). According to this reading of subjectivity, a consideration of death and dying suggests that identity is produced through 'interpersonal engagement via a conversational form within a world constituted by existential concerns' (Hallam; Hockey and Howarth 1999, 7). Thus subjectivity is intersubjective 'constituted within the existential spaces which link and divide us from one another' (1999, 7–8). Unlike some accounts of poststructuralism and symbolic interactionism, there is more than language to our experience, and death and decline suggest that we may know our own bodily experience independently of it. Seale comes to a similar conclusion via his empirical work with those in chronic pain, which more than most experiences threatens any sense of life as meaningful and worthwhile. Even here though, actors employ a 'narrative reconstruction of biography and self-identity, so that a sense of meaning and purpose in life is restored' (1998, 26).

Beyond the Limits

The analysis of identity in this chapter has suggested that there are two dominant viewpoints within the social sciences in general as well as the sociology of organisations and work in particular. There is firstly a humanistic view, currently most influentially represented by Giddens's writing, which is usually placed *against* a poststructuralist viewpoint, most commonly associated with the work of Foucault. The similarities of these approaches have been noted: the most significant of which are that the self has become an individualised responsibility or burden and the pursuit of a satisfactory sense of self has become one of the overriding concerns of individuals in late or postmodernity. For Giddensians, there is no necessary problem with such a pursuit. For some Foucauldians, this pursuit is the route to self-subjugation to socially dominant norms and discourses. The former approach privileges the ability of individuals to make choices and act upon them, contributing to the structural development of society as they do so. The latter approach privileges the arbitrary and inescapable determination of the individual by discourse, allowing little room for agency.

Weaknesses, some shared and some applying to one approach rather than the other, become apparent when placed against the complexity and richness of human experience, particularly the way we respond to the knowledge of our own mortality. The sociology of death suggests that there is more to be said about the relationship that exists between social structure, the formation of persons and the way we act upon and make sense of our worlds than is apparent from either of the two dominant approaches. Questions arise about the location of lives in historical time, the boundary between others and selves, possibility and choice, the role of biographical self-narration and the ethics of what constitutes a 'good' or authentic identity. In this chapter I have sought to delineate these debates concerning identity and used the sociology of death to evaluate the contribution they might make to an understanding of the narratives presented in this book. My main conclusion is that it is possible to move beyond the limits imposed by the two approaches highlighted in this chapter and that this is necessary both for the reasons discussed in Chapter 4 and because of my conviction that the stories told to me by my respondents call for a different sort of response, a response that includes a recognition of a shared struggle to construct a life against the certain knowledge of our own mortality.

Chapter 4
Narrative Identity and the Existentialist Quest

In Chapter 3 I presented a debate between what I termed a humanist view of identity and a view of identity associated with poststructuralism, particularly the poststructuralism of Foucault. I did this because, as I have already argued, these tend to be the predominant influences on identity theory commonly found within organisational studies and so of most relevance to understanding the life stories of managers.

I went on in Chapter 3 to attempt to go beyond the usual terms of this debate in order to open up some critical space. I did this because, whilst the poststructuralist critique of the rational, reflexive and self-constructing 'sovereign self' (Dunne 1996, 18), posited by influential humanist positions such as that of Giddens (1991) is persuasive, it also has limitations with respect to my own intentions for the narratives found earlier in this book in Chapter 2. I am largely persuaded by poststructuralism's critique of humanism's over-optimistic view of identity in late modernity but am reluctant to follow the more deterministic and pessimistic reading of Foucault that has sometimes dominated recent identity theory. Following Ricoeur, I wish to escape the polarised positions of 'exalted subject, humiliated subject' (1992, 16) and to move beyond this in order be able to answer the question 'Who is speaking?' (1992, 16). With this in mind, I moved on to try to destabilise the restricted nature of this polarisation by a consideration of the sociology of death, as this seemed to me to illustrate the particular problems of accepting an entirely negative and deterministic view of identity (McNay 2000). The sociology of death also points towards an alternative conception of what the self is and how it is constructed in its invocation of narrative, an alternative way of formulating the trajectory of the self, to borrow Gidden's phrase (1991). In addition, this analysis moved towards viewing the stories in Chapter 2 as accounts of 'acting and suffering' (Ricoeur 1992, 18) individuals, and this is where Chapter 2 finished.

In this chapter I pick up these nascent themes and begin to give them a more rigorous theoretical framework by a consideration of a self that is suggested by what I have termed 'existentialism' as represented in the work of Heidegger, Sartre and Ricoeur. It is perhaps more precise to refer to this work as phenomenology and existentialism (Kearney 1994) but, for convenience, I have truncated this to a term most often associated with Sartre. Despite the fact that Heidegger objected to being considered an existentialist, his work provided a jumping off point for Sartre's *Being and Nothingness* (Vogel 1994) and his central project of illuminating the nature of Being (or existence) would seem to mandate the use of the term in his case. Ricoeur's work falls less easily into such a classification and so I would not attempt to claim that he somehow forms part of an identifiable existentialist tradition. He does draw, however, on Heidegger's phenomenology of existence in attempting to denote the acting and suffering individual and in establishing the epistemology and ontology of selfhood. It is in this sense that I refer to the 'existentialist' aspects of all three thinkers in this chapter and elsewhere in the book where I use this term.

By considering the work of all three thinkers, I hope to show that, whilst not reducing the differences between views of personal identity based on humanism or poststructuralism to a simplistic amalgam, many of the insights of both can be integrated within a view of the self where choice is a possibility but determinism a probability. The systematic working through of the implications of finitude and death for the self, particularly by Heidegger, develops the ideas introduced in the last chapter and suggests that choice is always possible though always accompanied by anxiety.

There are other reasons for wanting to revive this rather unfashionable philosophical tradition, which I hope will become more persuasive as I discuss them below, but can be summarised here as part of my general introduction to the chapter. Firstly, existentialism has been described as being 'rigorously rooted in everyday experience' (Craib 1976, 20). Thus Heidegger writes that we can only understand the nature of human existence 'if we take as our clue our everyday Being-in-the-world, which we also call our "dealings" in the world' (1926/1962, 95). This attempt to understand who we are by a detailed analysis of everyday life is a major aim of this book and motivates my empirical analysis in Chapters 5 and 6. The categories of analysis that are shared by existentialist thinkers, and that are relevant to my own concerns, include: the nature of existence; the question of being; the working of consciousness; our relationship with others; the transcendence of environmental constraints; choice, freedom, possibility and action; and the quest for an authentic and secure self. Again these issues seem to resonate strongly with the themes that suggest themselves in the accounts my interviewees gave of themselves. In addition, these are the very issues that are contested or neglected within the debates presented in Chapter 3.

As mentioned above, a central theme in existentialist analysis is the significance of temporality as an essential aspect of being human and in particular our understanding of our own finitude. Thus death, which my previous discussion suggests poses significant questions for the bipolar debate, is integrated into a conception of identity that can also accommodate (or at least hold in creative tension) both the danger of lapsing into inauthentic self-determination by the 'they' (Heidegger 1926/1962; Sartre 1943/1957) but also the possibility, and in Sartre's view (1943/1957) the inescapable necessity, of transcending such determinations through a steadfast conscious pursuit of an authentic self, a pursuit that, according to Ricoeur, is mediated through the construction of intersubjective narratives (Kearney 1996b). Thus there is the strong suggestion of both an existential quest for an authentic self and of the existentialist hero who fashions themselves through a narrative that is enacted throughout their life in the world and with others. The resonance of this conception with my reading of the life stories in Chapter 2 is, I argue, striking, as is the promise of a fruitful way of incorporating some of the insights from both sides of the bipolar debate into a view of the self that allows for both coherence and fragmentation, choice and determinism, multiple identities and an enduring continuity of selfhood over a lifetime.

So, the twin aims of this chapter are, firstly, to extend and further interrogate the debate on identity already presented in order to arrive at a conception of the self that enables me to make sense of the narratives in Chapter 2. The narrative self also accords with my conviction that a more empathetic understanding of managerial identity in the context of whole lives is required. Secondly, I wish to ground the interpretations of the narratives in a rigorous theoretical framework. How successful this attempt is, and what its implications are for the framing of managerial identity and attempts to change it, are finally evaluated in the concluding chapter. Having already carelessly bandied about all sorts of existentialist terminology in this introduction, I next need to present a more systematic account of my reading of existentialism and the contribution to an understanding of identity that such a reading can make. I shall begin with an account of the relevant work from Heidegger, Sartre and Ricoeur. Following which, I will discuss the implications of this work for my understanding of managerial identity and provide some justification for the underlying ontology of my interpretative framework in Chapters 5 and 6.

Heidegger

As this account must of necessity be very selective, I shall restrict my treatment of Heidegger to his most well-known work *Being and Time*, published in 1926. Heidegger's main concern is the question of 'Being', a question that he argues has been disregarded throughout the development of philosophy but one that is central to Heidegger's project, the exploration of the mystery that 'there are beings rather than nothing, that things are and we ourselves are in their midst, that we ourselves are and yet barely know who we are, and barely know that we do not know all this' (Heidegger cited in Polt 1999, 1). The only way to provide an understanding of this question of questions is to access the nature of Being through a rigorous reflexive analysis of our own Being or *Dasein* as Heidegger terms it. 'Thus to work out the question of Being adequately, we must make an entity – the inquirer – transparent in his own Being ... This entity which each of us is himself ... we shall denote by the term "Dasein"' (Heidegger 1926/1962, 27). In other words, 'Human life, in all its concrete individuality and historical situatedness, is the origin of theoretical truth' (Polt 1999, 17). The link between Being and 'Dasein', Human Being, is instructive because it is only for Dasein that its existence is an issue for itself. In other words, although understanding selfhood is not the primary aim of Heidegger's investigation, it is an essential step towards understanding the nature of Being in general.

To begin there are two central themes to Heidegger's work of direct relevance to the view of personal identity being developed in this chapter. The first, as the title of Heidegger's book indicates, is the location of human beings in time, within a life that has a beginning, middle and end. An understanding of this temporality is essential in order to understand ourselves (Kearney 1994). 'Time must be brought to light – and genuinely conceived – as the horizon for all understanding of Being and for any way of interpreting it' (Heidegger 1926/1962, 39). Human existence is played out over the timescale of a lifetime and is inserted within the larger timescale of history.

Secondly, Heidegger insists that an essential part of our humanity is that we are responsible for ourselves. Our acceptance and consciousness of this responsibility, an attitude of being accountable for who we are, is at the root of the authentic individual according to Heidegger. Some have argued (Levinas, for example) that Heidegger over-individualises selfhood though others insist that this interpretation of his work is a result of Sartre's influence which 'gives the impression that the authentically free individual is a solitary private hero who makes his own decisions without regard for the demands of a larger public order' (Vogel 1994, 8). Indeed this solitary existentialist hero is fully realised in Sartre's novels (Craib 1976; Schroeder 1984). It is possible, however, to derive from Heidegger an ethics of selfhood based on his concept of *Mitsein* or being-with (Vogel 1994; Olafson 1998). For example, even where Heidegger writes of the individual existentialist virtue of 'resoluteness', he does so in the context of relations to others, their freedom to be authentic themselves: 'Dasein's resoluteness towards itself is what first makes it possible to let the Others who are with it 'be' in their ownmost potentiality-for-Being, and to co-disclose this potentiality in the solicitude which leaps forth and liberates' (Heidegger 1926/1962, 344).

When the temporality of the self is combined with our ability, indeed our responsibility, to make choices we arrive at Heidegger's theory of how the self emerges over a lifetime. We become ourselves through intentional acts 'because, from a phenomenological standpoint, there is no essential self or given *cogito* before there are intentional acts (of our concrete lived existence) which constitute the 'self' as a meaning project' (Kearney 1994, 32). Our future always offers us possibilities, though ones constrained by our pasts, that we must decide what to do with. By choosing and accumulating experiences we become ourselves. This gives rise to Heidegger's famous paradox 'that we cannot be reduced to what we actually are at any given moment – our present characteristics. I am not just what I am – I am who I am not' (Polt 1999, 69) and again 'Dasein does not merely have a past but lives its past, it exists in the terms that its past makes available for it' (Mulhall 1996, 20).

The throwing up of possibilities into our present by our futures presents us with continual choices which determine who we shall be, even though most of the time we choose not to choose.

> At every moment, I am following one possibility rather than a host of others – for instance, I go to the University today and teach my class, rather than joining the Army or shoplifting. Sometimes I choose carefully, but usually I just let myself fall into the most comfortable option. As I go on living, I build an identity. I become myself, I define myself as a professor, rather than a soldier or a criminal (Polt 1999, 34).

As we reflect on our choices, our pasts and our possibilities, so we gain an understanding of ourselves but this understanding is only possible by coming to an understanding of the world that we are in and the others we share it with. Thus our self is intersubjectively and instrumentally dependant upon and engaged in, our Being-in-the-world (Kearney 1994). This world is not a fixed reality, however, it is a world fashioned by the shared concerns of human beings, sedimenting as history and culture. Our world is thus historical through and through (Polt 1999). Heidegger describes our existence as being characterised by care or solicitude (1926/1962: 235–41). To understand ourselves and our identities is a project that is most meaningfully undertaken by rigorously describing our primordial engagement with the world in which we do things rather than by theorising *about* it. This essential engagement with the world suggests a self and its environment that interpenetrate each other to such an extent that the self cannot be reduced to the interior humanist *cogito* that can know itself through introspection in isolation from the world and others. It is also a self that departs from the discursively determined subject, in that choice is an essential feature of our humanity, even though such choices may be inauthentically repudiated, which is also a choice of sorts (Polt 1999).

Heidegger (1926/1962) explores his ideas on authenticity in relation to temporality in some detail in Division Two, Chapter One of *Being and Time*, through a discussion of the significance of death for Dasein. He starts with the notion that most of the time we avoid serious reflection on our choices; as such reflections are uncomfortable and generate anxiety. It is much easier just to be who others (the 'they') want us to be and so be spared the pain of working this out for ourselves. As argued in the previous chapter, our repression of the knowledge of our own mortality is perhaps the most significant example of our tendency to immerse ourselves in the everyday world and to thus avoid thinking about how we choose to live our lives. Although Heidegger also observes this tendency he argues that resolutely facing up to death has the potential to produce the sort of jarring anxiety that can make us acutely aware of these choices (Mulhall 1996; Polt 1999). It is through such repression that selfhood may be determined by the social and historical norms in the way associated with the idea of the passive subject as 'It is already a matter of public acceptance that 'thinking about death' is a cowardly fear, a sign of insecurity on the part of Dasein, and a sombre way of fleeing from the world. The 'they' does not permit us the courage for anxiety in the face of death' (Heidegger 1926/1962, 298). However, the certainty of our own deaths may be liberating as well as terrifying as it frees us from the pursuit of trivialities and forces us to come to terms with what our lives and our selves should be, freeing us from the 'they'. 'Death is Dasein's ownmost possibility. Being towards this possibility discloses to Dasein its ownmost potentiality-for-Being, in which its very Being is an issue. Here it can become manifest to Dasein that in this distinctive possibility of its own self, it has been wrenched away from the 'they' (Heidegger 1926/1962, 307).

As well as jolting us out of our unreflective absorption in everyday life, the fact of our deaths provides additional clues as to the centrality of temporality in the construction of a narrative of the self. As long as we are alive we have possibilities and so our existence can never be grasped as a whole: 'As long as Dasein *is* an entity, it has never reached its "wholeness" (Heidegger 1926/1962, 280). Until our deaths, we do not know whether our story should be considered as tragedy, epic or farce. In bringing choice to an end, death completes us. Death also confirms us in our uniqueness as individuals. Heidegger's odd phrase is that death is our 'ownmost possibility' (1926/1962, 307). I only can die my own death when my life ends, no-one can do this for me and, at the moment of my death, my life for the first time takes on its definite final shape (Polt 1999). The only authentic approach to death is to embrace the liberation its steadfast contemplation brings us from trivialities and make our choices of who we should be in the full knowledge of our finitude, indeed of the fact that every moment of our lives could be our last. The pressures to become who the 'they' would have us be are thus lessened, for death shows us that our lives are inalienably ours to do with what we will, even as our death is also our own.

Although the future is an open horizon of possibility bounded by death it is also constrained by the past. Our awareness of our mortality produces an anxiety that 'confronts Dasein with the knowledge that it is thrown into the world – always already delivered over to situations of choice and action which matter to it but which it did not itself fully choose or determine' (Mulhall 1996, 110). A striking instance of this is our births: Ricoeur notes that Heidegger's student, Hannah Arendt, observed that we never experience ourselves as being born, rather our entry into the world is experienced by us as already having happened, as *having already been* born, thus our earliest experience is of 'thrownness' (Ricoeur 1985).

Heidegger's concept of authenticity also has a temporal dimension, that of self-constancy. He writes of the call of conscience reminding us of the responsibility we have for our pasts and our need to be true to them even as we consider our futures (1926/1962, 313–48). Both resoluteness towards our future and constancy towards our past are essential Heideggerian virtues and are contrasted with our usual state of inauthentic unreflective absorption in the present. We pretend to ourselves that our choices are mandated by our present situation. The self-fashioning authentic individual contrasts strongly with the determined Foucauldian self apparent from Chapter 3 but one has an uneasy feeling that Heidegger's thinking on authenticity and resoluteness is only the sketchiest guide to how one should actually live one's life. In making resolute choice itself the prime ethical goal we are left with a vacuum when it comes to deciding what choices are good choices, although

Heidegger defends this on the basis that our existential choices cannot be limited by the rules of others. Heidegger's own choice to support National Socialism casts a long shadow on this moral relativism (Polt 1999) and some, most famously Wolin (1990), have argued that Heidegger's political choices were immanent in his philosophy though others, Zimmerman (1990) and Vogel (1994) for example, have sought to make a distinction between his thought and his unarguably disreputable conduct during the Nazi era in Germany.

This cautionary note aside, the authentic self that is emerging from these ideas does so in response to the world around us. We are active agents in its production according to how we make use of our pasts in making choices about our future. This is not a constant unchanging self, it is rather a dynamic self characterised by a conscious steadfastness towards our past, present and future. The process by which these choices are evaluated and accounted for suggests a narrative model of identity, as the sense we make of our past depends upon our projection of the future. For example, in deciding about a change of career, I may narrate stories to myself about my past that illuminate for me how to make a decision concerning what sort of job I would be good at and whether this will enable me to be the sort of person I wish to be. Thus, counter-intuitively, the future is a source of our narrated past. 'We might say that because of our historicity, our lives form *stories*, dramas that unfold from birth to death' (Polt 1999, 101, italics in the original). The source for such possible projects of the self 'is the heritage that I share with others in my community, the wealth of possible self-interpretations that my culture has accumulated over millennia' (Polt 1999, 101). In particular we work out these possibilities with our peers, within the particular historical and social circumstances shared with others of our own generation. Heidegger's authentic self has some affinity with the possibility of choice and self-fashioning in humanism but with Heidegger this is only achievable as a result of resolute and anxiety-ridden choices and so comes at a high price. His concept of the self differs from that of poststructuralism also, in that it allows for the possibility of choice but he would concur that the determination of the self from outside by the 'they' is the 'normal' state of human existence. This necessity for painful choice is also at the heart of Sartre's thought on the self to which I now turn though he has a much more pessimistic view on the relation of the self with the other.

Jean-Paul Sartre

Jean-Paul Sartre shares with Heidegger a phenomenological method put to work for a clarification of the ontology of existence. However Sartre is concerned with human existence *per se* rather than seeing our existence as a special case that allows access to a meta-theory of Being (Schroeder 1984; Kearney 1994). In the introduction to *Being and Nothingness*, 'The Pursuit of Being' (Sartre 1943/1957, xxi-xliii), he outlines his investigation, making his key initial distinction between two types of being 'in-itself' and 'for-itself' on which the rest of the book depends.

Sartre shares with Heidegger the conviction that we cannot escape the imperative to recognise our own existence and to fashion ourselves through choices: 'To be authentic is to embrace our existence as an open-ended field of multiple possibilities of self-identity from which we choose' (Kearney 1994, 54). Again, this is not to say that we are utterly free of environmental constraints, rather we always have a choice as to how to respond to them.

According to Sartre, this freedom to choose is not a blessing but a curse.

> Thus we are perpetually engaged in our choice and perpetually conscious of the fact that we ourselves can abruptly invert this choice and 'reverse stream'; for we project the future by our very being, but our existential freedom perpetually eats it away as we make known to ourselves what we are by means of the future ...Thus we are perpetually threatened by the nihilation of our actual choice and perpetually threatened with choosing ourselves (1943/1957, 465).

The result of recognising our freedom is 'anguish', which results from our consciousness that possibility is always *our* possibility and so no objective criteria can reassure us that our choices are good choices (Kearney 1994), we are also always fearful of who we will become as a result of our choices. In Sartre's words: 'I have to realise the meaning of the world and of my essence; I make my decision concerning them – without justification and without excuse' (1943/1957, 39). In addition:

> Anguish in fact is the recognition of a possibility as my possibility; that is, it is constituted when consciousness sees itself cut from its essence by nothingness or separated from the future by its very freedom. This means that a nihilating nothing removes from me all excuse and that at the same time what I project as my future being is always nihilated and reduced to the rank of simple possibility ... I await myself in the future ... Anguish is the fear of not finding myself at that appointment (1943/1957, 35–6).

As with Heidegger, it is in our steadfast acceptance of the inevitability of this anguish that authenticity lies. Sartre's distinctive contribution to a narrative conception of identity lies in his critical re-interpretation of psychoanalysis, particularly his belief that the workings of consciousness are fundamental to an understanding of human existence.

Sartre's theory of imagination, worked out in detail in the eponymous book, preceded his presentation of many of his key ideas in *Being and Nothingness* (1943/1957) and provides a more concise rendering of his deployment of the concept of 'nothingness' in his later work. According to Sartre, imagination is always an intentional activity of consciousness and enables us to go beyond what is already presented to our consciousness by our senses. In Sartre's terminology, imagination is the negation or nihilation of perception in order that something not immediately present can be the object of our consciousness (Barnes 1957). Thus imagination means that we are always transcending our present with a future self that we are not and thus re-casting a past self that we are no longer, 'Consciousness confronts its past and its future as facing a self which it is in the mode of not-being. This refers us to a nihilating structure of temporality' (Sartre 1943/1957, 34). In other words 'As soon as I realise myself as I am now, I am already imagining myself as I am no longer (my past self) and as I am not yet (my future self) ... To imagine is, therefore, a temporal act in which I constitute myself as both nothingness ... and freedom' (Kearney 1994, 59).

Sartre sees human existence as a dialectic between 'nothingness', the ability of imagination to negate reality and 'being', the perception of, and absorption by, the facticity of the world around us. As outlined above, our consciousness operates in two modes based upon these concepts. The 'for-itself' mode 'negates the given world in order to project itself towards a new horizon of possibilities' (Kearney 1994, 62). 'It is the obligation of the for-itself never to exist except in the form of an elsewhere in relation to itself, to exist as a being which perpetually effects in itself a break in being' (Sartre 1943/1957, 78). In the 'in-itself' mode our consciousness is reduced to a thing amongst things, objectified by the necessity of living in the world with others. To seek to live 'for-itself' involves the anguish of responsibility for what we are, to live 'in-itself' is to be objectified by the gaze of the Other and thus to experience shame (Kearney 1994).

> I have just made an awkward or vulgar gesture. This gesture clings to me; I neither judge it nor blame it. I simply live it. I realise it in the mode of for itself. But now suddenly I raise my head. Somebody was there and has seen me. Suddenly I realise the vulgarity of my gesture, and I am ashamed....By the mere appearance of the Other, I am put in the position of passing judgement on myself as on an object, for it is as an object that I appear to the Other (Sartre 1943/1957, 221–22).

From these two modes of consciousness follows an additional argument that the 'I' or self, only exists intermittently as it does not exist in our original pre-reflective consciousness or when our consciousness is absorbed in the 'in-itself'. In this argument, Sartre follows both Hegel and Heidegger (Schroeder 1984) in concluding that our consciousness must become an object for itself for the self to emerge which is, therefore, the product of intentional and reflective action (Barnes 1957).

This intermittent and intentional self, at any given moment, may be reconstituted by consciousness, making it precarious and unpredictable (Barnes 1957). This makes Sartre's self closer to some poststructuralist notions of selfhood, although we have a potentially unstable *series* of unrelated selves rather than simultaneously existing multiple selves, thus Sartre's fragmentation does allow for the possibility of a coherence built up between selves by a process of biographical construction. However, for Sartre, a refusal to step beyond a past self constitutes an act of 'bad faith', his version of 'inauthenticity', 'demanding the privileges of a free consciousness, yet seeking refuge from the responsibilities of freedom' (Barnes 1957, xii). His best known illustration of the concept is of a young woman who goes to dinner with an older man who wishes to seduce her. She hides her knowledge of this from herself, preserving a past in which she was unaware of such a knowledge, by pretending that his intentions are honourable, thus she avoids either choosing to accept or to reject his advances (Sartre 1943/1957, 55–6).

As with Heidegger, Sartre sees identity as an ongoing ethical project or quest that can only be laid aside and completed at one's death, when the for-itself becomes lost in the in-itself. 'Death reunites us with ourselves. Eternity has changed us into ourselves. At the moment of death we are; that is, we are defenceless before the judgements of others ... By death the for-itself is changed forever into an in-itself in that it has slipped entirely into the past' (Sartre 1943/1957, 115). Until death human beings are 'never complete, never self-sufficient, always empty and self-transcending; hence, they must constantly sustain what they have been in order to continue being it. To achieve or retain identity is a *task*, a project. At any point persons can break from their past and define themselves anew' (Schroeder 1984, 175). As I will go on to show in Chapters 5 and 6, such attempts at reinvention are a repeating motif in the stories presented in Chapter 2.

Analogically similar to the role of imagination is the role of emotion in Sartre's work. We make use of emotion to 'magically' transform the world according to our desires. In many cases we know how to make use of the world to achieve our wants. If I wish to eat, I know how to go shopping and prepare food. Our imagination enables us to draw on prior experience to plan 'routes' to future achievements. We are frequently frustrated in our plans or unable to cope with the complexity of some situations, thus emotion can be deployed to transform the world so that it conforms with our own desires (Barnes 1957). Sartre (1939/1962) uses the example of 'sour grapes' to illustrate his point. One rendition of this might be that having failed to get a job I applied for, my disappointment and anger enable me to change the world to one where the job was not really worth having in the first place and where the job was, in any case, already promised to a friend of the boss. Sartre's theory of emotion indicates that the narrative construction of identity should not be seen as a rational cold-blooded process but rather one that is full of emotion and that seeks to transform the world of impossibility around us into one that answers to our needs and desires, a theme developed by Ricoeur, in his exploration of the links between historical writing and fictional writing with respect to personal identity (Rabinow 1984; Ricoeur 1985; Ricoeur 1992). It is obvious though that an emotional transformation of our perception of the world is just that, and emotion gives us no direct power to alter the environment or the perceptions of others. Such an idea does, however, indicate why narratives of the self must be continuously renewed and re-told, seeking affirmation in the face of the knowledge that our view of ourselves is built on shifting sands.

Sartre has a particularly bleak view of intersubjective relations, unlike either Heidegger, whose concept of 'Being-with' is essentially non-conflictual or Ricoeur, who sees relations with the other as positively constituting an authentic individual (Schroeder 1984; Kearney 1996b). Sartre sees relations with others as a win-lose game, we can only be free at the expense of the freedom of others and *vice versa*. 'While I attempt to free myself from the hold of the Other, the Other is trying to free himself from mine; while I seek to enslave the Other, the Other seeks to enslave me' (Sartre 1943/1957, 364). Sartre believes that we are always driven to seek the affirmation of others for our self-projects because there are no objective justifications for our choices but as soon as we do this there is a conflict with one individual always objectifying or being objectified by the other. Thus attempts to overcome our essential isolation are self-defeating and contradictory. 'By virtue of consciousness the Other is for me simultaneously the one who has stolen my being from me and the one who causes "there to be" a being which is my being' (Sartre 1943/1957, 364).

We also have to live with the knowledge that our self, as perceived by the Other, is beyond our power to determine or even to know. No matter how hard we try to influence the view of the Other, in the end we experience guilt and shame because their view of us is always independent of our attempts. It is perhaps not surprising that the central theme of Sartre's 1944 play *No Exit* (1989) is predicated on the idea, voiced by one of his characters that 'Hell is other people'. Again this view contrasts strongly with Heidegger where

> Others are not experienced as distinct from oneself in any significant sense, but rather are typically experienced as similar to, even inter-changeable with, oneself. More generally, one's basic experience of other persons is *not* that they are present, self-subsistent beings whose minds are hidden, but rather that they are *engaged*, accessible beings who share the same instruments and gathering places and function much like oneself (Schroeder 1984, 130).

Schroeder (1984) takes exception to the bleakness of Sartre's vision of relations with others, attempting to retain the insights of his arguments whilst denying that there is any absolute necessity for relationships to always be of this win-lose nature. He argues that there are ways of relating to others that are not always conflictual and that, in any case, we do not always stand completely exposed to the gaze of the Other. We have many psychological defences against feeling completely objectified, all of the time, in the presence of others. Schroeder argues from writers such as Goffman that, for most of the time, we exhibit combinations of 'being-as-subject' and 'being-as-object' as we mediate the gaze of the Other through the filters of memory and social convention. Instead Schroeder suggests we take Sartre's view as an extreme case to be contrasted with Hegel's concept of reciprocity, which is much closer also to Ricoeur's thinking. If the Other recognises our own sense of self and affirms it, then one's subjectivity is strengthened rather than weakened. 'Mutual recognition elevates and unites both; each discovers himself in and through the other' (Schroeder 1984, 189).

In summary, with Sartre, as with Heidegger, we see many of the features of the poststructuralist self such as precariousness, contingency, dislocation and a lack of agency. We also see that the humanist self that depends upon some essential human nature that can stand outside of its world is refuted. Although the possibility of social determinism is allowed for, even presented as the most likely outcome for most lives, it is not featured as an inevitable part of our attempts to become a person. The role of agency is not only significant but is laid upon us as an ethical imperative, as the only way of having a fully human existence. The human capabilities of solicitude, imagination, resoluteness and self-awareness are able to transcend determinism and make choices out of the myriad possibilities that our future makes available to us. This transcendence becomes a matter of urgency when we are aware that death could overtake us at any moment. The language of Heidegger's and Sartre's existentialism suggests a heroic quest and the need for self-narratives to make sense of our pasts and to provide genres that can enable widely divergent human lives to be seen in common terms. It is to Ricoeur that I now turn in order to develop this aspect of the existentialist self, not only to narrative as a sense-making heuristic, but to Ricoeur's claims that human life itself is imbued with narrativity.

Ricoeur

Ricoeur's work on narrative identity was produced some forty years later than Sartre's writing and the ensuing linguistic turn in the social sciences is strongly represented in his approach. This brings certain issues to the fore of his intellectual project 'such as meaning, intentionality, interpretation and understanding', leading to 'a model of selfhood that privileges a narrative ... identity emerging cumulatively and intersubjectively, always mediated by others' (Rainwater 1996, 100). Ricoeur rejects both the Cartesian *cogito* of the humanist self and the poststructuralist subject as exclusive positions and seeks to find a middle way that enables him to take account of insights from both, a way that 'can claim to hold itself at an equal distance from the *cogito* exalted by Descartes and from the *cogito* that Nietzsche proclaimed forfeit' (Ricoeur 1992, 23). Ricoeur's work can be summarised by his statement that we should be 'aiming at the 'good life' with and for others, in just institutions' (1992, 172). This neatly brings together the three important and inseparable aspects of his view of identity, those of ethics, relationships with others and political and social justice.

Unlike the rather isolated existentialist heroes of Heidegger and Sartre, Ricoeur argues for a self that is intimately connected with others. 'The selfhood of oneself implies otherness to such an intimate degree that one cannot be thought of without the other, that instead one passes into the other' (Ricoeur 1992, 3). Thus 'the shortest route from self to self is through the other ... the self is never enough, is never sufficient unto itself, but constantly seeks out signs and signals of meaning in the other' (Kearney 1996b, 1). Rather than a Sartrean conflict between competing selves, Ricoeur sees no conflict between the assertion of ourselves and an ethics of care for others (Waldenfels 1996).

> To self-esteem, friendship makes a contribution without taking anything away. What it adds is the idea of reciprocity in the exchange between human beings who each esteem themselves. As for the corollary of reciprocity, namely equality, it places friendship on the path of justice, where the life together shared by a few people gives way to the distribution of shares in a plurality on the scale of a historical, political community (Ricoeur 1992, 188).

This view of the mutuality at the heart of identity projects is derived from Aristotle's teaching on friendship, where the necessary engagement with others as part of our striving for the good life enlarges what is good for me into what is good for us and concern for oneself takes on the form of concern for the other (Ricoeur 1992).

Ricoeur's ethics of reciprocity regards persons as unique, suffering, self-creating beings suggesting both a desirable plurality and a call to mutual respect and solicitude, a contrast with the 'scattered and heterogenous fragments of life, incapable of sustaining self-constancy' (Pucci 1996, 126), that is a feature of the poststructuralist self.

Temporality, as with Heidegger and Sartre, is a key aspect of Ricoeur's identity theory. In his case a distinction is made between 'real' or cosmological time and our own lived time. Our experience of time is discordant with the impersonal aeons of cosmological time and so narrative devices are used to relate one to the other, such as the mapping of the succession of generations onto cosmological time (Kearney 1996a). One device that Ricoeur discusses is the calendar, a contrivance that divides unstructured cosmological time into periods such as days, weeks and years that our own experiences (the narratives of history, for example) can be related to. The calendar 'cosmologises lived time and humanises cosmic time. This is how it contributes to reinscribing the time of narrative into the time of the world' (Ricoeur 1985, 109).

In common with Heidegger and Sartre, Ricoeur views our finitude as an essential aspect of the building of a personal identity. 'To be a self, a finite *cogito*, and to grasp one's own way of being in time are inseparable tasks. Becoming aware of oneself occurs within the reappropriation of the past, while the future discloses new possibilities' (Pucci 1996, 125). However, Ricoeur's concept of narrative is intended to resolve what he sees as an aporia arising from 'the mutual occultation of phenomenological time and cosmological time' (Ricoeur 1985, 244–5) in Heidegger's work. Narrative identity invokes narrative time, a time that bridges the 'fictionalisation of history' and the 'historisation of fiction' (1985, 246), for 'to answer the question "Who?" ... is to tell the story of a life' (Ricoeur 1985, 246).

Ricoeur's middle way between the humanist and poststructuralist self rests on a distinction between two meanings commonly attached to the word 'identity' and has commonalities with Mead's 'I' and 'me'. 'I shall henceforth take sameness as synonymous with *idem*-identity and shall oppose it to selfhood (*ipseity*), understood as *ipse*-identity' (Ricoeur 1992, 3). *Idem* can usefully be linked to the word 'identical': it is *idem* identity which incorporates the idea of the continuity of the self over time, the individual recognised by others and denoted with a name and place in the world. Ricoeur uses the example of a person who enters a room and then leaves, later returning: 'We have no trouble recognising someone who simply enters and leaves, appears, disappears and reappears' (1992, 116–7). Over a greater period of time the principle of *idem* identity still persists so that an individual at 80 is still identified as being the same individual (for legal or biographical purposes) as at the age of six, despite the immense changes that will have taken place to that person. Opposed to *idem* identity is that of *ipse* identity or 'self-hood', by which Ricoeur denotes my sense of myself as an 'I', rooted in the present, the answer to the question 'who is speaking?' which may be very different from the past and is characterised by 'diversity, variability, discontinuity, and instability' (Ricoeur 1992, 140). The distinction between the two forms of identity is not a simple one as both may share temporal persistence in different ways. For *idem* identity, sameness is guaranteed by the social and official recognition of the individual but *ipse* identity may also remain constant through choice as with a promise where the 'I' commits itself to remain the same with respect to another over a period of time, echoing Heidegger's concept of self-constancy. It is through the narrative element of 'character' that the paradox of identity being both sameness and difference is resolved 'a dialectic of sameness and selfhood' (Ricoeur 1992, 141). Thus our character provides a continuity by which we are recognised as individuals (thus we talk of individuals acting out of character when this sense of sameness is violated) but this character is also dynamic and changes according to the decisions of the self, which form the plot through which the character develops through action.

Thus Ricoeur is going further than simply arguing that narrative is a way of making sense of ourselves, rather human existence is only possible through narrative. 'Narrative is a universal feature of social life: it is the fundamental mode through which the grounding of human experience in time is understood' (McNay 2000, 85). As with Heidegger and Sartre, the Cartesian consciousness, transparent to itself is rejected (Rainwater 1996). Rather we can only understand ourselves by interpretation, mediated to ourselves through language, symbol, culture and history. Ricoeur's theory of the essential narrativity of existence rests on two ideas taken from Aristotle, 'emplotment' and 'mimēsis'. Emplotment refers to 'a productive and dynamic process that synoptically orders its material under a model of concordance. The logical and dramatic unity of beginning, middle and end provides the ordered background from which discordance emerges' (Rainwater 1996, 103–4). Mimēsis may broadly be understood as 'representation' and Ricoeur identified three modes of it that, in total, can encompass the complexity of the term. Mimēsis 1 is the 'prefigured world of action', Mimēsis 2 is the 'creative act of configuration' and Mimēsis 3 is the 'refiguration back into the world by spectators or readers' (Rainwater 1996, 104). From experience, we configure narratives about its meaning which we narrate to others who make their own sense of and then refigure their interpretations of ourselves back into the world, reflecting ourselves back to us thus stimulating another round of configuration. This is a model of narrative that once more illustrates Ricoeur's stress on intersubjectivity as mimetic activity requires a dialogue between configuring and refiguring that in turn foregrounds the ethical and political concerns that Ricoeur works through explicitly in ways not obvious in Heidegger's and Sartre's work.

It is not just in representing ourselves to ourselves and others that narrative comes into play. Our actions in the world also involve narrative. No action is an isolatable event. All actions are shaped by our pasts, through the sedimentation of our characters and all actions look forward in that they attempt to shape an unpredictable future, thus the future may be different from the past. Not only is narrative the only way of making sense of our actions but 'living is itself the enactment of a narrative' (Dunne 1996, 146) and 'stories are lived before they are told – except in the case of fiction' (MacIntyre 1985, 212). The distinction between 'real' lives and fictional ones is significant in Ricoeur's work. Although the structures of fictional and historical narratives are similar (Ricoeur 1985, 180 –92). As Dunne puts it:

> No-one can have the privileged perspective on his own life that an author has on her fictional creations; the enacted narrative of my life meshes too finely with the narratives of other lives ... for it to be subject to my sole construction: I am the main protagonist in, but not the author of, it (Dunne 1996, 147).

The embeddedness of narrativity in our lives and selves is further illustrated by the linkage between the idea of constructing narratives and giving an account of ourselves.

> Accountability is inherent in the very living; giving an account of it, to others or to myself, is not something discretionary, apart from the living, which I may or may not indulge in. If *no* account can be given of my life, it can scarcely be called a *human* life ... and if *I* cannot give an account of it, it can scarcely be said to be *my* life (Dunne 1996, 147).

The notion of giving an account can be further extended into that of accountability, one's life as inescapably a moral quest as we attempt to discern the direction our lives are moving in, in comparison with our solicitude to pursue some 'goods' rather than others. This quest always involves struggle because of the way our lives intersect with other lives and with our environments. The unpredictability of events in our lives, the unintended consequences of our and others' actions, the complex of influences from family, gender, class, ethnicity, education and so on, provide all of the attributes of emplotment, but our storied lives are the result of a dialectic between this plot and our questing *characters*, as constructed and made sense of by narrative (Dunne 1996).

The presentation of Ricoeur's narrative conception of identity has thus far concentrated on narrative as a heuristic device for making sense of lives and selves. It has also outlined that narrativity is embedded in the very act of living, which in turn is refigured into further narratives thus constructing our characters through struggle as we pursue our interconnected quests for the good life. There is also a third aspect of narrativity in Ricoeur's thinking to do with the significance of the act of narrating itself. What difference does telling one's story make (Dunne 1996)? The first obvious answer to this question is that telling self-narratives makes connections between events and so produces a certain unity in one's life. The poststructuralist view of such a project would be that this production subjects the self to domination via dominant discourses or social practices. The Ricoeurian concept of narrating seeks to avoid this accusation by claiming that it 'seeks to supersede sheer succession, heterogeneity and discordance' and whilst it 'has recourse to established genres and narrative conventions' is not thereby 'committed either to a substantialist notion of the self or to a static notion of narration' (Dunne 1996, 149). Rather the act of narration invokes a 'whole' life, including lives that may be dislocated and fragmented. Narrativity suggests that actors may be protagonists in multiple collective stories rather than one self-enclosed story and that 'self-identity can include mutability and transformation within the cohesion of one lifetime' (Kearney 1996a, 181).

The second answer to the question regarding the significance of telling one's story is to do with arriving at an understanding of ourselves and others which then informs our actions and relations to others. Once more, ethical concerns are inseparable from this concept of narrative because self-understanding is not an isolated accomplishment but is part of the dialectic with others by which we form ourselves. It becomes a way of standing up to be counted on by others, being true to our self-understanding and, as we pursue the 'good' life, demonstrating constancy for others. Despite the unpredictability of our plots and our own personal struggles there should be 'a fidelity of which I am capable' (Dunne 1996, 153). In a re-working of Heidegger and Sartre, we have a moral duty to be reflexive about our own stories so that we do not disown aspects of what we are and so that we resist the attempts of others to make us what they wish us to be. This moral duty extends beyond the living to previous generations in our commemoration of them: 'Everything takes place as though historians knew themselves to be bound by a debt to people of earlier times, to the dead' (Ricoeur 1985, 100).

This debt to the past can take on the nature of 'testimony', the need for which is particularly important when preserving the collective memory of human sufferings such as those suffered at Auschwitz. Not only this but the techniques of constructing fictional narratives may be appropriate in order to generate an emotional intensity of reaction equal to such extreme suffering, acting as a warning of what can happen and should not happen again. In less extreme circumstances, one can see narratives of more mundane lives, such as those presented in this book, as testimonies to the hopes and sufferings of those who also deserve empathy and understanding and are also worthy of being recorded and re-told (Kearney 1996a). Such a view of testimony may raise the suspicion that critique has been abandoned for the cosy desire to 'like' everybody. However, the term 'testimony' also invokes the idea of a cry that justice be done, that evil deeds also be remembered, judged and explained. Critique and empathy do not necessarily preclude each other.

Despite the possibility within Ricoeur's narrative conception of identity for a form of coherence and agency, as with any story that is constantly re-told in changing circumstances, it is still precarious and discordant for 'narrative identity can be made and then unmade, since it is possible to weave different plots through the same personage, even if these plots oppose one another' (Pucci 1996, 126). Narrative identity also departs from the sovereign self, looking out from its splendid isolation of consciousness, in favour of a self that 'lacks the substantiality and discreetness of an object which is amenable to direct description or explanation … Its reality is peculiarly dispersed, it is always partly outside or beyond itself' (Dunne 1996, 143). There is then no inevitable guarantee of coherence and constancy. The possibility of these are rather ethical achievements as exemplified in the idea of the promise that Ricoeur takes from Levinas, that friendships rely on the implicit promise of self-constancy over time (Kearney 1996a; McNay 2000).

Finally, the ethics of narrative identity compel us to understand and affirm each other. We are always echoing Christ's question to his disciples 'Who do you say that I am?'

> The narrative imagination opens us to the foreign world of others by enabling us to tell or hear other stories, but it can never be sure of escaping the hermeneutic circle of interpretation, which ultimately strives to translate the foreign into the familiar, the discordant into the concordant, the different into the analogous, the other into the self. (Kearney 1996a, 185).

We reach across the gulf of our self-narrations to ask 'Where are you?' and the other responds 'Here I am!' (Kearney 1996a).

Narrative Identity and Identity Narratives

How can the philosophy of being and selfhood contribute to understanding the lives of managers? This question is answered (I hope) by the sense I make of the life stories from Chapter 2 in the next chapter. In the way of a summary of this chapter, I shall identify the key points that provide the theoretical foundation for my analysis. Although the above discussion makes it clear that there are important differences between the three writers, I want to draw attention here to the broad areas of convergence in their work as it applies to the understanding of identity that informs my approach to interpreting the life histories presented earlier. Firstly, all stress the centrality of temporality and finitude: on the relationship between past, present and future and the necessity of making choices that arise out of the biographical narrative implicit with being thrown by our past into the bounded possibilities of our future. Death becomes a guarantee of individual existence in that each of us awaits our own particular, unique end. Secondly, all three see the construction of identity as an ethical quest and one that, in different ways, involves other selves with whom we share the world. Thirdly, although all three insist that individuals possess the agency required for the construction of their own identities, this task is always incomplete, uncertain and precarious. Most of us spend most of our lives fleeing the terror of our self-responsibilities and take refuge in allowing ourselves to be determined by the 'they', thus the total structural or discursive production of selves may indeed be the norm but it is not inevitable, for it rests on our failure to choose rather than on a lack of capacity so to do.

This view of identity seems to me to be both attractive and persuasive. It appears capable of encompassing the poststructuralist critique of humanism with its suggestion that, in conditions of postmodernity, selves are indeed mostly subjects of individualistic consumerist discourse. In doing so, however, it does not negate the very categories required to make such a critique matter. The narrative self retains the possibility of possibility, that human beings have choices, even if to pursue such choices requires struggle and, most likely, suffering. The accumulation of countless choices that each individual makes, as their lives unfold, also provide an explanation for the heterogeneity that marks members of societies whose identity is made up both of 'sameness' and of 'self-hood'. Additionally, the intense ethicality raised by the insistence on choice and intersubjectivity provides a possible foundation for emancipatory projects that seem scarcely worth pursuing as merely reactive power effects of discursive systems.

One could reasonably object that lives are more than stories, that the significance of embodiment, the brute materiality of existence, argued in the last chapter when considering death, is not reflected in narrativity and this is, I think, true to an extent as is the charge that power and social structure are not given sufficient attention in an approach that stresses the individual assertion of the will so heavily. On the other hand, no one theoretical approach is likely to be able to encompass every aspect of the human condition, even assuming that this is not itself a moving target. I would argue that narrativity enables an opening up of debates on managerial identity and hope that I will further demonstrate this in the analysis of life histories that is to come.

What are, then, the implications for understanding managerial life stories that a narrative conception of identity gives rise to? It firstly might be thought to validate the entire approach of presenting individual life histories as having a significance in themselves and thus of being placed in prime position within this book. Additionally, in such stories we should be able to discern both the intentionality and the process of narrative identity construction. For all three philosophers, the phenomenological method suggests that an imaginative and empathetic identification with the lives of others is more likely to yield insights than abstract forms of theorisation (though one might be forgiven, after reading Heidegger, for wondering what abstract theory would look like if such writing is merely the rigorous description of experience). It gives me a basis for arguing that part of the value of this book may be simply as a collection of stories, a recounting of 'ordinary' lives to set against the more abstracted representations of managers in organisation studies. Thus I hope that this may stand as a 'refiguring' of what it has been like to forge an identity as a lower-middle-class citizen of the United Kingdom at the end of the twentieth century. Such managers are a group continually written 'for' and 'about', in the pages of management textbooks or work on identity within organisation studies (Brown 2001; Alvesson; Ashcraft and Thomas 2008) but rarely does one read attempts to represent their experiences using the conventions of storytelling outside of fiction. This is despite the fact that the literary resources available for the writing of 'fictive truth' (Stanley 1992) have been developed over the entire history of humanity for the empathetic communication of the experiences of others. From the standpoint of Ricoeurian ethics, the narratives in Chapter 2, stand alone in their own right both as commemoration, bearing witness to our shared lives and as a claim to understanding on the part of readers.

In this book, however, I also hope to answer questions as well as provide a testimony. Firstly, does the narrative construction of identity convince as a way of making sense of managerial identity? Can its theoretical claims be verified by working through the experiences that they are meant to be derived from? The analysis of my managerial life histories in the next two chapters is just such an attempt to test how credible this view of identity is and the plausibility of this attempt is a question returned to in my final chapter.

Chapter 5
My Generation: Life-Stories as Historical Narratives

In the previous three chapters I discussed a theoretical approach to identity that sees it as a narrative achievement. In Chapter 4 I suggested that this narrative conception of identity has many points of connection with existentialist philosophy and provides an alternative to the somewhat polarised debate that has characterised identity within organisation studies. I argued that existentialist theory suggests that identity is historical through and through but yet not altogether determined by it. In other words, that we still possess both choice and responsibility which, though agonising to face up to, provide a degree of freedom from the discursive forces that shape modern individuals. In this sense, identity becomes an ethical quest to live the good life. In this chapter I begin to interpret my life histories in the light of these insights, specifically I examine the historical context out of which these particular lives emerge and which make them distinctive and unique. I explore the specific conjunction of events, aspirations, opportunities and social structure that has enabled one set of selves to emerge rather than another and that, for reasons discussed below, seem unlikely to recur.

It might be objected that a theoretical analysis of the stories is at odds with the aspiration to let the stories stand in their own right. I have argued, following Ricoeur (1992) that the narratives in Chapter 2 should have an intrinsic value as a testimony to what my respondents believe is significant about their own lives. Bochner, an influential voice within autoethnography, would certainly see the two as incompatible arguing that 'when we stay with a story, refusing the impulse to abstract, reacting from the source of our own experience and feelings, we respect the story and the human life it represents, and we enter into personal contact with questions of virtue, of what it means to live well and to do the right thing' (Bochner 2001, 132). He goes on to lament the way in which theoretical critique privileges 'rigor over imagination, intellect over feeling, theories over stories, lectures over conversations, abstract ideas over concrete events' (Bochner 2001, 134). According to this viewpoint it would seem that the act of theorising represents a Sartrean objectification of the other.

I have a good deal of sympathy with Bochner's arguments but would not agree that theorisation must always destroy narratives as story and, in the analyses that follow, my intention has been to understand both the context and construction of the stories in order that they can be appreciated as the rich accounts I take them to be. In Ricoeur one finds just such a rigorous theorisation of identity combined with an insistence on an ethics of representation. In any case I also wish to answer some of the questions I have posed in the preceding chapters about identity and specifically to evaluate my claims that the model of identity outlined in the previous chapter can indeed contribute insights to an understanding of what being a manager means for this group of individuals in the context of their wider lives. I hope that my approach will enable my readers to understand, and empathise with, the struggles, failures, triumphs and dilemmas of this group of fellow human beings.

With these intentions in mind, I have deployed three modes of interpretation that treat the stories as 'historical' narratives but, as discussed in Chapter 4, also as narratives that make use of a plethora of fictive devices to communicate their 'truths'. The first mode, which takes up the remainder of this chapter, is based on seeing the narratives as referential of a particular historical context. The second and third modes are both concerned with interrogating the stories as performances and analysing how and why different narrators produce distinctive stories from a common pool of available narrative resources (Watson and Harris 1999).

The need for the first mode of historical referentiality was forcibly impressed upon me when I began to listen to the tapes and read the transcripts of the interviews. It struck me that I had stumbled across an account, albeit partial, of my generation's experiences of work, rooted in the history of the United Kingdom in the second half of the twentieth century. It was all the more surprising then that seeing such accounts as a collective generational history was entirely absent from the academic writing on managerial identity that I had been reading.

The phrase 'my generation' perhaps needs some qualification, for I do not mean by this *all* those now in the 35 to 50-year-old age bracket. Indeed, for reasons that were initially unclear to me, I was taken aback by the number of parallels between my own story and that of my interviewees. On reflection it seems to me that this is due to a coincidence that has brought together members of a distinct social sub-category. One might describe this group crudely, in class terms, as 'upper-working/lower middle'. To restate this in terms of occupation, my respondents are drawn largely from skilled-craft and the lower ranks of supervisory occupations at one end, to public sector administration and public sector professions at the other. As time has gone by, many of these original occupations have been transformed into middle or sometimes senior management positions.

The coincidence that brought us together was, therefore, the increased but temporary upward social mobility of this group in the 1960s and 1970s. One important source of this mobility was the rapid post-war growth in the public sector, particularly teaching, healthcare, and social work. Public sector employment in the UK hit a peak at just under six million employees in 1992 and has remained (with some fluctuations) at about this figure to the present day (ONS 2007). This has been combined with a more general expansion in technical and managerial work (Hobsbawm 1995; Rosen 2003). Access to the public sector professions or the higher echelons of management has increasingly required degree level education. All but one of my story-tellers missed out on a university place but keenly felt that they could and should have had a place, responding to the way in which 'education has become an increasingly important determinant of class' (Rosen

2003, 75). They came on the course that I was teaching in order to make up for what they saw as this deficiency and the part-time nature of the programme enabled them to obtain access to a university degree without the traditional attendance requirements. This coincided with my own trajectory of a teacher turning himself into an academic, which included my own years of part-time postgraduate study. Nearly all, including myself, were members of the first generation of our families to obtain a degree. Thus nearly all have had to struggle to become included in this expansion of opportunity in the last decades of the twentieth century, indeed they may be seen as scrambling to get through a doorway which was becoming increasingly narrow once more.

Richard is an exception to these generalities and the only interviewee to have had a public school education. He chose, however, to reject the expectations of his more secure middle-class background and, in this sense, it could be argued that he is an 'honorary' member of the group that I am describing. It is interesting to speculate whether the fact that he alone has become an entrepreneur and chief executive of his own company, rather than a salaried manager, indicates that his different class origins have made a difference despite the rise of what is generally perceived as a more meritocratic society.

I am jumping ahead a little here though and, to return to my original point, one of the key ways in which I wish to make sense of these stories is through their historical and social referentiality. I wish to start my analysis, therefore, with a more detailed look at how the identities of my interviewees and myself have been influenced by our location in a particular space and time. The significance of our historical location is a key element of the existentialist approach to identity. As explained in Chapter 4, Heidegger, Sartre and Ricoeur all stress that identities are specific to the particular historical and cultural circumstances into which we are 'thrown' by our pasts and which determine the possibilities of our future, although not our choices concerning how we respond to these possibilities. This implies that the location in space and time brings to bear particular social, political and economic developments that all converge on the characteristic shape of the managerial identities adopted, with varying degrees of enthusiasm and success. The play of choice with possibility emerges as my storytellers deploy the idea of being a manager in a variety of ways that at least partially enable them to carve out a space to be someone they wish to be, albeit that this is often only precariously achieved with accompanying tensions and contradictions. To conclude this discussion of the importance of temporal location it only remains to explain that I have treated the narratives for this mode of interpretation as histories, albeit ones shot through with fictive techniques. I have therefore made use of themes typical of historical analysis: for example, those of location, significant shared events, economic and social status and the membership of significant groups such as class and family. In this way I also stress Ricoeur's first element of identity, that of *idem* or sameness.

My Generation

I shall start by outlining the broad social and political factors which appear to have the most relevance to my own experience and that of my interviewees, drawing in examples from the narratives found earlier in the book. In this endeavour I shall draw upon the work of a number of social historians of the twentieth century. To begin, Hobsbawm, as do many other historians (see Brower 1988; Erickson 1996; Calvocoressi 2001, for example) characterises the post-war period as consisting of two distinct parts: the 'Golden Age' of the 1950s, 1960s and early 1970s followed by 'The Landslide' which began around the same time as the International Oil Crisis in 1973 which has in turn been followed by a series of economic, political and social crises. The Golden Age was a period of 'high growth rates, low unemployment and low inflation' (Howlett 1994, 320). Of course, it has to be acknowledged that such a characterisation only applies to certain groups mostly restricted to the wealthier parts of the globe but it does apply to the individuals represented in this book. This *caveat* aside, it is reasonable to argue that, by the 1960s; times were better than anyone remembered, or had expected. This sense of unparalleled prosperity and optimism is evident from Harold Macmillan's claim in 1957 that 'most of our people never had it so good' (Sandbrook 2005). Indeed by most economic indicators this was self-evidently true. Unemployment in Europe was 1.5 per cent throughout the 1960s (Hobsbawm 1995) and in the UK 'unemployment averaged only 1.67 per cent during the 1950s' (Rosen 2003, 12). Personal affluence and consumption also rose at an extraordinary rate. To give just three brief illustrations, up until the late 1950s, Spain had no mass tourism, 30 years later it was visited by just over 54 million foreign tourists (Hobsbawm 1995). In 1956 only 8 per cent of British households had refrigerators, a rate that is virtually 100 per cent today (Rosen 2003). In 1950 less than three in ten households owned their own home, by 1973 more than half did (Howlett 1994).

Solutions for all the political and economic problems of the past seemed to have arrived or to be imminent. The technological sophistication of the Golden Age, Harold Wilson's 'white heat of revolution' (Sandbrook 2006), of which new management techniques were a part, offered apparently boundless possibilities for both high rates of consumption combined with unlimited leisure. Even the intractable conflict between capital and labour seemed solvable by the ability of many developed economies to fund improving wages and conditions of work at the same time as providing generous welfare states. Thus the Golden Age is often referred to as a 'post-war settlement' between capital and labour, characterised as a period dominated by Keynsian economics, expanding welfare provision, dedication to full employment and acceptance of a large measure of state direction (Davies 2000).

The world of work was also changing with a huge expansion in technological, administrative, and scientific work matched by the equally large expansion in public sector jobs in the new welfare states (Rosen 2003). The enlargement of these sectors more than compensated for the decline of heavy industrial jobs (Davies 2000) to such an extent that ex-colonisers sought to top up their labour supplies by encouraging large scale immigration from their ex-colonies. 'Between 1951 and 2000 the number of members of ethnic minorities resident in Britain rose from under 100,000 to 4,039,000' (Rosen 2003, 89–90). Again higher education has proved a route to upward social mobility for many of the children of these immigrants with a higher proportion of ethnic minorities entering higher education than the indigenous population by 1991, although this tends to be unevenly distributed between different communities. This expansion opened up vast new areas of opportunity for the sons, and increasingly the daughters, of the lower middle and upper working-classes in teaching, nursing, engineering, administration, finance and the lower levels of management.

The increasing complexity of work and the egalitarian impulse of post-war left-wing governments led to a massive expansion in the availability of higher education, further boosted by moderately generous state financial support in the UK, for those who would not have been able to afford to put their children through another three years of full time study. According to Hobsbawm (1995), Germany, France and the UK, the big three European economies, had only one tenth of one per cent of their populations attending university before the Second World War. Rosen notes that Britain had proportionately fewer university students than any other European country and as recently as 1954–55 there were still only 122,000 full time students in higher education (Rosen 2003). By the 1980s 1.5 per cent of the *total* population were in higher education in the educationally conservative UK (Hobsbawm 1995) and by 1999–2000 there were 1,259,700 students, a tenfold increase in 46 years (Rosen 2003). For the upper-working/lower-middle-class, a university education was almost a guarantee of a better life than their parents and a ticket to entry into relatively rewarding new public sector professions.

The traditional markers of class lost much of their symbolic power during the Golden Age as inequality narrowed and higher rates of consumption and educational achievement reached lower down the social structure (Brook 2001). Accent and appearance tended to become much less visible badges of identity for most people than they had been. The wearer of a Burton's suit was not obviously different from the wearer of bespoke Saville Row. The collectivism and public nature of working-class life was increasingly replaced with a new individualism as homes became more comfortable, with entertainment provided within them by the radio, record-player and television, instead of outside them at the cinema, pub and music hall. Better futures became available via individual meritocratic competitive effort rather than by communal struggle (Benson 2003). However, although the economic actualities of class have become less obvious it has not disappeared, rather it remains a powerful source of collective identity but one which is incorporated into more individualistic and voluntaristic identity projects, whether in defence of an increasingly precarious middle-class identity (Lawler 2005) or the constant re-interpretation of a desired working-class identification (Woodin 2005). Indeed, as some of my storytellers illustrate, 'nostalgia became embedded in the conception of being working-class' (Brook 2001, 773) due to these changes.

Ties to the place of one's birth were also weakened for the upper-working/lower-middle-class; partly by the tradition of attending a university away from one's home town but also by the pursuit of careers, rather than simply jobs, for firms that were larger, more geographically dispersed and more likely to require mobility on the part of their key employees (Dex 2003). The experiences of the group analysed in this book bears out this trend, but only partially, as many narrators did still think of the area they grew up in as 'home' even when they actually lived hundreds of miles away.

The presence of women at work, particularly in administration, the caring professions and teaching, was also a marked change that became widespread in the Golden Age. 'The employment rate of women of working age in the UK rose from 47 per cent in 1959 to 70 per cent by 2000' (Rosen 2003, 103). Increasingly this has meant a high proportion of women within management and the professions. By the end of the 1990s, for example, half of all entrants to medical school were women (Rosen 2003). Hobsbawm argues that, at first, for middle-class women, this was more about an assertion of independence from the domestic sphere, rather than for economic motives. As wage differentials between men and women narrowed and the cost of living a comfortable middle-class existence increased, however, double household incomes have come to be seen as a financial necessity (Dex 2003). All of the women in settled relationships that I interviewed earned the main household income and every interviewee that was part of a couple was a member of a double income household.

Of course, as with all Golden Ages, it did not last and the problems that have arisen since 1973 are all too familiar to us as we continue to live through them with no clear resolution in sight. According to a report by the New Economics Foundation which sought to measure overall quality of life '1976 had been the best year to be alive' (Garnett 2007, 4) Since then there has been a reversal of many of the gains of the Golden Age, leading to immense nostalgia for this period from many anti-capitalist commentators (see Klein 2000; Monbiot 2000; and Frank 2001, for example). The welfare state has shrunk leaving the upper-working/lower middle-classes to pay for dental treatment, eye tests, university fees, higher public transport fares and so on (Joseph Rowntree Foundation 1992). In addition the security and desirability of many of the occupations to which they had access has decreased (Scase and Goffee 1989; Dex 2003), not least because of the impact of globalisation (Castells 2004). Intensified global competition in manufacturing and the ability of firms to relocate at will in search of lower labour costs has meant huge culls of middle ranking managers and technicians in developed economies (Sennett 1998). The previously dull but secure careers of banking, accounting and insurance are arguably not much less dull but are infinitely less secure. The upper-working/lower-middle-classes have had to work ever longer hours in less secure jobs (Dex 2003) simply to hold on to the gains that came relatively easily to their parents in the Golden Age. Any public sector professional who has been working for the past twenty years or so will have experienced large cuts in funding and increases in central government control, working hours and job insecurity, perversely ostensibly via 'the discipline of the market' (Pollitt 1993; Clark and Newman 1997). Private consumption has continued to increase but anxiety increasingly gnaws at the middle-classes about the ability to afford access to 'good' universities or whether a comfortable standard of living can be maintained into the extreme old age which is increasingly likely to be our fate.

Class, Family and Location

What does this probably familiar account of the last few decades have to do with the narratives found earlier in this book? As already observed, all but one of my storytellers, including myself, fall fairly neatly into the upper-working/lower-middle-class category, although many have secured much more obviously middle-class occupations and lifestyles than their parents. Class also provides a vivid illustration of the way in which aspects of identity are transmitted from one generation to the next. One of the keys to the self-identity of the group under consideration is that many of the narrative resources they draw on to define themselves are based, in turn, on narratives that precede their direct remembered experiences. Several of my interviewees used the term 'working-class' to describe aspects of their identities that they considered important and enduring, despite the leaving behind of many traditional markers of such a class identity. There appears to be an intuitive commitment to Ricoeur's (1985) argument that we have a debt to those who precede us. I will now consider some examples of such class identifications both in terms of family background and in terms of self description.

My father started out as an accounts clerk and finished as group accountant, my mother did not work for many years after which she became a teacher. Janet's father was a clerk at a power station; Ethan's, a construction worker and later a policeman; Mary's father was a steel worker; Alex's father was a lorry driver; John's father was a technician in the RAF; Mona's father worked as a labourer and her mother as a secretary; Elaine's father was a production manager and her mother, initially a housewife, worked later in a bakers, before they both changed occupation to become pub landlords; Rob's father was an aviation engineer. In most cases, mothers stayed at home as housewives, particularly while their children were young. These are clearly the occupations of the working or lower middle-classes and the changes to them reflect the wider historical changes outlined above.

The obvious exception is Richard who is difficult to categorise according to social class in this way at all and provides a good illustration of the limitation of class as a sole means of understanding the identities of the storytellers. His father was a rather Lawrentian figure, the son of a coal miner whose radical convictions had propelled him into contact with other social classes and who subsequently married a member of the disappearing minor rural gentry (they were clerics and small landowners). However, both parents escaped their respective class backgrounds to run a 'delinquent' childrens' home. Richard receives the classic middle-middle-class training of a minor public school, in his case a Quaker foundation. His route into management, unlike other narrators, is not driven by the desire to 'better' himself. It comes about because he drops out of school and rebels against parental expectations. His account creates the impression that his family thought that engineering was only a glorified form of 'trade' and so not a fit occupation for him.

There are other complexities to be considered as well. Ethan is from the US and clearly does not think of class in the same way as other interviewees. He thinks that he was brought up in disadvantage and poverty but does not indicate that this confers a collective identity upon him. This suggests that the element of class-based identity in the others is a very specific discursive element rooted in the British historical context. Similarly, Mona's parents were Asian immigrants, which cross-cuts a class-based identity and confounds simple categorisation. She describes her upbringing as a 'middle-class' one, in leafy suburban Surrey but her father works all hours as a labourer to provide this. We also do not know what social status her parents left behind them in Mauritius. From the description she gives, though, her experiences are closer to other interviewees than Richard's, although learning to cope with racial abuse is, of course, unique to her. What creates this commonality is that the expanding opportunities for ordinary people also became available to some overseas immigrants, usually via educational achievement (Rosen 2003). In Mona's case, her parents were determined to give her a British middle-class identity from the outset, at the cost of severing the intergenerational transmission of a distinctive ethnic identity.

These class identifications suggested by family background are reflected in many accounts as self description. As I have argued above, the increasingly precarious position of the upper-working/lower-middle-classes through the Crisis Decades has often made upwardly mobile members of this class acutely aware of their ambiguous social position, in, but not of, the middle-classes. One reaction to this is to value and continue to claim a strong working-class identity as a metaphorical 'home' in which one can both feel a secure sense of belonging and an inverted sense of superiority in relation to the usual social hierarchy. Janet, Mary, and Rob all claim a strong and continuing sense of being working-class and regard it as a positive aspect of their identity. They all stress the communal aspects of their childhoods based around church, school, extended family and friendship.

Others though make no such self-identifications, either as working or middle-class. For them such a category holds no attraction as positive self-description and is either alluded to in terms of relative poverty to be escaped from or is simply effaced in their stories entirely. Elaine describes herself as 'semi-privileged' and places her family as ordinary but better off than many around her. Alex, whose narrative positions her as a victim rather than hero, finds nothing positive in her family's social origins, regarding it simply as a scene of deprivation to be escaped from. Mona describes her *upbringing* as 'middle-class' but does not claim any specific class identity for herself. John also makes no use of class as self-description. Richard, arguably the most middle-class of my group, is proud of his father's working-class origins and as a young man rejects his middle-class destiny. His adoption of a strong Yorkshire accent and a certain bluff bloke-ishness (he refers to himself as a 'bloke'), strengthen the impression that he has embraced a working-class persona, in preference to the more middle-class one which his upbringing, education and relative wealth might suggest.

It may be that there is an effect of age emerging here. As already remarked, a strong collective working-class identity has been in decline since the Second World War. For younger interviewees with perhaps younger parents, class may have simply been a disappearing narrative resource with which to build their identity. The discourse of the 'classless' society, so beloved by recent centre-right politicians, promotes the idea that class inequalities and antagonisms are a thing of the past and so class identifications are archaic, reactionary and irrelevant. To use such a discourse in order to construct one's sense of self may be thought of by some interviewees as antithetical to the new meritocratic mobile society of which managerialism seems to be such an indispensable part.

Whether interviewees talk in terms of class or not, the family was an important institution for all and most interviewees were at pains to trace the origins of who they are now to their upbringing. What is striking looking back from the new millennium, where, in 2004, the number of divorces was over half of the number of marriages (ONS 2007), is the stability and solidity of family life described in the narratives. Only Alex experienced the divorce of her parents. Janet's father dies and her relationship with her siblings and mother is problematic but nevertheless the family remains a solid unit. For all the other interviewees, and for myself, the family was the bedrock of our developing selves and the site where social traditions were passed on, modified and sometimes rebelled against. In particular, the narratives paint a portrait of parents that both expected and desired that we should have a better life than them. Their hard work, sometimes their social ambitions, and their love for their children ensured that all of the stories *are* stories of social and material advancement.

All of the interviewees (and again myself) to an extent measure the success of who we have become by our family origins and our parents' aspirations. In Richard's case he rejects his parents' aspirations in his youth but then spends much of his later adult life trying to redeem himself through business success. He seeks to match the achievements of his parents by becoming, in his turn, a public benefactor and pillar of the community, still sharing their Quaker convictions. For Janet, her father's attributes, convictions and hopes are the cornerstone of her upbringing and he is powerfully present in her account of her childhood, even after his death. Mary stresses her links with her extended family but it is her parents, solicitous of her success at school and of her going to university, that propel her into a public sector professional career. It was Alex's mother that insisted that the family moved to York in order to give her children more opportunities for education and work, at the cost of her marriage. John's family life was also an island of stability in the troubled seas of military rootlessness, although he blames his mother for making what he sees as the mistake of going into the RAF rather than aiming for university.

Mona's awareness of the sacrifices her parents made is augmented by her knowledge of the hardships of leaving their homeland for the uncertainties and discrimination of England in search of a better future. It is clear that she felt that she had let her parents down because of her poor academic record. Her desire to do well in her career and later studies is partly a reaction to this. Rob is also acutely aware of the sacrifices his parents made to provide him with a comfortable and stable home. He also feels that he let his parents down by doing badly at school, although, like John, there is some ambivalence towards them for discouraging him from continuing his studies past the school leaving age. Ethan is an exception here; his account of himself makes almost no reference to his parents or the area he grows up in. His Polish descent is described but forms no part of who he sees himself as. With so many siblings his parents are unable to give him any sort of springboard into a better life. It is the army and good luck which do this.

Related to attachment to family is attachment to place or at least the desire to put down roots and call somewhere 'home'. Many of the interviewees still live and work where they grew up despite the trend towards geographical mobility particularly in search of better economic opportunities. In my case I have ended up 200 miles away from North London where I grew up. As with some other narrators, this was partly due to a wish to be near family when children were young. After a brief spell away from the Northeast, Janet settled in her home town in order to look after her mother. Mary, after spells of work elsewhere, has ended up within a few miles of her childhood home. She wanted to be near her parents when she became a mother herself. Alex has stayed in York, partly to be close to her mother and friends and partly because it simply feels like home. Her unhappiness at her last job was partly due to not liking to be constantly away.

John's longing for a place to call home is based on a sense of rootlessness, suggesting that he cannot be a 'whole' person without this attachment. He also blames his mistake of going into the forces partly on the lack of a place to call home. Mona has lived for several years in Hull, a long way from Surrey, both geographically and qualitatively. Now that she is thinking of having children she too is planning to return 'home' and is very clear that Surrey will always represent this to her. Elaine has always worked and lived within a few miles from where she grew up. Rob, much to his own surprise, left his family behind when he fell in love unexpectedly one day in Manchester but still expresses a strong attachment to Kent. Richard and Ethan are again the exceptions. Richard seems to have turned himself into a full-blooded 'Yorkshireman'. Perhaps his unconventional family home and its early truncation when he went to boarding school lessened this attachment but it is clear that he has put down roots in North Yorkshire instead. Ethan expresses no attachment to, or desire to return to, the Mid-West or any indication that he regards where his family live as home but he does end his narrative with a wistful portrait of settling down permanently by the English coast.

Education and Occupation

Whether or not these managers make use of class as a narrative resource, it can be argued that their membership of it governed many aspects of their experience and thus the form their self-descriptions take. Experiences of education and how narrators came to find themselves in their occupations were significant elements in all of the stories: the former not determining but certainly constraining the latter. It should be remembered that the expansion of higher education offered the upper-working/lower middle-class unparalleled access to the training ground of professional and managerial groups.

For all of my group, including me, the route to a better life was success in the state education system and the great watershed for many was the 'eleven plus', which determined whether one went to a grammar school, originally oriented towards the lower ranks of the less prestigious professions such as banking and insurance. As the sixties turned into the seventies, grammar schools increasingly facilitated the entry of the academically able members of the upper-working, lower middle-classes into the universities (Rosen 2003). The striking thing about all of my interviewees is that, for one reason or another, they just missed out on the benefits of these new opportunities, even when they had gained that prized grammar school place. All came on the Masters to make up for what they keenly felt as a lack. There are, however, differences between the experiences of interviewees and their failure to get into university. Some narratives talk of promising academic careers cut short by difficulties caused by moving, isolation, bullying, poverty and so on. Others simply admit that at the time they were not able to pass the exams.

I went to university, having got into grammar school, without being required to sit the 'eleven-plus'. Janet refuses to go to grammar school, despite having a place, because she does not want to leave her friends. She later dropped out of sixth-form college and so never went to university. Richard drops out of boarding school and so misses university, pursuing vocational qualifications in agriculture and engineering instead. Alex, her education disrupted by moving and the divorce of her parents, does badly at her 'O' levels and leaves school without taking 'A' levels. John, despite being academically able, misses university because he follows his father into the RAF, pressured to do so by his mother. Mona fails her 'eleven-plus' but still does well at her 'O' levels. She abandoned being the dutiful studious daughter while studying for her 'A' levels and so does not get the grades to enable her to do a degree. Elaine fails to get into grammar school and her education is disrupted by her parents moving into town to run a pub, she goes out to work at 16. Rob passes his 'eleven-plus' and gets into grammar school but is socially isolated there and fails to do well and so his parents insist that he leaves at 16 and get a job. Mary goes to grammar school, does well in her 'A' levels and goes to university but is so embarrassed of her domestic science degree that she feels compelled to lie about the subject she took and make up for it with a Masters degree. Ethan, not growing up in the UK, does not experience this 'sheep and goats' division at 11 but family poverty means that education past high school was simply not an option.

Thus, for nearly all, the career options open to them are limited. Only Mary and I are able to enter the public sector professions of housing management and teaching. The rest of the group have to overcome this initially keenly felt obstacle to the social betterment that both they and their parents have come to expect. It is part-time study for vocational qualifications which both enable them to climb into managerial jobs and give them access to higher level management qualifications. Janet, Alex, Mona, Elaine and Rob all follow this route to their managerial status and Master's degree. Richard follows a similar route into engineering but becomes an entrepreneur rather than a salaried manager. John and Ethan use military service as a substitute for college; John succeeds in carving out a managerial identity within the military, again studying part-time. Ethan's specialist security experience enables him to pursue a career within the United Nations, albeit one that is restricted until he becomes a graduate. This is upward social mobility the hard way, working enthusiastically enough at one's job in order to make oneself a candidate for promotion and then going home and studying in the evenings and at weekends, a route I also took but to *escape* a managerial career. It is interesting to note that because management has developed as a professional-technical occupation, it has spawned its own academic discipline and educational qualifications (Ivory, Miskell, Shipton, White, Moeslein and Neely 2006). As a result, those who entered it without this status are able to claim their places at university on the basis of their experience of work. Thus a management career has provided its own particular route to upward social mobility, both in terms of material success and in terms of access to higher education.

It is also significant that the public sector, including the military, provides career opportunities for most of the group, whether graduate or not. Mary, Janet, John, Ethan, Alex, Rob and I all work in, or began our careers in, the public sector. Elaine, Richard and Mona though, carve out managerial careers via the private sector as client account manager, engineering entrepreneur, and training manager respectively. All, except me, would currently describe themselves as managers, no matter what route they chose to get to their jobs. I would have described myself, reluctantly, as a manager until I left the further education sector to work in universities. In other words, for this group, a managerial identity has by and large been the means by which they have fulfilled the expectations of a better life derived from their parents' generation.

The reasons my narrators gave for studying the Masters bears out this interpretation that a managerial identity represents a successful transcendence of humble origins, or even a route to self-redemption from a sense of shame and failure arising from youthful mistakes. Janet undertakes the Masters both to give herself more credibility as a management developer and to overcome the sense of failure caused by dropping out of school. Ethan undertakes the Masters because he cannot get promoted without a degree. Mary is trying to efface the shame of having a first degree in domestic science and because it is increasingly expected of someone at her level of seniority. Richard wanted to prove that he was intellectually capable of a degree, to make up for what he saw as deficiencies in his management skills and to legitimate his new role as external consultant/business advisor. Alex wanted the qualification primarily as a way of being able to move upwards in her career but also because it made her feel more secure as a manager. She also felt it would give her the option of alternative occupations such as teaching or freelance contracting. John wanted his Masters as part of his escape plan from the military. Although Mona had her arm twisted by her employer, she valued having completed the Masters because it both made her feel more secure as a manager and because it increased her chances of promotion.

Expectations and Attitudes

Finally, and perhaps more speculatively, it may be argued that the upper-working/lower middle-classes in the last few decades of the twentieth century have a particular outlook on life, influenced by and reinforcing the social and economic changes that were occurring post-war. For the first time, the idea of pulling oneself up by one's bootstraps must have seemed plausible to large numbers of adults from the working and lower middle-classes, for the reasons discussed above. No longer would collective mass action seem the only feasible route to improvements in individual lives (Brook 2001). This shift in outlook is nowhere more vividly represented by the desertion of the prosperous working and lower middle-classes from the British Labour Party and their willingness to vote for Conservative governments, devoted to the idea of individual enterprise and famously hostile to any form of collectivism (Garnett 2007).

As the prophetess of neo-liberalism, Margaret Thatcher opined 'There is no such thing as society – only individuals and their families'. Even though Janet, Rob, Mary, John, and Richard identify themselves as having left-wing sympathies, no narrative assumes anything other than that life is a quest for individual betterment and self-development, although what these terms mean differs between each narrative. One thing that is worth noting is that such an assumption does not mean that my interviewees have embraced a 'red in tooth and claw' competitive careerism. For all of them being a manager is deeply concerned with moral decisions. Their narratives assume a fundamental link between ethics and effectiveness when they invoke the ideal of the 'good' manager.

All assume that their working lives should exhibit the traditional 'puritan' virtues (including the Catholic storytellers) of hard work, fairness, commitment to employer and family, sobriety in its archaic sense, and thrift (Anthony 1977). Their pride in their career success is presented less as a celebration of consumerism and affluence than as the outward manifestation of the exercise of these virtues. It is another indicator of the influence of earlier generations that Christianity was such an important factor in many narratives. My own upbringing was deeply involved with the church. Janet and Mary's childhood stories also reflect the importance of religion for their families and communities. Richard's Quakerism, despite his unhappy schooling, had continued to strongly influence his sense of how he should deal with his relative wealth and his authority as a company chief executive. For the rest, there is little evidence that formal religious observance has been an important part of their lives, but nevertheless, its influence on education and on the moral background fabric until very recent decades should not be underestimated.

Age and the Stages of Life

All of my narrators, myself included, are old enough to look back on their lives and contemplate childhood and youth as stages already past. The idea of life stages is deeply embedded in western culture (Miller 2000; Rosen 2003) and how we place or find ourselves within an age category is an important aspect of our self-descriptions and thus identity. Where the boundaries between such stages lie, and the significance of describing ourselves as in one or the other stage, is largely socially determined and has varied considerably over both historical and personal time horizons. It is a cliché that teenagers only came into existence in the 1950s but it illustrates the point. There has also arguably been a homogenisation within British society of the once varied experience of life stages for different social groups and genders. For example, it is no longer as common to talk of women being 'left on the shelf' to become 'old maids' or to sneer that older women are 'mutton dressed as lamb'. On the other hand one now talks of women's rather than men's 'biological clocks' ticking, as many now defer having children for career reasons (Dex 2003). It is only men, though; who become 'dirty old men', the phrase 'dirty old woman' has quite different connotations. All of these distinctions rely on an unconscious awareness of what is appropriate behaviour for various life stages and express disapproval or pity when individuals violate these norms. Orwell (1942) remarks, in his analysis of McGill's postcards, that in the 1940s the working-classes moved straight from the first bloom of youth to late middle-age, whereas the middle-classes were able to prolong their youth into a much slower decline. Such class distinctions are much less evident today, largely perhaps as a result of the welfare legacy of the Golden Age.

Leaving aside the obvious exceptions of birth and death, my narrators draw on widely shared distinctions between childhood, youth, maturity, early vigorous old age, and later frail old age. Individual life stages are mapped against historical time as the crisis decades impact on the aimed at upward trajectory of these career stories in the case of Rob or myself, for example. Narrators also use expectations about what one 'should' have obtained or achieved by certain life stages as a way of measuring their own achievements and planning their futures. Early promotions or successes (a claim to distinctive talents based on earlier than usual achievement) are a common feature of the stories. To illustrate some of the ways in which narrators make use of age in constructing their identity in a little more detail, I shall now discuss the broad categories of youth, maturity and old age.

Narrators look back on their naïve and sometimes irresponsible childhood and youth with indulgent nostalgia. There is a shared assumption that childhood and youth are essentially preparations for mature adulthood, that the child is the father/mother of the man/woman. There is a marked gender division between men with 'sowing wild oats' stories (Richard, Ethan, and John, for example) and women who stress a continuity of devotion to duty, particularly to family (Mary, Alex and Janet, for example).

Several narrators look back with some regret, shame and guilt, mainly as a result of a mature realisation of ingratitude and thoughtlessness towards their parents. When I became a parent I re-assessed (and by extension, re-narrated) my own childhood: I found that I could more closely identify with my own parents' experiences and a similar re-assessment takes place with other parents in the stories. All who express these feelings take pains to present them as gentle reflections on a past self rather than as current emotional storms. This 'distancing' from a past self is a narrative practice used alongside others which stress continuity (presenting one's youth as part of a progressive self development, for example) and provides a glimpse into the continuous but precarious performance which must be undertaken within the narrative construction of identity. It illustrates vividly Sartre's portrait, discussed in the last chapter, of a self that must be shielded from objectification by the gaze of the Other, even when it is a past self. The strategy of disassociation, on the other hand, risks cutting one's self off from the past and so losing the desired narrative coherence that enables us to view our past lives as still our own.

The way in which careers are thought of is associated with how we define ourselves as being 'of a certain age'. All of the stories assume that one's youth is the time for rapid career advancement and the struggle to establish ourselves as adults that slows as middle age sets in. This link also illustrates the fine gradations in how narratives are constructed. Younger interviewees were still looking forward to further promotions (Mona and Elaine, for example) but slightly older ones presented themselves as having arrived at their peak and as 'old-hands' (Janet, Mary, and Rob, for example). Finally, Richard looking back over his working life, presents his work identity as more about mentoring and guiding the next generation of entrepreneurs. Thus managerial identity appears differently depending upon life stage. Elaine and Mona, in presenting themselves as being in transition from late youth to early middle age, discuss whether to have a family or not and how to balance the desire for family with the desire for further career success. In talking this through in their interviews they rehearse narrative options that will enable them to construct a self where a managerial identity becomes less significant than in the past and can only be retained by finding a balance with competing claims on how they and others see themselves (Wajcman and Martin 2002).

All assume that later life will be about repose and the pursuit of non-work based identities, although with Richard it is impossible to disentangle leisure and work. Unlike Richard, many express a desire to escape from work completely so as to enjoy an untrammelled and vigorous late middle/early old age. Few contemplate late old age, a life stage that has few positive connotations in our society, being seen as a time when identity is attenuated by physical incapacity, isolation, and disengagement from the world, an antechamber to the oblivion of the self (Bauman 1992; Clark 1993; Hallam, Hockey and Howarth 1999; Cicirelli 2001; Rees 2001).

As this section of empirical analysis is concerned with the referentiality of narrative, rather than treating it purely as free-floating text, it is worth concluding this discussion of age and identity by reflecting on the sheer physicality of age. Age is not simply a social convention (although our understanding of its significance may be), it is a process that happens to our bodies over time. We expend ourselves in the act of living and being. The demands of managerial work have grown in the Crisis Decades with its accompanying processes of privatisation, de-industrialisation, de-layering, longer working hours and work intensification (Gorz 1982; Thompson and Warhurst 1998; Dex 2003; Castells 2004). For most of my interviewees such demands are combined with parenthood, social activities, family duties and socially sanctioned forms of care of the self (such as my trips to the gym or the organic farmer's market). This intense existence places increasing demands on a diminishing stock of energy as individuals move from youth to maturity. There is a sense of weariness in many of the narratives and a longing for a future when these demands will lessen. The Faustian bargain struck by these story-tellers for upward social mobility has required that they are consumed by work even as it provides their lives with meaning.

The Twilight of Management Identity

To summarise the key points of this chapter, in their different ways, the narratives presented in this book demonstrate that identities are not free floating constructions which present endless possibilities for self-invention. All bear the marks of their particular location in history and are constrained by physical and social circumstances and by the attitudes and beliefs that are part and parcel of such circumstances. I have argued that the experience of growing up in upper-working/lower middle-class families and pursuing careers as the Golden Age gave way to the Crisis Decades has been a significant aspect of how my narrators see their work identities.

Future generations may not regard a managerial career as part of a multi-generational project of upward social progress or think that a university qualification confers anything very special on its holder. The symbolic value that my narrators place on material affluence as a measure of their personal achievement may also lessen for their successors. Such speculations cannot be verified except by time passing but engaging in them again underlines the conclusion that there is no such thing as a constant managerial identity. It is something fashioned out of the existing and historically specific circumstances of managers' lives in pursuit of a life that can be narrated to themselves and others as worth living. In only two of my stories had this attempt ended unsuccessfully, although even then not in total failure. Alex has had her fingers badly burned in pursuing her consultant-manager aspirations but has not given up hope that a managerial identity that makes her happy can be achieved. I was only ever a very reluctant manager and never sought being one as a positive self-description, preferring a more traditional public-sector professional identity. Nevertheless, for most of the group under discussion, being a manager can be plausibly presented as a success story enabled by the legacy of the Golden Age and the love and hard work of their parents. These unique circumstances have allowed a convergence between personal aspiration and managerial work which has meant that a managerial identity has been a largely positive route to them feeling reasonably satisfied with who they are and what their lives have become. There are numerous indicators that this convergence is now in reverse and that therefore a managerial identity may be becoming a steadily less attractive one in the future, a possibility that has serious implications for individuals, organisations and society. In the next chapter I turn to *how* my story-tellers incorporate such a managerial identity into their life stories and their sense of themselves.

Chapter 6
Telling Tales

In Chapter 5, following the existentialist insight that individuals are historical through and through, I outlined the historical context that both enabled and constrained the narratives of self presented in Chapter 2, treating them as a collective generational history and locating each account within this historical context. One striking result of this approach for my thinking about managerial identity has been the way in which managerial careers have provided a vehicle for the achievement of the post war aspirations inherited from the parents of my story tellers. In this chapter I shift my focus from the collective to the individual, echoing Ricoeur's dialectic of *idem* identity (sameness) with *ipse* identity (selfhood) (Ricoeur 1992). In other words I will examine how the content has been utilised by each story teller in order to construct a unique narrative of selfhood out of the common discursive resources and aspirations provided by a shared historical context.

In order to analyse the content and process of each narrative it is necessary to find a method of comparing and contrasting each of them and this presents a number of problems, the first of which is, that although the existentialist theory presented in Chapter 4 supports treating these stories both as an instance of the narrative construction of identity and of identity as an ethical quest it does not suggest a ready-to-hand method for analysing individual stories. The challenge then has been to find a method which is compatible with, but not directly a product of, these theoretical insights. Such a method should enable the stories to be compared and contrasted as well as enable the identification of the building blocks within each story and shed some light on the significance of utilising these elements rather than others.

I have sought to achieve these aims in this chapter by treating the narratives as analogous to folk stories and analysing their narrative elements in a way suggested by the work of the folklorist and Russian formalist, Vladimir Propp (1968), whom Ricoeur (1992) also draws upon as part of his theory of the self and narrative identity, particularly the insight that human beings are either acting or undergoing (suffering) the actions of others. Even before reading Propp, I was struck by the way my stories reminded me strongly of traditional tales both in their plots and in the way in which the storytellers presented themselves (mostly as the heroes of their accounts) and other protagonists. In addition, this way of approaching the stories is congruent with the idea of a self constructed over a lifetime as an existential quest that I outlined in Chapter 4. Of course, for Heidegger and Sartre the aim of human existence is not 'and they all lived happily ever after' but rather authenticity, their version of the 'good' life.

There are some pretexts within organisation studies for classifying narratives according to such generic schemes. Gabriel (2000), for example, has recourse to a typology of narrative genres and functions, although based on classical literature rather than folk stories. This suggests that generic categorisations based on narrative elements are a useful way of making sense of stories, enabling analysis of both commonalities and differences. For all of these reasons, Propp's work seemed to promise an engaging and relevant way of analysing how my narratives are constructed whilst still treating them as stories and thus enabling me to retain my treatment of these accounts as 'whole' stories rather than depersonalised fragments.

As well as analysing performance in terms of the functions of textual elements, insights can also be generated by analysing how these elements are deployed differently across a number of narratives. How the story is told may be as important as its contents, particularly when the story-teller is telling us about him or herself. Accordingly, I complete this chapter by examining the process of narrative construction via a framework suggested by Holstein and Gubrium (2000). They suggest a method of analysing this aspect of narrative performance through what they term 'narrative practices'. Firstly they highlight 'narrative linkage', the way in which links are built between 'what is available to construct personal accounts, the biographical particulars at hand, and the related work of contextualising who and what we are' (2000, 108). Secondly, they draw attention to 'narrative slippage'; the way in which seemingly standard discourses are differentially employed by different individuals or by the same individual in different circumstances, even to the point where a completely different meaning and projected identity could be conveyed. Thirdly, Holstein and Gubrium turn to 'narrative options', noting that stories frequently present alternative and competing meanings which are deliberately contemplated within the narrative itself. Finally, they consider 'narrative editing', the decisions which occur during story-telling about which direction the story should take, often by presenting alternatives in their stories, gaining a reaction from their listener, and then developing the story in a certain direction as a result. Such an approach is consistent with Ricoeur's work, particularly in its assumption that narrative accounts of the self are continually adjusted as a result of the dialectic between recounting and enactment (Rainwater 1996).

In using these two methods in this chapter I am also seeking not to lose sight of the historical context explored in the previous chapter. After all, none of the three methods of interpretation I have utilised work well in isolation. It is impossible to identify functional narrative elements without drawing upon an understanding of social and historical context. For example, if a narrator compares their boss to Adolf Hitler, some basic historical context is helpful in deciding whether the story-teller is likely to be deploying the functional role of 'the villain' or that of the 'inspirational/powerful helper'. In just the same way it is impossible to make judgements about how individuals link their own stories as managers to prevailing social discourses about management without any knowledge of how this discourse comes to occupy its influential position at the start of the twenty-first century. It is then inevitable that no clear division of modes of interpretation can be sustained but by attempting to foreground each in turn, I hope to have drawn attention to different aspects of the narratives and to generally demonstrate the validity of narrative identity as an interpretative approach. Bearing this in mind I shall now go on to discuss the way in which Propp's work can yield worthwhile insights regarding the nature of contemporary managerial identities.

Propp (1968) sought to classify and understand the cultural significance of folk stories through a functional analysis of their common narrative elements. With conceptual similarities to structuralism (Kearney 1994), Propp asserts that stories have a limited and consistent sub-structure of basic elements which can be combined and presented in different ways to yield different stories. This assertion is based on four principles. Firstly, 'functions of characters serve as stable, constant elements in a tale, independent of how and by whom they are fulfilled' and secondly, 'the number of functions known to the fairy tale is limited' (1968, 21). Thirdly, 'the sequence of functions is always identical' (1968, 22) and finally 'All fairy tales are of one type in regard to their structure' (1968, 23).

Now it might be reasonably suggested that, doubtless interesting though Russian Formalism is to the literary theorist, it does not have much relevance to contemporary accounts of working lives and management careers. I would argue that such principles *are* of interest, not least, because autobiography/biography is an identifiable genre with its own conventions. As Stanley has pointed out 'the autobiographical archetype is the *Bildungsroman*, the tale of the progressive travelling of a life from troubled or stifled beginnings; in which obstacles are overcome and the true self actualised or revealed' (1992, 11). This archetype also applies to traditional stories which are frequently rooted in the chronological sequence of childhood, youth, early struggle, establishment, aging, disengagement and reflection on the past, and death, as discussed in more detail above. In other words, the conventions of this genre tend towards correspondence with Propp's four principles. In addition, an important shared convention of autobiographical life stories with folk stories is that they are also frequently accounts of the lives of individuals (*Beowulf* [Heaney 2001], *Cinderella, Robin Hood*, or *Dick Whittington*, for example).

A moment's thought will suggest that this similarity is no coincidence. Folk tales embody a view of what a human life is that has considerable historical continuity. They concentrate on how 'ordinary' people achieve extraordinary successes through extraordinary endeavours combined with extraordinary qualities. Much modern drama follows the same conventions; television soap operas might be thought of as a form of folk story and lend themselves to a similar formalistic deconstruction. Two of Propp's folk story narrative elements illustrate their applicability to a wide range of both modern and historical story-based genres: 'The victim submits to deception and thereby unwittingly helps his enemy' or 'interdictions are addressed to the hero but always violated' (1968, 30, 26–7). These plot devices can be applied equally to Shakespeare's plays and to every Hollywood blockbuster one cares to recall. For many of us our only experience of how people should and do behave when faced with life's more serious crises is through such fiction, which provides us with a ready-to-hand language for describing our experiences in our own stories. In this sense such generic stories provide one instance of Heidegger's notion of how we manage to immerse ourselves in the 'they' rather than making our own authentic choices.

In short, life-stories are analogous to folk stories, with the distinction that they are more complex, messier and usually less conclusive. However both draw on a communal repository of narratives that spans both centuries and cultures but, despite their diversity, consist of familiar and often limited elements in their construction. In the following pages, I attempt to draw attention to the generic narrative elements employed in the stories in this book as a way of evaluating the idea of narrative identity construction. Of course, it might be objected that all I have done is to re-tell my earlier narratives in a different form and this is perfectly true, one cannot easily escape textual conventions and still communicate with one's readers. My argument is though that life-stories strongly lend themselves to such a treatment which exposes the underlying assumptions and processes out of which managerial identities are built. My approach then has been to illustrate the shared narrative elements and their distinctive deployment in each story by drawing analogies with various folk, fairy, traditional or deeply culturally embedded myths and stories. This has sometimes included films, contemporary stories and biblical stories as all seem to me to provide deeply culturally embedded examples of common elements of the life histories in Chapter 2. I begin with my own biography.

Management Folk Tales

The Researcher

I present myself as a self-deprecating slightly diffident hero: A detached and superior observer of my own life and circumstances. The opening consists of a description of my parents and family and is heavily nostalgic; it conveys something of the stereotypical 'happy childhood' which is to be disrupted by commencement of the quest. In folk tales this frequently follows upon some catastrophe such as the death of a parent or the theft/abduction of something/someone of great value. The portrait of a slightly eccentric and certainly 'different' family also positions me as different and the claim to uniqueness has parallels again with traditional storytelling. The hero has attributes that set him or her apart, such as unusual strength, beauty, character or cunning. Sometimes this individuation can be achieved through the possession of magical objects or by help from a powerful supernatural figure (Propp 1968). In my case, the nearest elements to this are the implicit claims to a superior intellect, echoing the unparalleled importance of education achievement for social mobility in the post-war years for members of my social class.

The element of the quest is apparent throughout my story, although it takes two forms. It involves both the overcoming of an obstacle and the search for something that is lacking. The first of these is the inability to understand my own unwillingness to apply myself to my studies and later employment. The second is the search for my *metier* or perhaps even my 'vocation', which stresses both the idea of a 'calling' and a profession. The objective of arriving at a happy and successful life, including work, lies in achieving both parts of the quest. I will not be able to overcome my inability to commit myself to work unless I can find the right career, and the right career will result in failure unless I learn to apply myself to it. The narrative thus develops as a picaresque journey searching for the right job and along the way encountering temptations from my inner demons of diffidence, laziness and boredom. Thus the quest is both about its eventual destination and the journey. The end can only be reached when I have both learnt to recognise it and developed the moral worth and maturity to be able to benefit from it. There is a parallel here with the Arthurian story of the quest for the Grail. Galahad achieves the Grail because of his essential purity and the trials he undergoes finding it, but Lancelot cannot, despite discovering its whereabouts, because of his moral failings. In many respects both elements of quest can be incorporated in the idea of a search for my self, or at least the self I wish to be.

Other than these internal enemies, the external enemies and trials encountered are numerous; from a father who discourages me from going to university, the recurring motif of the bullying boss, and a right-wing government that lays waste the further education system where, until forced out, I thought my quest had ended. As with many stories (Bunyan's *Pilgrim's Progress* comes to mind here), when I take a wrong turning I am corrected by disasters which both teach a moral lesson and serve to set me back on the right track. For example, work in an insurance company seems a good idea at first but results in my realisation that this is an immensely boring dead-end job and so I return to my studies. University serves as a peaceful interlude between trials but also one that prefigures the career destination at the close of the story. It also serves as a contrast that makes the unhappiness of my first job as a journalist more emphatic, the hero deceived by false promises. Entering the seedy world of journalism also represents a moral failure that is punished by suffering but that drives me on to train as a teacher. There is a sense of destiny here, all episodes must have meaning and play their part in the realisation of the overall story.

Another important element that recurs in all of the narratives, and is present here, is the 'lucky break'. The moment of fate that decides one's future. In my case this coincides with the partial achievement of the search aspect of the quest – I find my vocation in teaching, a job that I can sustain. In one sense I have found my 'self' in the identity of teacher, although in another the quest starts again as I realise that I have to be a particular sort of teacher, an academic. As with other heroic stories, the achievement of one success simply paves the way for more difficult tasks and obstacles leading to more self-knowledge and moral development.

Unlike most fictional stories there is no finale, autobiography can never be complete. Becoming an academic has not proved to be the equivalent of marrying the princess, inheriting half the kingdom and living happily ever after. Achievements are ambivalent; they always have the potential to turn out to be disasters later on, recalling Sartre's insistence that consciousness can always reform our interpretations of ourselves. As Heidegger stresses, a 'real' as opposed to fictional life is only ever completed by death but after my death, my story can no longer be autobiography. As long as the life story *I* tell carries on, my life must continue to have a meaning for me and so the terms of the quest must be constantly revised and renewed.

The NHS Manager

When I first heard Janet's story I was immediately reminded of Cinderella. She is the favourite youngest child but her father dies leaving her at the mercy of a much less loving mother and resentful older brothers and sisters. Janet even gives herself a decidedly folkloric name when she calls herself 'Second Hand Rose'. In its invocation of Cinderella, Janet's narrative foregrounds her qualities of patience, virtue and dutifulness that enable her to overcome the setbacks of her childhood. This is clearly a highly gendered story. Her self-description also positions Janet as an innocent victim of both cruel fate and cruel relations; there is no suggestion that her siblings' resentment has any grounding in her own conduct. Janet, as with many other interviewees, stresses the difficulty of her circumstances in order to emphasise the scale of her later achievements and the determination required to obtain them.

Janet, unlike Cinderella, is not more beautiful than her siblings but she does imply that she is more clever, when she describes herself as being more independent minded and insightful than the rest of her family. She alone can 'see through' Catholicism. The youngest child with special qualities is a familiar folkloric motif, think of the clever and handsome youngest miller's son in *Puss in Boots* and how he is contrasted with his two doltish older brothers. In Janet's case these special qualities are her rationality, her intellectual ability, her courageousness (which enables her to take on irksome people and circumstances) and a highly developed sense of justice and morality. This motif of the unique person who is set apart by special qualities is evident throughout all of the narratives. It establishes the narrator as having the requisite characteristics to qualify as the hero of their own story.

Religion appears in Janet's early narrative as a 'dark force' to be overcome in much the same way that enchanted forests or other places of supernatural danger are in folk stories. Janet's family are in thrall to the spell of religion but Janet herself is liberated by the power of her rationality. As well as her rationality, Janet presents herself as having a stronger sense of what is right than those around her; whether they are her family or, later on in her story, her fellow managers. In metaphorical terms she is a knight in shining moral armour. However, Catholicism, along with Socialism, is also deployed as a positive influence in giving Janet a strong sense both of justice and the primacy of service to others, which is how she later endows her work with meaning and moral significance both as nurse and manager. In this sense Catholicism plays a dual role as both enemy and helper.

The motifs of entrapment (sometimes with overtones of having been deceived) and escape also figure strongly in many of the narratives. In Janet's case this entrapment is sometimes linked to romantic attachments. Persuaded by a boyfriend she begins her working life as a trainee technician. Only after starting this job does she realise that it is not equal to her abilities. She can only escape to London to do voluntary work if she leaves behind the 'hostage' of a promise to her mother to return to take up nursing. Later on she is forced to give up full-time work both because of an alcoholic husband and because an old vanquished enemy (Catholicism) rears its head again in the form of persuading her to submit herself to an inappropriate marriage.

The role of luck and the lucky break are also apparent in Janet's story as it is with nursing that Janet finds her vocation and her managerial self even though she originally has no intention of taking up her training place. A separate but related element can be identified as the importance of fate or destiny. Story-tellers are frequently affected by luck, good and bad, which can both blow them off course or enable them to achieve part of their quest. Such luck is not entirely meaningless or arbitrary. It serves both moral and functional purposes in advancing the pilgrim's progress or teaching lessons. To believe that we are not simply victims of capricious fate but rather that 'all things work together for good' is a strong consolation and prop to a secure sense of self. There is also an implication, in the way that lucky breaks are recounted, of a resourceful and adaptable self. Janet's story is no exception to this and once she finds her destined path it becomes an account of upward progress into management.

The last great trial in Janet's narrative is a combination of promotion, doing the Masters degree and acquiring a boss who is, as with Janet's other villains, corrupt. Janet is now the experienced manager in her prime, who overcomes the problems she faces by the familiar combination of straight talking and moral courage. She is no longer 'Second Hand Rose', but a successful senior manager in control of her destiny. There are some intimations that she is about to start a new stage of 'questing', leaving hospital work and starting a new career in teaching. There is also an oscillation between a desire for new adventures and a desire that they should come to an end with a long passive 'living happily ever after', or at least a desire to be the older story-teller, entertaining and edifying younger members of the organisation as she looks backwards rather than forwards on her own story.

The United Nations Security Manager

For an English reader, the metaphor of folk story seems less apt for Ethan. Rather, his story suggested a Hollywood movie but, as I argued above, the links between these genres can be close. His story begins as a child in a large poor family and so, as soon as he grows up, he has to go into the wider world to seek his fortune. For Ethan, travel and adventure are frequently cited as major attractions of all the jobs he undertakes. His first job as a US Marine deploys the motif of the young naïve hero who is tricked by the wily older recruiter. The narrative then becomes a story of how he escapes from this unpromising start. Once more the 'lucky break' figures when he is selected at random for presidential security duties. This stroke of luck not only enables him to escape from the irksome life of troop training but it also sets him on his career path. His quest does not consist of a search for his vocation, rather it becomes an adventurous journey that his special security skills take him on. Ethan, along with some other male narrators, stresses his physical strength and courage as heroic qualities that, as with Samson or Hercules, enable him to emerge victorious from trials. In Ethan's case, he must survive as an infantry commander and as a Kosovan war-crimes investigator in the face of violence and Conradian horror.

Ethan's time in the army coincides with his final stage of preparation for adult life. He has passed through the trials of physical and moral strength and has assumed the mantle of leadership. Unlike the AWOL-prone 'grunts' he leaves behind, he is destined for better things. After adventures in the hostile land of Soviet Russia he finds himself the loyal retainer of the kingly figure of UN Secretary General. The outsider who works their way up to becoming the valued and highly capable servant to powerful figures is another familiar motif from traditional stories, for example the Old Testament stories of Joseph and Daniel. Ethan downplays the fear and emotion that his adventures might be expected to give rise to and so presents himself as the cool, controlled, self-contained, detached, guarded and typically masculine action hero from a thousand Westerns.

A strong feature of Ethan's narrative, but one which is also evident in many others, is the implicit dualism between the site of the quest on the one hand and family, home and repose on the other. For Ethan there is little room for juggling between the two as his career unfolds despite his having married in his early days at the UN. A desired domesticity, symbolised by returning to the UK and living quietly by the sea is firmly assigned a place in his future, after his travelling is done and his adventures come to an end. Perhaps one can detect here a parallel with Odysseus, a parallel which would frame the story as principally a quest to reach home itself.

It is in Kosovo that Ethan's story shifts from an account of personal advancement to one that is imbued with moral significance. He descends into chaos, a realm of death and violence, in order to help bring restoration and justice. His special qualities of physical courage and resourcefulness enable him to face the challenges presented. He alone of his colleagues volunteers to return to the field to investigate war crimes on the ground. He infuses these heroic 'manly' qualities into his idealised view of a 'good' managerial identity. A good manager is someone who is prepared to put themselves in danger for others, to set an example to those he leads, to see justice done and to foster the idea of collective endeavour in order to get the job done. As the result of another lucky break, Ethan finds himself in charge of war crimes tribunal security and so his questing is rewarded with a senior management position. One of the noteworthy aspects of managerial identity that begins to emerge from this form of analysis is its sheer mutability. Different narrators plausibly reinterpret what it means to be a 'good' manager in pursuit of sometimes very different desired selves.

Ethan's new job requires that he obtain a degree and he chooses that this should be a management degree. He now extends his quest to include the figure of the transformational manager, championing change in his organisation. Ethan appears to see a managerial identity as a way of making the transition between action hero and a quieter type of quest, one that he can pursue now that he is in middle age. Ethan's narrative closes with a wistful reflection on the desire to return home (defined by Ethan as the UK) and to enjoy complete repose, watching the waves break on the coastline, a reminder of journeys past.

The Mental Health Charity Manager

Mary's story is presented in anti-heroic terms and, at first sight, yields less than other narratives to this mode of interpretation. It is an un-dramatic account of a life that has run smoothly and has itself been effectively managed. Mary is at pains not to stress either the depth of the difficulties or the heights of her achievements but this 'no-fuss' story is as archetypal as other more 'heroic' narratives, drawing on a gendered sense of virtue that has its roots firmly in the past. Mary is the person who gets on with quietly doing things while others panic or whinge. She is the plain speaking yet discreet heroine of Jane Austen novels; a self-effacing 'ordinary' person who nevertheless achieves extraordinary things through the power of common sense. The term 'heroine' is deliberate; instead of a macho, heroic, and self-promoting sort of quest, Mary's has been one of idealised domesticated care, characterised by dutifulness, resourcefulness and a desire to quietly succeed rather than draw attention to her difficulties and achievements. Mary was the only female interviewee to link her motherhood to her work, as maternal care for her subordinates. Her narrative stresses the role of organisation as a way of minimising the unpredictable and so the ups and downs of adventure would be inappropriate to the construction of her own vision of the good manager. In other words this is more an exemplary moral tale than an adventure yarn.

These important distinctions aside, Mary's narrative does contain some similar structural elements to the others. She comes from humble beginnings but her special qualities of dutifulness, cleverness and diligence enable her to succeed at school and obtain a place at university. These qualities also ensure that her progress is smooth and unproblematic. There are no grounds for conflict with her family or with her school. She carries the hopes and expectations of her parents for a better life without demur or resentment and there are no lapses or failures to disappoint them or lead her into unexpected trials. Perhaps the only villains in Mary's account are the 'un-respectable' working-class which provide a symbolic focus for the fear of failure that is the other side of the coin of the hope of social advancement. Mary's family are respectable and hard-working upper-working-class. Her horror when she comes face to face with skinhead yobs at school or conditions on an inner London housing estate is palpable. It is from these symbols of failure that she must distance herself if her quest to meet the aspirations of her family is to succeed.

One of the things that *does* go wrong is that her naivety about the middle-class world she is moving into means an embarrassing choice of degree subject and this mistake must be redeemed by her studying for the Masters degree later. The 'lucky break' in her narrative is her interest in housing which unexpectedly leads to a first job in London, although at the time this also seems a setback. The theme of entrapment and escape runs through the narrative as Mary moves from one job to another to escape the various problems that unexpectedly emerge. Perhaps not surprisingly, given her preference for a rational un-emotive basis to her identity, Mary displays a marked affinity for a managerial identity.

Mary's love of quiet efficiency should not be taken as implying passivity. Her choice of jobs is usually governed by wanting to be able to take action and get things done, thus her preference for organising housing projects over straightforward administration. Her idealised management identity stresses the ability of managers to get things done in a bureaucratic/social service organisational setting. She also uses her managerial status as a measure of her success, a marker of the distance travelled from her self-description as 'working-class lass'.

As with the other narratives, being a manager is imbued with moral purpose and various villains are implicit in contrasting models of bad managers who do not care for their staff, or never get things done because of their enslavement to bureaucracy. Where organisations are hopelessly infected with these faults then Mary must leave in search of the organisation that will allow her to become a 'good' manager. Determination and doggedness are constantly stressed as ordinary characteristics that enable her to overcome obstacles at which others fall. She also imbues herself with moral virtues through identifying herself as a champion who fights for the cause of her clients against the enemies of complacency and bureaucratic sloth. Towards the end of the narrative Mary, as with other narrators, looks forward to the end of her quest. There is a wish that her new senior management job will be her last and that in ten years time she will be able to retire. She is the mature hero whose main concern is to survive to her homecoming and rest but she worries that she might 'burn out' like her predecessor, now that she has achieved her ambition.

The Engineer

Richard's narrative is presented as a combination of adventure yarn and redemption story. He is a self-made man in a number of respects, both as an entrepreneur but also as someone who struggles to create himself anew from his failure at school. He begins by describing a happy carefree childhood that is disrupted by his being sent away to boarding school, where he is made miserable. The story suggests the sort of childhood reversal of fortune familiar from Charles Dickens (*Oliver Twist* (1838/1982) or *The Old Curiosity Shop* (1841/1997), for example) following the death of a parent or a sudden descent into poverty. Richard escapes from this misery by running away and seeking his fortune, which initiates a series of adventures. His quest is to overcome the disaster of his boarding school education and to become the sort of man both his family and he can be proud of. This is no mean task as he portrays both his parents as exceptional individuals from exceptional families; their radicalism, dedication to charitable work and intellectual abilities place a heavy burden on Richard to emulate them.

As with Ethan and Rob, Richard claims the traditionally masculine heroic qualities of physical strength, toughness and physical skill. From being a bullied weakling Richard changes himself through sport and so is able to take on tough construction workers at sea. This toughness also takes the form of sheer endurance and a capacity for hard work that dwarfs those around him. His other claim to a special quality is as a 'naturally' gifted engineer and inventor. This skill is elevated in his story to the status of a magical power. It enables him to travel and experience many adventures, in the process performing miraculous acts of engineering that no-one else can do. The discovery of his special skill happens almost by accident. Just as the future King Arthur discovers who he 'really' is by accidentally pulling the sword from the stone, so Richard 'discovers' himself as an unintended result of settling on casual farm work for want of anything better to do.

This early part of Richard's story is a story of growing up, his picaresque adventures are a typical 'sowing wild oats' story including the girl in every port, fighting to defend himself and the physical risks of his job. This is not a story of aimless dissolution though, all of Richard's experiences are recounted as having a purpose and of contributing towards his later success. The skills he acquires will form the basis of his business. The physical toughness and ability to deal with all sorts of different people will also stand him in good stead. Richard's wild life is, however, a dangerous one in both a physical and moral sense. It is only a lucky escape from a nearly fatal accident (another instance of the 'blessing in disguise') and the love of a good woman that redeems him from both sorts of danger and sets him on the right path to business success. This in turn enables him to become a Quaker philanthropist and so the man he should always have been.

Another important heroic quality that features in Richard's account of himself is his incorruptibility. His is a world where others have their snouts in the trough but Richard walks like Bunyan's Christian in Vanity Fair, in the world but not of it. He makes a point of eschewing the trappings of wealth and status. Richard portrays himself as a champion of good sense and moral rectitude in a corrupt world, fighting against greed, snobbery and incompetence, righting the wrongs that he became acutely aware of at school. He undercuts this epic atmosphere by his reflection on the double-sidedness of his heroic traits. His aggression, ruthlessness, competitiveness and complete obsession with his work are presented at times as damaging and corrosive; a second level of struggle with inner demons and temptation which must also be overcome if he is to become the 'balanced' and mature human being he aspires to.

The second phase of Richard's story marks the end of his wild-oat sowing and his transformation into a paternalistic entrepreneur. His extreme assertion of individuality and competitiveness seem to make running his own business inevitable. One can simply not imagine Richard as a docile corporate middle manager. Again his special qualities as an engineer and his powers of endurance enable him to succeed where others fail. He is also driven by the compulsion to seek redemption, a need to atone for his young man's selfish rejection of the sacrifices his parents made for him. His pursuit of a management qualification contributes to this quest to become a person his parents can be proud of and to confirm him in his position of the wise elder who can advise younger managers or struggling businesses.

Richard's story concludes from the viewpoint of someone who has largely achieved the quest he set out on. He can return 'home' and reflect on his past with satisfaction. In his relinquishment of his CEO post there is something of Prospero's repudiation of magic, enabling him to return to 'civilised' family life. He has become an upstanding philanthropic member of the community, enabling him to feel that he is what his parents wished him to be. There is also some poignancy to his realisation that he no longer has the strength for the titanic struggles of his past. He is, then, a bloody and bowed hero who has now become, in his own words, a 'wise old owl' and is at last, he hopes, finding some peace at journey's end, albeit a peace combined with resignation.

The Information Systems Consultant

Alex's story contrasts strongly with most others which present themselves as positive epics. In Alex's case we have more of a tragic story in which she positions herself as undeserving victim, as the vanquished not the victor of the struggles that her life has presented her with. Unlike other narratives, Alex tends to repudiate her own agency, seeking some consolation for her unhappiness in the thought that it is not her fault.

Her childhood is not an idealised happy and secure time which becomes disrupted by the start of the quest of adult life. It is merely a time of misery and difficulty emphasising the undeserved misfortunes that are heaped upon her and which disadvantage her from the start. Her life seems to consist of almost achieving the good things she deserves only to have them snatched away at the last minute, like Tantalus. There is an element of the tragic in her story of early promise and success destroyed by her falling to the temptation of her current job, deceived by the glitter of a consultant's title and company car. All the things she loved; her work, her home, her friends and her boyfriend have one by one been lost as a result of her disastrous decision. Alex invites us to share her sense of the unfairness of it all, to accede to her conviction that she deserves better because of her hard work and abilities, to pity rather than admire her.

Structurally, however, Alex's story bears a strong resemblance to the others. It starts with an account of her childhood which is disrupted, as she approaches adulthood, by her mother's decision to move to a better area for the sake of her family's future. As with so many other decisions in Alex's tale, this results in disaster and the opposite of what was hoped for. The family are plunged into strife and poverty. Her quest is expressed as an attempt to overturn these initial disadvantages and to secure for herself an entirely different life from that of her miserable childhood. Again there is the 'lucky break' in that, when she begins work, she realises that she is both good at it and finds it enjoyable. She has found her vocation and, as promotions follow, her developing managerial identity becomes a source of affirmation and pride. It also enables her to successfully embark on management qualifications, however, this is Alex's story and so these successes go sour.

House purchases, friendships and love affairs all go wrong. The thing that Alex is most unhappy about is how her working life is made miserable by her subordinates, a group of 'bickering women', who are lazy and obsessed with their children. These harpy-like tormentors are contrasted with her own qualities of hard work, commitment and motivation and her belief that work is a central, not a peripheral, part of one's life. This contrast also stresses her moral worth, a worth that is confirmed by adversity rather than disconfirmed by failure. Domesticity here seems to represent a place of misery and confinement, a place that she must escape from, in order to achieve her quest.

The crux of Alex's story and a structural element that is unique to her narrative is a fateful choice. In other narratives the protagonists appear to be at the mercy of events, often ending up where they do because of luck. Their agency consists in the resourceful way in which they make the best of the circumstances they find themselves in. Alex's story hinges on a terrible practical and moral dilemma about what to do with her life. She must choose between using her Masters degree, and the critical awareness it has given her of the world of management, to become a teacher, a morally worthy and self-denying option. Alternatively she can become a business consultant and obtain all the material rewards and status she has desired for herself. This choice is presented as a fall; she is all set for a virtuous career in teaching when temptation in the form of a job offer takes her by surprise. She yields and punishment follows as her new glittering career turns into a personal and professional nightmare, a classic Heideggerian lapse into inauthenticity at the behest of the 'they'. As with all temptation there is a strong element of deceit and trickery. She is promised all sorts of good things in this new job; useful experience, challenging work, more pleasant colleagues and autonomy. All of these promises turn out to be deceits and in fact her job gives her the opposite of all these things.

In this story of a choice one can see another instance of the moral weight interviewees attach to the idea of management. In embracing a morally questionable management identity she risks becoming a 'bad' manager. The horror of what she has risked becoming is embodied in her account of her bullying, shouting, callous boss, a classic villain who must either be escaped from or overcome.

This is a more complex tale, however, than a straightforward account of personal disaster solely designed to elicit the sympathy of its hearer. Unless Alex is to give in completely to despair she must be able to find a positive aspect to her experiences, to fit them to a narrative that looks forward to better times in which a sadder but wiser Alex is able to avoid the mistakes of the past and rediscover the path to the achievement of her quest and this is what Alex goes on to consider. How can she escape back to the virtuous path of a career in teaching? By the second interview this problem is resolved. She has repositioned herself as less the helpless victim and more the battered but determined hero, again in pursuit of her quest. She has intervened in her story by handing in her notice and returning to her old employer, albeit on a short term contract. For her to be able to claim that her experiences have in fact been at least partially positive she must do more than simply tell a story of a return to the point where she took a wrong turn. Alex achieves this with her new identity of freelance contractor and consultant which enables her to present this next move as a progress towards her goals, a step forward not backwards. In her reversal of her temptation through her resignation she finds a moral redemption as she recounts how her friend tells her that she 'has made more progress in two weeks than in the last year'. Anything is now possible once more.

Of course, this is not a neat fictional story and she has not reached a 'happily ever after' conclusion. As she says, 'my Prince Charming has not turned up'. Her hostility to domesticity has disappeared to be replaced with a fear that she may never be able to have children if no-one turns up soon, nevertheless her story can now end on a note of optimism.

The Squadron Leader

John's story might be characterised as an endurance story, one of patient but not passive suffering. John makes a naïve mistake in his youth which has consequences that must be lived with for many years. It is a story of exile, or even enchantment. His rootless disturbed childhood and his desire to belong somewhere cause him to be deceived by the attractions of a career in the RAF. The glamour (at one time a word synonymous with the deceit of enchantment) of being a pilot mysteriously fades away as soon as he joins up and realises that he is different from the other trainees. John's quest can also be read as the interrelated search both for his 'true' self and for his vocation invoked in other narratives.

This is also a story of heroic resistance against the crushing weight of the military machine, as John carves out an un-military self and the magic talisman that enables him to do this, that protects him, as if by a cloak of invisibility, is a managerial identity. This identity enables him to resist the absorption of his self into the machine and so keeps the quest alive, in the sense that he can continue to discover more about himself. However, it does not by itself give him a hope of final success. To do this John needs a powerful helper and in his story this is provided by his master's degree. For no other narrator is the masters course a central functional element in the story. For John his studies unlock the doors of his inner self and so enable him to know who he is. Obtaining the qualification enables him to pursue what he now believes to be his vocation, an academic career.

John's childhood is recounted as both happy and difficult. His family are loving and close but constantly on the move, because of his father's job in the RAF. He portrays himself as a sensitive and intelligent child who loves art and literature, nevertheless his desperation for somewhere to call home deceives him into joining the RAF and denying these aspects of himself. In keeping with the sense of a slow journey of self-discovery he has no regrets at first and as a young man enjoys the adventure and travel. As he matures he becomes 'desperately unhappy' and begins to deeply regret his choice. Even in the early days he knows that he is different. He reads different books to his colleagues and cannot get excited by the technology of aircraft in the same way. His eyesight prevents him from training as a pilot but this turns out to be another 'blessing in disguise' as, by the time this problem is resolved, he has decided that he does not wish to become that 'sort' of person.

By becoming part of personnel administration, John is able to carve out a self-identity as a manager that enables him to insulate himself against the encroachments of military life. This resistance comes at a price. John keenly feels a sense of imposture: a sense that is evident from many of the narratives and for which the achievement of management qualifications provides some relief. In John's account, he is pretending to be someone he is not and feels guilty about taking the money under false pretences. Unlike most of us, for John putting on a business suit represents taking off, not putting on, a uniform. His sense of himself as a morally worthy manager is troubled by guilt at this performance of a 'false' identity. He does not leave at the various 'option points', however, because he is tempted by promotion. He is also tied by the promise of his pension. John is thus trapped, a prisoner amongst strangers, and part of his construction of a heroic self rests on his qualities of patience and endurance, given moral value by the fact that his remaining in the RAF is partly done for the sake of his wife and family. The story thus far presents us with an *impasse*, he is trapped in the RAF and fights to preserve a sense of himself that is constantly under threat from military life but he also knows that he will have to leave at some point and then his lack of a degree or a clear knowledge of what he wants to become will leave him unable to pursue his existential quest.

The 'lucky break' for John is the Master's course itself. It gives him a qualification that will enable him to find satisfying work but it also explains himself to himself.

It enables him to make sense of his past and gives him a direction for the future. He has discovered what it is that he wants to be; a management academic. It is a 'lucky' break because it is unplanned and unexpected that the course will have this radically transformatory effect.

John defines his future self as a thorn in the side of the establishment. Once he is on the outside of the RAF and is 'armed' with an academic position he will then be able to take on the forces of reaction and complacency, ironically retaining a rather military conception of his post-military career. He is constructing a future quest with an appropriate heroic identity which he hopes will enable him to write the next chapter in his narrative. This future provides him with continuity as it makes a positive thing of his suffering. It provides meaning and significance for what might otherwise be felt to be a wasted life. Suffering must be developmental and for a purpose, the purpose of achieving the quest of becoming the person he wishes to be.

The Human Resources Manager

With Mona's story we have another version of the dutiful daughter who is trying to pay back the sacrifices made for her by her parents and make up for letting them down with her poor 'A' level results. She chooses not to make extensive use of the heroic possibilities of her ethnic origins, although racist insults do figure as an early trial that develops her special qualities of forthrightness and sticking up for herself. She does, however, speak of a particular sense of not knowing who she is, of not belonging anywhere, adding pathos to the usual story of a search for one's self.

This story once again portrays an idyllic happy childhood where all goes well until a disruption triggers the start of the quest. In this case the disruption is also a moral failing on the part of Mona herself. She abandons being the dutiful studious daughter and neglects her college work, with the result that she fails to get onto a degree course. This fall from grace might also be read as partly the result of deception. She is tempted by the hedonism of life in the 'city', in itself an archetype for moral hazard, after her life of rural simplicity at school. This failure is all the more poignant because of the sacrifices and hardships her parents have undergone as immigrants to give her a good start in life.

It is her managerial career which enables her to redeem herself and give herself a positive identity after this serious personal setback. Mona learns from her defeat and goes on to other hard fought victories which eventually give her a second chance at a degree when she studies for the Masters. There is some suggestion that her failure results in exile. She has to pursue her career far away from the leafy suburbs of Surrey in a factory in Hull, only being able to think of returning home when her job offers her a chance of a transfer back to Surrey.

There is a great sense of urgency about Mona's quest. She fears that time is short and that, with the fading of her youth, her ability to succeed in her career will also fade. One is reminded of the folkloric convention where maidens with magical powers lose them along with their virginity, see William Morris (1894/1980), for example. As with many other narrators, Mona's desire for career success emerges from a wish to meet her parents' aspirations that she should have a better life, partly as a repayment of a debt of gratitude to them and partly because she wants to avoid how hard their lives have been. This is not only an existential quest for identity but also one for material comfort and security.

Mona presents her career as a series of battles that require her special qualities of courage in challenging the status quo and her ability to make things happen and see things through to the end. One is reminded by this self-portrait of the archetypal heroic manager who features in popular management books such as *In Search of Excellence* (Peters and Waterman 1982). She is an instigator who can bring things out of nothing, a training department and policy where there had been none. These qualities are sometimes destructive for Mona as when her determination to succeed at work, and on the Masters, lead to the break-up of her marriage. Unlike Alex, Mona manages to make her marriage break-up part of a positive upward progress; things went wrong because she had matured and outgrown her husband as she had matured and outgrown previous jobs. By the second interview her strong assertions of centring her life on career success and being a manager had been modified. Her recent re-marriage had caused a re-evaluation of the object of her quest. She now wanted to return home to be near her parents and have children, to love and be loved. To become again the dutiful daughter she was before her fall.

The Insurance Account Manager

Elaine's story can also be characterised as a quest to escape unpromising beginnings and establish herself as a successful person through her career as a manager, although she expresses no obligation to her parents unlike Mona and Richard, for example. Once more she portrays her childhood as particularly idyllic, using the freedom of the countryside to contrast with the later bleakness of the inner city. As with some of the other stories, this happy idyll is disrupted by a disaster. In Elaine's case the disruption is caused by her father (something of a villain figure in her account), who throws away his own managerial career and drags his unwilling family to life running an inner-city pub. There is a strong impression of abandonment in a hostile environment, another common folkloric theme (*Babes in the Wood* or *Snow White*, for example). Further disadvantages follow on from this disaster. Elaine's education is disrupted and she ends up in a dead-end job as a seamstress. It is here that her special qualities begin to show themselves, stimulated by the difficulties of her situation. The qualities suggested by the narrative tend to be those of determination, forthrightness, competitiveness, shrewdness, a need for challenge and a knack of dealing with others and building relationships.

There is a clear 'lucky break' for Elaine when she is chosen for a Rotary Club exchange to the US, she is recognised as special by this event. This epiphany seems to mark her out for a managerial career and provides a clear division between a non-managerial and a managerial self. Rather than a slow self development, the trip to the US represents a 'road to Damascus' experience, a sudden coming into her own. It convinces her that her quest should be to reach for the senior levels of management, not just stop at being a supervisor. She is adamant in her first interview that her quest lies solely in her career, she cannot see herself as a mother, 'baking buns'. Other than the clear lucky break episode, there is not much room elsewhere in Elaine's account for fortune. Things happen as a result of her own determination and decisions. She is an instigating, not a reacting hero.

Part of her upward progress is to demonstrate to herself and to her parents that she is capable of being the first person in her family to get a degree. This task is used to illustrate all of her particular qualities, as it takes her ten years of part-time study of vocational qualifications to reach her masters degree. Once achieved, she hopes that her masters will confer extra powers on her and that it will give her an 'edge', as she puts it, to compensate for what she sees as the disadvantages of her relative youth in her senior position and of being a woman; it will cloak her in the robes of a legitimate managerial status, enabling her to appear different in the eyes of those who have known her before her transformation.

As well as its importance as a marker of successful achievement, Elaine too imbues being a manager with moral qualities. She describes a number of her previous managers as villains because they abuse their authority and oppress their subordinates. Elaine, on the other hand, aspires to be a 'good' manager, one who is capable and effective but also kind and caring. Despite her unequivocal ambition, Elaine's projected end to her story is of early retirement at 50, leaving her time to travel and pursue other interests, followed by the repose and rest of the hero who has successfully fought her last battle. By her second interview she is also rehearsing a different future plot development and self; that of combining career with motherhood.

The Airport Security Training Manager

With Rob we begin with another idyllic but poor childhood, in a happy and warm family where all goes well until the inevitable disruption occurs, setting off the start of his quest to become a manager. With Rob the disruption seems like a success, the opposite of a blessing in disguise and more like the poisoned apple in Snow White. He gets into the local grammar school, but this turns to disaster when he does badly at his 'O' levels, bringing shame on himself and his family. The result is that his parents forbid him from what seems like the obvious next step in his progress, 'A' levels. Instead he becomes a shipwright and again all goes well until, unexpectedly, the shipyards are closed. Although this seems a disaster, resulting in an unsettled and unsuccessful period in Rob's life, it is also a classic 'blessing in disguise' reversing the earlier 'disaster in disguise' as it eventually leads to Rob becoming a manager.

This is a story of a resourceful, determined hero who is forced into action by events rather than being the instigator. The early part of the story consists of a series of setbacks which must be overcome: the death of his grandfather; the failure at school; the poor apprenticeship exam; the closure of the shipyards and so on. The 'giant' that Rob must vanquish is as much his own sense of early failure as anything else. This is the story of the 'ordinary', even humble, man who becomes swept up by larger forces which conspire against him, but who overcomes them to reach his goals of prosperity, happiness and self-respect. The qualities Rob stresses most about himself are those of decency and straightforwardness and his willingness to work. He shares the assumption of many a traditional story that, in the end, good will prevail, and in his case, 'good' means the puritan virtues of hard work, honesty and thrift. Like Richard, though with more modesty, he also reveals considerable pride in his physical strength and skills, needed for his work on ships and submarines. Unlike Richard, this pride in strength is not rooted in the ability to defend himself from violent attack but is part of his claims to stoical effort that wins out in the end. In keeping with this low key form of heroism, there is a less obvious sense of an adventurous quest, of ambitions that Rob wants to achieve; he simply wants to live a decent quiet life, although even this modest ambition requires more than simple passivity.

Rob's story at first appears to be following a conventional pattern, youthful adventures as he tries out different ways of making a living followed by settling down with his fiancé, a mortgage and a steady job. At this point the 'lucky break' emerges in a highly unexpected way. In a three day trip away with his friends in Manchester, expecting only to watch cricket, Rob falls in love and for once instigates radical changes in his life. This has associations with the story theme of the 'calling'. The hero must abandon his home and loved ones to follow a leader or achieve a task. It also suggests that love frees him from the shackles of his previous inauthentic relationship. There is an assumption that his previous life was something that he just drifted into whereas the lightning-bolt of true love illuminates the path that he must now follow. Momentarily, Rob's task becomes a romantic quest. He seeks to be with his new-found love and leaves everything he knows behind for her. This rather romanticised portrayal of his actions enables him to remain the hero of his own story despite the morally questionable overnight abandonment of his fiancée for someone else.

One's expectations that such a story will develop from this point into a full-blown series of adventures, a break with his previous humdrum existence, are disappointed when this reluctant romantic hero settles back into dealing with the everyday tasks of life as they present themselves. His narrative presentation of his earlier self would become implausible were the transformation to be too violent. It is, however, from this break with his past that Rob's transformation into a manager begins and it is his new partner who supports him and then suggests that he apply to the airport for a job.

One should also not assume that the very quality of 'ordinariness' stressed in Rob's story means that there are no elements of a heroic quest. Completing his education and gaining his masters, after a weary struggle, were clearly of great significance to him. He mentions in a number of places in his story his conviction that he is not very academically able. This both stresses his virtue of modesty but also makes his achievement of the Masters more heroic. His satisfaction in establishing his children as prosperous and successful gives his career and life a meaning beyond its everyday banality, endowing it with moral purpose and again, heroic achievement. His narrative also makes it clear that he makes a conscious decision not to follow his peers into semi-skilled work (the kind of work expected for someone from his background) even though it paid so much better than his own early jobs. He saw himself as going somewhere different, being more successful in the longer term, being marked out by destiny in some way.

Rob uses his narrative to make sense of the various events in his life as steps along a journey to the destination of his current self. Everything contributes to who he will become and prepares him, through the accumulation of experience, maturity and skills for the next step. He projects his managerial self backwards to the shipyards, tracing an emergent manager in his coordination of more specialist trades and linking his love of working with his mates as a security guard with his previous love of football and the dockyards. Rob's study for the Masters represents a way of redeeming his failure at school and he imagines his old head-teacher's reaction on being told that he had a masters degree. However, his struggle with the inner demon of his sense of failure continues. He must overcome the fear of failure, of not being good enough, the fear of letting down his employer as he once let down his parents. When talking about his studies, Rob defines his quest as one of self knowledge, a search for the truth, of discovering where his limitations lay even if this meant moderating his career ambitions.

As noted with other narratives, the final hoped-for happy ending of Rob's story has to be deferred until the struggles of his working life are done. He stresses his sense of continuity with his past self, symbolised by his still being able to apply his skills as a shipwright. This is not an altogether positive idea as this past self is partly an enemy, a shameful failure, who has been overcome as Rob has matured but who now 'is still lurking there, under the surface, just waiting for the ideal opportunity to pop out.' Rob's story ends in his contemplation of his success and in a desire for an eventual homecoming, the return of the successful hero and dutiful son who has fulfilled his parents' aspirations and redeemed his earlier failures.

With this final interpretation of Rob's story I have completed my analysis of their content in terms of their functional elements. I have drawn on generic stories that provide a vast range of narrative resources made available for the task of self narration. In the final section of this chapter, I concentrate on the 'how' of the deployment of these elements rather than on the content of them.

Performing Narrative

As I outlined at the start of this chapter, I have divided this concluding section according to Holstein and Gubrium's (2000) four narrative practices of narrative linkage, narrative slippage, narrative options and narrative editing. The last two of these I have combined as, in practice, it was difficult to make clear distinctions between the consideration of alternative meanings within stories and points where stories 'branched' in different directions. My intention in this section is to draw attention to the strategies employed by narrators as they selectively and creatively employ the various narrative elements identified in the preceding section.

Narrative Linkage

Narrative linkage refers to the links story-tellers make between the presentation of themselves and the narrative resources available to them. The emphasis of this type of narrative practice is on commonalities and its consideration can also usefully serve as a summary, in this chapter, of the shared historical context discussed in Chapter 5, in terms of Ricoeur's conceptualisation of narrative identity, the emphasis here is on *idem* identity or sameness. At the heart of all of these narratives one can discern the impact of the aspirations and struggles of a generation of upper-working, lower middle-class families, for themselves and their children. For my interviewees these aspirations have increasingly found expression and fulfilment in managerial careers as the Golden Age gave way to the Crisis Decades. This insight may help to explain the persistence of traditional forms of attachment to family, place, and class-based social identities that are such a feature of these stories. The very forces of globalisation and de-traditionalisation, may make such attachments even more important as refuges from economic and political uncertainties in the future (Giddens 1991; Castells 2004).

In such uncertain times, it may be that my story-tellers are looking to their work organisations as the communities in which their lives take on meaning, providing sources of self-identity that are affirmed by daily contact with others (Holmes and Robinson 1999), a new form of the sociality of labour more evident at the start of the twentieth century than at its end (Hardt and Negri 2000). Castells (2004) has suggested that globalisation is moving us beyond Giddens' 'late modernity', indeed beyond postmodernity, into an information age where individuals seek even stronger forms of communal identity as the nation state declines in importance. In this sense organisations may be the new villages, places where lives are lived out. The importance in the accounts above of the notion of vocation, the need to find one's primary identity through work and organisational membership seems to indicate this as a possibility. The role of manager, in particular, seems to be able to satisfy the criteria that were important to my narrators. In brief these were: individuality; self-development; material comfort and public success; economic ability to provide similar opportunities for their own children; advanced educational attainment; upward social mobility in terms of class; moral legitimacy and purpose and a heroic purposeful life. The links that narrators made between being successful and being 'good' also imply that these are rewards for the exercise of the virtues they identified as central to their self projects. In addition, for the women in the group, there was at least a partial escape from the traditional constraints of their gender. The fact that this existential project can plausibly be presented so positively within these stories poses a serious challenge to critiques of managerialism that imply that managers are either dupes or villains (Reedy 2008). A management identity, if one takes such stories at face value, would seem to have delivered both psychic and material gains on a large scale.

Of course, this apparent enthusiasm for the benefits of becoming a manager is too crude a generalisation. Attitudes to being a manager do differ markedly between stories and the overall impression one gains is that there is a downside, a price that has to be paid for the undoubted gains, as discussed above. The duality between the 'work' self and the 'home' self causes tensions and contradictions that are not easily managed, particularly for the women, an experience that seems to be a common one in twenty-first century Britain (Dex 2003). However, I would argue that these tensions go beyond the idea of 'work-life balance' and reflect more profound existential tensions that narrators expend some effort in trying to resolve within the stories. Emotions such as feelings of imposture, not being taken seriously, educational inferiority, fears of being unpopular, fears of slipping back and losing what one has gained, worries as to the consequences of both gaining and not gaining promotion, guilt at the treatment of subordinates or neglect of family and so on, figure frequently in the stories. In Heideggarian terms, one can see a struggle for a sense of authenticity on one hand and a desire for approval from, and belonging to, the 'they' on the other.

The constant reiteration of the importance of luck in the stories demonstrates a high level of awareness that they frequently lack control over their own lives. It hardly needs pointing out that in the Crisis Decades, job security has become a thing of the past, and most of the stories demonstrate the difficulties caused by frequent job changes, constant travel, insecurity, and long working hours. Investing so much of one's identity in work means that not only is one's livelihood at constant risk but one's very self may also be at stake. Alex's story is a vivid illustration of how this investment in a consultant identity threatens her entire sense of herself as a worthy individual or that she is pursuing a life worth living. Much of the latter part of her narrative exhibits the considerable existential task of re-building this sense of self on an alternative set of discursive foundations.

Finally, one strikingly common feature of all the stories is their positivity. Orwell wrote that any life seen from the inside is simply a series of failures but one would never guess this from these accounts. The suppression of unpleasant memories is a commonplace of psycho-analytic theory (Freud 1914) but the concept of the narrative construction of identity suggests that something else is happening. This positivity can be linked with the question of whether there is something ridiculous in these stories being presented as heroic quests. Am I indulging in the triumph of hyperbole over plausibility? What is heroic about the comfortable lives of insurance managers, airport security trainers, and (most mundane of all) university lecturers? There is something plausibly heroic about Ethan's experiences in Kosovo or Richard's fights for his life on-board ship, but this has little to do with their subsequent lives as managers. On reflection it struck me that all of us were making use of the powerful consolatory and life-affirming possibilities afforded by story telling (Gabriel 2000). By placing ourselves at the centre of our own lives as heroic agents, able to respond to, and possibly improve upon, what life throws at us, we are able to make life a bearable and sometimes even joyful experience. Our determination to find meaning, sense, continuity and progress in our lives acts as a defence against being overwhelmed by meaninglessness, shame, disappointment and despair. It may be that this constitutes a form of inauthenticity or bad-faith but it seems closer to me to a dialectic between making individual resolute choices and seeking to live in the world as we find it.

Perhaps, as Bauman (1992) believes, there is real heroism in the attempt to cheat life and death of their horror and meaninglessness through the constant insistence on meaning, development, morality and the ties of affection and love. Even if there were some objective measure by which it could be demonstrated that such a narrative construction was deluded and that reality was as bleak as we sometimes fear, the ability to construct and maintain an illusion that gives meaning to our lives in the way the stories here suggest represents a heroic triumph in its own right. The real surprise is perhaps the unlikely conscription of management careers into this project. The implications of this conscription are discussed further in my concluding chapter.

Narrative Slippage

The second of the two categories of narrative practice is that of narrative slippage which foregrounds the way in which different individuals adopt and modify standard discourses to produce their own unique narrative, a shift in focus towards Ricoeur's *ipse* identity. It can also refer to the same individual using the same narrative elements in different ways within the same narrative. One way to think about narrative slippage might be to produce a typology of the stories and then discuss the implications of the classificatory process. For example, the stories that have been presented in this book suggest the following types: adventure stories (Richard and Ethan), where claims are made of performing great deeds; heroic protagonists (Mary, Janet, and Elaine) who make their own lives by their own actions; heroic reactors (Rob) who respond as events happen to them in unique and resourceful ways; dutiful/rebellious children (Richard, Janet and Alex) who express their lives in terms of service and perhaps even redemption from the effects of early rebellion; endurance stories (John) where one sticks out uncomfortable circumstances for the sake of others and even longer term self-development and finally; tragic stories (Alex) where the protagonist is the heroic victim.

Such a classification helps differentiate stories and draws attention to one important aspect of narrative slippage, whereby similar discourses, not least that of management work, are used to present very different qualities and identities. It can also, however, obscure the way in which stories switch to and fro between different story types. For example, the fulcrum of Rob's story is when he suddenly acts against type and becomes a protagonist not a reactor. Equally, Alex ends her first interview as a defeated and despairing tragic victim but by the end of the second interview has become a heroic protagonist.

Perhaps more useful than a discussion of type is to consider how aspects of narrative linkage are employed differentially within stories. As has already been noted, class is a central resource for self-description on the part of some narrators but completely irrelevant for others. Where it is important it is always a working-class identity that is looked back on with nostalgia as a spiritual home, a link with the past. Middle-class identities are claimed by no-one, and rejected outright by some, even though this might also act as a badge of success in terms of upward social mobility. Beyond a nostalgic desire for continuity, though, class affiliations are weak across all stories in terms of any serious collective solidarity or class-based politics.

Religious affiliations work in a similar way to class. Where they are claimed it is as a way of retaining links with one's origins as well as signalling a certain set of values. For some religious affiliations are irrelevant. Those who claim them most strongly (Richard as a Quaker and Janet as a Catholic) belong to minority belief-groups and so religion acts as a mark of distinctiveness. For Janet, at different times in her story, a religious upbringing is something to be repudiated and then something that provides the moral bedrock of who she is. It may also not be a coincidence that it is the oldest interviewees who claim religious affiliations. The decline in religion as a marker of identity for this group is also indicated by the fact that no-one made any claims for continuing personal religious beliefs.

Family and home both appeared as important in all narratives but not in the same way. In most cases they are seen as sources of happiness, moral purpose, rest, sanctuary and love but at times they are seen as places to be escaped from. Elaine and Ethan hardly mention them once they begin to talk about their adult lives. The social location of family origins does act as an important way of measuring the success of narrator's lives in terms of social and economic distance travelled and the achievement of parental expectations. The failure to meet these expectations is also a source of regret and shame in some accounts. Early educational failure is almost always linked to family circumstances. Where one comes from is important in some narratives and several story tellers have not, in the end, strayed very far away from home. Home in the present is usually presented as a counterweight to work that must be protected from its encroachment but sometimes something made possible by work. Home in the future is the destination, a place to be reached once work is done, although some narrators found difficulty in imagining a future entirely composed of 'home' rather than 'work'.

Gender is also differentially employed as a narrative element. Not surprisingly, male narrators are mostly oblivious to its implications as they have rarely experienced it as a disadvantage. The women all incorporate an awareness of the additional difficulties that being female has caused them, some to great effect as a way of emphasising their achievements. In some accounts, particularly Mary's, being female is seen as a positive attribute enabling her to be a better manager.

Most also feel a sense of representing their gender and providing examples of how women can succeed in the masculine world of management.

Attitudes to being a manager itself vary from narrative to narrative. My own story entirely rejects the label of manager and others show differing degrees of ambivalence towards it, from Mary's enthusiastic appropriation of the label to Richard's preference for self-descriptions such as engineer or inventor. All tend to interpret their 'pre-managerial' lives as in some sense a preparation or training for their later managerial roles. In this sense they conflate being a person with becoming a manager, although in my case, this identity has subsequently been repudiated.

What these various examples of narrative slippage indicate is both the infinite possibilities for self-differentiation within stories and the skills of narrators in making use of this differentiation. The stories do not suggest that a managerial discourse is producing a homogenisation of identity, rather they suggest the resourcefulness and skill of story tellers in making use of sometimes contradictory narrative resources to maintain a sense of themselves as unique individuals with worthwhile meaningful lives. Whether such efforts merely trap subjects within discourses and act as self-disciplinary techniques, thus producing inauthentic lives, is a debate returned to in the concluding chapter.

Narrative Options and Narrative Editing

Narrative options and narrative editing refer to the related practices of considering alternative meanings within narratives and decisions within narratives as to which direction the story should take, perhaps as a result of the reaction of their audience. The desire to present continuity and harmony in oneself within life histories perhaps explains why I found it difficult to identify a significant element of these practices, although there is evidence that both processes take place. For example, many narratives consider the possibility that pursuing management careers may be a good or bad thing, often found in the form of a dilemma as to whether further promotions should be sought. Alex and John actively consider options for their next career choice. Elaine and Mona discuss options of career versus motherhood in their first interview and then choose to take a much more positive approach to having children by the second interview. Mary backtracks somewhat on her matter-of-fact 'just get on with it' persona in her second interview when she considers that such traits might also be unattractive, morally wrong even, through her reflections on her lack of grief over her mother's death.

The significance of these practices lies in the suggestion that they provide of active on-going processes of identity construction through narrative. Narrators do not appear to be simply passively parroting discourses. The processes by which they intervene and make decisions about how they present themselves are indicated by the examples identified above. Thus the fact that individuals tell a different story at different times may suggest the difficulties and imperfections of this process rather than indicating multiple identities clashing. The narratives recall

Heidegger's and Ricoeur's assertion that identity is a task that must be continually worked at. The desired continuity and self development is thus a narrative project. Sometimes work must be unpicked when it does not meet with affirmation from others and alternatives suggested. This editing process re-writes the past as well as constructing alternative futures. However, such editing is always constrained by those biographical details that one cannot altogether change. I can characterise my family as loving or as harsh but not as Peruvian, without my sanity or veracity coming into question.

Finally, some last words about my stories before I close this chapter and move on to my conclusions, where I seek to bring together the various ideas in the book thus far. Management identities have been seized upon by my narrators because they offered an opportunity to realise their aspirations which were derived from their location at a particular historical juncture. This also means that the current understanding of what it is to be manager has partly been determined by these aspirations. Thus managerial identity is also in flux as social and historical processes bring about change. In fact, the English upper-working/lower-middle-class narration of a managerial identity represented here is only one way amongst many possible ways of narrating being a manager. The continuation of the Age of Crisis may, in turn, sweep away this currently accessible identity and leave it as anachronistic as that of the colonial administrator, although this too was a once favoured route to social advancement for the lower middle-classes well within living memory.

Chapter 7
And They All Lived Happily Ever After?

The Story So Far

This book of stories has now to be brought to a close and so I face the familiar difficulty of all story-tellers. How do I come up with a satisfying ending for myself and my readers? If this was a novel I would set about tying up the loose ends produced by the interaction between my characters and the plot, and in some ways this comparison is apt. This book has been built upon the stories of a number of individuals; Janet, Ethan, Mary, Richard, Alex, John, Mona, Elaine, Rob, and me. So the book does have 'characters' about whom it is natural to feel some curiosity, concern even. As well as wishing to satisfy this curiosity, I also need to return to the original questions I posed myself. In these conclusions, therefore, I will suggest some answers to these questions particularly the ways in which management identity can be understood as part of a historically contingent life project, rather than simply a role confined within the boundaries of a work organisation.

Given the above, I shall first remind the reader of the aims that I started out with and of the journey that pursuing these aims has taken me on through the earlier chapters in the book. I will evaluate to what extent the various theoretical and narrative discussions in earlier chapters add to our understanding of what being a manager means to those who partly construct a life out of their management careers. In addition I want to explore some of the implications of my view of management identity for future research. Finally, what of the storytellers, what are the prospects for managerial identities, including their identities, in the future?

In order to achieve these objectives I shall divide the chapter into three sections organised according to Ricoeur's statement that being an individual should be concerned with 'aiming at the "good life" with and for others, in just institutions' (1992, 172). If one considers this statement in the context of the narrative self as a product of interlocution, then three questions arise around which these conclusions may be organised. The first section poses the question that lies behind every chapter in this book, 'Who is speaking?' The section thus evaluates the usefulness of treating the accounts of my interviewees in the way that I have. What, if anything, is added to an understanding of managerial identity by this approach? The section also returns to the stories themselves and a consideration of what more might be done with research based on extended life histories.

The second section poses the question 'Who is listening?' which shifts the emphasis from the interior of the self to its relationship with the 'other' that Ricoeur suggests we ought to be 'for' and 'with'. As I argued in my introduction, other than the pronouncements of celebrity chief executives, the voices of individual managers are rarely heard. They are spoken for and about. If ever there was an identifiable Heideggerian 'they', it is the vast army of those who make a living out of defining what managers ought to be, this includes business school academics such as myself. Outside of academia there is an equally extensive cadre of consultants, trainers and populist management writers. Finally there are the frequent cultural representations of corporate managers, whether as grey-suited automatons (men in suits), self-delusional buffoons (*The Office* [2001–2003]) heroic go-getting entrepreneurs (*The Apprentice* [2001–2008]), or sinister amoral self-seeking manipulators (*Michael Clayton* [2007]) or even the devil incarnate (*Devil's Advocate* [1997]). How can the experiences of managers themselves be heard over this and what might be achieved by taking their accounts of themselves seriously? Finally, I finish the chapter by discussing what might constitute 'just institutions' and to what extent the pursuit of management identities enables or obstructs their creation. If management work has become the most accessible route to a reasonably prosperous and self-affirming life what are the wider societal implications of this conjunction between aspiration and opportunity? Of course, as I argued in my first chapter, all biography tends to be autobiography, and these enquiries are those at the heart of my own existential concerns, my own ambivalent relationship with the world of work and career, and so are likely to be central to my own research and writing as an academic in the future.

Before launching into these discussions then, it might be useful to remind the reader of my initial aims and how the book took shape over the preceding chapters. In Chapter 1, I located the research as being both about stories but also constituting a story in itself. A story where there could be no clear dividing lines between the managers' biographies and my autobiography, between researcher and the researched, and between the research methods employed and the theory of how we come to be ourselves. The aims of the book were then to treat all of these issues in an integrated way by looking at how they interpenetrated each other. The ensuing chapters sought to develop these central themes, by deploying a methodological and theoretical framework derived from what I have for convenience termed 'existentialism' but that specifically drew on the work of Heidegger, Sartre and Ricoeur.

In Chapter 2, therefore, I presented the stories that are the heart of the book *as* stories, in other words unadorned with either analysis or theoretical reference. This was done for the reasons explained in my introduction and further examined in Chapter 4, I wished to draw attention to their status as narratives and enable the reader to respond to them as both fictive truths (Stanley 1992) and as testimony (Ricoeur 1992), in other words it was an attempt to listen to, rather than speak for, the managers whose stories I had collected. In this chapter I also presented my own story, partly as an additional narrative of the trajectory of a manager. Together with my interviewees we shared many similar constraints and opportunities in the construction of our lives and selves and I did not wish to create the traditional but artificial division between objective researcher and research subjects. Following

Sartre, I wished to avoid the objectification of the other inherent in such a division.

Chapter 3 was the first of the theoretical chapters that developed my position on identity and its implications for the issues I began to discuss in my first chapter. I explored the way in which identity tends to be written about within the social sciences in general and organisational studies in particular. I discussed some of the problems with what I saw as the resultant polarisation of identity theory and its consequences, via a consideration of the implications of the sociology of death. In Chapter 4, I argued for an alternative theoretical framework for understanding identity as narrativity, founded upon the work of Heidegger, Sartre and Ricoeur. I sought to demonstrate that this work provided new possibilities for exploring the issues raised by the discussion in Chapter 3 and suggested methodological and ethical principles that could be used in interpreting the accounts in Chapter 2.

Chapters 5 and 6 sought to apply the theoretical insights of Chapter 4 by analysing the stories in Chapter 2, according to three modes of interpretation suggested by Ricoeur's narrative model of identity. In Chapter 5 I emphasised the insight that narrative identities are located in specific times and spaces and can therefore be taken as referential of, as well as derived from, their historical context. In Chapter 6 I treated the narratives as built from identifiable elements drawn from the cultural repository of available narrative resources. Thus the work of Propp (1968) was utilised because of the affinity of the narratives with traditional tales and particularly with the ubiquitous element of the quest. The final mode of analysis, used in my summary to this chapter was suggested by Holstein and Gubrium (2000), and foregrounded the strategies that different individuals employed (narrative practices) in order to construct their particular stories from the more generic elements suggested by the first two modes. How successful has this development of my initial questions been and what can now be understood about the nature of managerial identity as a result? In the following sections I try to suggest some answers to this question.

Who is Speaking?

What sort of people emerge as managers in this book? One obvious answer that emerges from the book is the sheer heterogeneity and extent of what counts as managerial work at the start of the twenty-first century, a trend also noted by others (Grey 1999). From RAF Squadron Leaders to IT consultants the narratives in the book illuminate the variety of work that is now classified as managerial. This would certainly not have been the case thirty years ago, particularly for those of us working in the public sector. I have also represented the managers presented here as a cohort, as belonging to a particular generation of the post-war upper-working/lower middle-class British. Finally I have tried to let the individual voices of my interviewees, as unique experiencing and acting people, emerge. Is this sufficient to answer the question 'Who is Speaking?' It might very reasonably by objected that in reality only one voice is 'really' speaking in the book and that is mine, the author. All other voices have been subjugated, edited, distorted, parodied, idealised and arranged to suit my own purposes and my own identity project; a Sartrean assertion of myself that instrumentally pushes others into the background, rather than being 'with' and 'for' the other potential voices. How then is the reader to know whether they have read an authentic polyphony of voices or a form of personal propaganda? Thus the question 'Who is Speaking?' sounds an immediate caution and requires that I evaluate my attempt to present several different voices in ways that are preferable to the fragmented use of stories common within organisational studies.

My first response to the sceptical reader is that they do have some points of anchorage in this sea of relativism. For a start I could not have made up everything, even assuming I had wanted to. Placing the stories within a historical context, as I do in Chapter 5, grounds these accounts in generally accepted events, such as the post-war boom and the expansion of professional and managerial work. It almost goes without saying that there may still be widely varying interpretations of the *significance* of these events. More fundamentally, my research suggests that the reader can also make judgements on the basis of plausibility that arises from a shared understanding of our use of a common world (Heidegger 1926/1962). The Other is accessible to us because they are like us, we recognise their voice as distinct from our voice and that of others. It certainly prevents me from claiming that some of my interviewees had wings, came from a parallel universe, or had three heads.

Notwithstanding these limits, there is still considerable scope for one voice to drown out possible others. I have adopted, therefore, an ethical stance to this research that required me to make a strenuous effort to be as true to my understanding of the accounts given to me and to present them in a way that was empathetic to their original narrators. Of course there can be no final certainty and, in the end, the reader has no alternative but to make their own judgements, to decide for themselves 'Who is Speaking?' For me I can still hear the distinctive voices of these managers in the accounts presented here and hope that something of this communicates itself to my readers. Again, preserving their stories in a longer form than is usual in much academic writing should help in this regard.

There have, however, been some limitations on rendering different voices accessible to the reader. I have had to balance my desire to present satisfying stories, in a literary sense, with the need to satisfy the requirements of academic research. It may well be that the genre of academic writing is simply an inappropriate way of telling stories as stories, that the requirement to analyse and theorise is incompatible with this purpose in the way the some US auto-ethnographers argue (see Bochner 2001, for example). Perhaps the novel, or a simple, less 'academic' presentation of more extended first person accounts, would have achieved this aim better. There may be a case to commemorate the lives of others through a return to the style of Studs Terkel (1970) and Ronald Blythe (1972), whose work I discussed in my introduction.

I would argue for a more personal and empathetic style of academic writing about living individuals rather that still allows for the use of theoretical analysis rather than seeing them as mutually exclusive. The work of Ricoeur (1985; Kearney 1996a) suggests that that the use of fictive techniques is proper to the task of generating an appropriate empathy for the suffering and hopes of other human beings. History may thus be 'truer' when told with the skill and passion of the storyteller. It was in this spirit that I recast the narratives as folk stories in Chapter 6 and this revealed the way in which managerial identity may be experienced as an existential quest, part of a life-project that involves many motivations, emotions and desires that extend well beyond the world of work. The aspirations of this group, often inherited from their parents, for status, material comfort, and security were thus grafted on to the ethical values of love for, and duty towards, one's family, self-development, and respect for others. This combination becomes typified by an ideal of the 'good' manager, even when being a manager seems often to conflict with being a good father, or daughter, or colleague. This insight seemed to me to be largely unrecognised by other academic accounts of management identity but is one that is important in understanding why individuals have been so prepared to buy into the idea of being a manager. Even with all the tensions and contradictions that accompany a managerial identity, it has proved highly amenable to the crafting by my respondents, into a desired sense of authentic selfhood.

There is another aspect to the question 'Who is Speaking?'. One must also address the question of whether the theory that is expounded in Chapter 4 helps shed any light upon it. The first point to be made is that there is an embedding of a Ricoeurian sensibility in the very question: 'Who?' rather than 'What?' The terms of the question insist upon dealing with others as unique individuals who we are accountable to and who are accountable to us. Likewise, as MacIntyre (1985) points out, being held accountable requires that we are changing but single characters. It is not a defence for murder that a different past self committed it. The exceptions to this principle, such as a plea of insanity, a temporary 'loss' of one's self, confirm the strength of this sense of biographical continuity and accountability. In other words this question forces us back to questions of responsibility to others and the politics of identity in a way that can sometimes be lost when we only think in depersonalised terms of subjects who are no more than nodes on networks of power relations. The adoption of this theoretical framework leads to the impossibility of separating ontological questions about identity from those of ethical questions. If we narrate ourselves into being through choices, albeit constrained choices, then, as Sartre (1943/1957) stresses, we cannot escape from our responsibility for these choices and their effects upon ourselves and others.

I would also conclude that, without the concept of narrative, no real sense can be made of ourselves at all. I would agree with MacIntyre that 'narrative history of a certain kind turns out to be the basic and essential genre for the characterisation of human actions.' (1985, 208) and that 'there is no way to give us an understanding of any society...except through the stock of stories which constitute its initial dramatic resources' (1985, 216). My treatment of the life stories in this book illustrates their value as a way of understanding managers but this is an approach that can be extended to many different groups, including those who have not had access to managerial careers. The use of extended narratives analysed within their particular historical and social contexts and presented and interpreted as stories has become relatively neglected since the heyday of the Chicago School, perhaps because of its time-consuming nature, but it is one that enables other voices to speak. For such work the philosophy of phenomenological existentialism provides a rich source of interpretative possibilities.

To return to the stories as stories, more specific conclusions can be suggested regarding the nature of managerial identity. The first is the remarkable way in which *managerial* identities provide such rich narrative resources for heroic self-description. Gabriel (2000) identifies four generic 'modes' of organisational story frequently used by their members, as being 'comic', 'tragic', 'epic' and 'romantic' from which can be derived what he terms the 'secondary' modes of 'humour', 'cock-up', 'tragi-comic' and 'epic-comic'. When recounting their lives, however, the story-tellers in this book tended to draw only upon the 'epic' mode, sometimes oscillating with the 'tragic'. My storytellers positioned themselves as the heroic/tragic figure who recounts how he or she achieved/failed to achieve success and become the person they are through a process of development occasioned by tests and trials. This process of becoming is located within the arena of the management career.

One can trace here the effects of influential and pervasive social discourses such as those of the career (Grey 1994) or the heroic inspirational leader (see Peters 1987, for example) that encourage the epic mode of managerial self-definition and suggest that a managerial identity provides an accessible route to the self-developmental quest typical of 'late modernity' (Giddens 1991). Indeed some see this heroic-entrepreneurial self as the predominant discourse of our times (du Gay 1996; Armstrong 2001), and an oppressive and politically suspect one at that. Certainly a brief scan through popular autobiographies of prominent and successful managers (see Iacocca 1986; Welch 2000; or Branson 2007, for example) reveals archetypal heroic stories that can, without rhetorical exaggeration, be described as modern myths. These pervasive stories of heroic management identity suggest another reason why folk stories are surprisingly apt in the interpretation of managers' life histories.

Existentialist theory may provide some clues as to why managers seize upon and are, in turn, seized by these characteristic discourses. Heidegger's work suggests that our historical location provides and constrains the range of possible self-interpretations available to us. Within this work, the possibility of an authentic existence, one that does not passively adopt such discourses, is not closed off, but there is a high price to pay for resisting the 'they'. This price consists of constant anxiety and self-doubt; typified by Heidegger's exhortation that authentic selfhood requires a continual facing-up to our own deaths as we make decisions about our possible futures. This uncomfortable freedom is also a feature of Sartre's version of the autonomous self. There is no chance, according to Sartre, of security or contentment in individuality, only anxiety, isolation, doubt and a zero-sum struggle for our freedom at the price of that of others.

Management identities could be interpreted as an attempt to find a compromise between this bleak, lonely, individuality and total absorption in the mass. The adoption of characteristic discourses of self-development such as the managerial, or for that matter, the professional academic career appear to offer a ready-to-hand set of narrative resources (Watson and Harris 1999) that provide possibilities for a degree of autonomy without totally isolating oneself from the main currents of modern society. One is reminded once more of Ricoeur's dialectic of *idem* (sameness) and *ipse* (selfhood) within narrative identity (1992).

Managerial work, at this historical juncture, has been a highly accessible way for my story-tellers to make their livings and meet the aspirations of their parents' generation for them. If such work has been selected, or drifted into, to satisfy these material aspirations it has also been invested with other qualities required for the contradictory quest of becoming an individual but an individual who is like others. For Sartre, one of the problems of striving for autonomy is the impossibility of there being any legitimating criteria for our decisions. The managerial self, though, hints at such legitimating criteria as the discourse of the 'enterprising individual' promises both a form of heroic individualism as well as the security of a graded measurement, through organisational hierarchies, of the success of the existential project.

The work organisation therefore provides a source both of belonging and a site where individualism may be practised making it highly attractive, given the widespread desire for both, as a primary source of meaning for lives. To give one example, promotion brings the outward markers of a successful life in terms of material reward and social status, which interviewees endow with huge significance in terms of distance travelled from the starting blocks of their family origins and aspirations. Such validation goes beyond a purely materialistic conception of competitive success as narrators tend to conflate this with their desire for a ethically valid 'good life'. Their quests had to be worth pursuing for reasons that transcended purely individual gain. Once more a managerial identity could be made to accommodate this desire through the rhetoric of the 'good' manager, who combines professional effectiveness with a caring and nurturing attitude to subordinates. Sometimes, mostly in the case of the public sector managers, there was also a strong sense of performing a duty or a service for the good of others. All narrators contrasted managers who were morally deficient with their own aspirations to 'make a difference' in terms of transforming work for the better for those around them. Sometimes, as in Janet's case, this was expressed in the sense of being moral crusaders, rooting out hypocrisy and corruption. The extent to which such ethical aspirations are seductive illusions rather than even partially achievable is worthy of further debate.

One must, however, be careful not to overstate the pull of managerial identity in terms of its heroic possibilities. The epic 'atmosphere' one might expect to be a feature of such stories is constantly undercut by elements of self-deprecation, humour, shame and regret. Narrators demonstrate that they are aware that they are often not, in fact, very heroic. Their stories show that they frequently fell short of success because they were too lazy or not clever enough or were taken in by false promises. These failings are not presented as the grand flaws of great tragic heroes, rather there is the stoical and resourceful heroism of ordinary people responding to circumstances not of their own making and usually beyond their control. There is a heavy emphasis in all the narratives on luck, both good and bad. Events are usually recounted as just happening to my narrators in a way that de-centres them as active heroes of their own story and positions them as often rueful responders to events. The element of 'throwness' identified by Heidegger features strongly in these accounts but even these less heroic elements still tend to resonate with the insistence of existentialist theory that, whatever the constraints of circumstance, we always have choices about how we respond to them. The stories frequently repeat the theme of narrators drifting with the crowd until they decide to intervene in some fateful way in their own lives and so differentiate themselves from the similar others around them. The narrators appear to have come to an intuitive understanding of the theoretical insights of Heidegger and Sartre. Choice is possible but terrifying and so only rarely to be exercised when absolutely necessary. A lack of agency may not be inevitable but it is the norm as a result.

The resemblance of these stories of managerial lives to folk stories is again underscored by this self-deprecating element that both undercuts and reinforces the heroic qualities of the stories. Both types of story tend to deal with the fate of 'ordinary' people, miller's sons, or poor widow's daughters in the case of folk tales; steelworkers, soldiers, engineers, and teachers in the case of the narratives in this book. In other words both deal with ordinary people who have to deal with the extraordinary events imposed upon them. The role of magic and the supernatural in folk stories underscores the capricious, unpredictable and uncontrollable aspects of lived reality. There is clearly a strong element of fantasy wish fulfilment in the way in which these unpromising beginnings end with marrying princes and princesses and such fantasies are mirrored in ideas of getting to the top, retiring relatively young and rich, and then living a life of repose and comfort that figure in the managerial stories found here. Thus another appeal of management careers is the almost unlimited possibility of self-fulfilment and reinvention as measured by social and economic success. Where the stories of management careers differ from fairy stories is that it *has* proved possible to at least partially achieve these fantasies. It may not be quite 'half the kingdom' but all of my storytellers reflect with some satisfaction on their affluence, status, education and careers and look forward to comfortable and healthy retirements with some degree of, possibly misplaced, confidence, given the deterioration in occupational pensions, social welfare and economic and political stability (Hobsbawm 2007). Despite these anxieties for the future there is no doubt that, thanks to management careers, their lives have been better in almost every respect to that of their parents.

Another aspect of managerial identity that surprised me but that seems pervasive in the stories is illustrated by a divergence between them and folk stories. The moral codes of folk stories are often far removed from those in the narratives. For example, the use of violence, theft, and deceit are as often practised by folk tale heroes (Jack, the Giant Killer or Puss in Boots, for example) as by the villains. I was reminded rather of another influential literary instance of the quest, equally deeply embedded in our culture. Bunyan's *Pilgrim's Progress* (1685/1907) an example of a life quest where the more modest puritan heroic virtues of humility and resignation are central. Here, the living of a 'good' life, is meant in the sense of a virtuous life and is contrasted as being superior to more outwardly successful lives. I have already commented on the survival of puritan moral attitudes to work, including thrift, sobriety and honesty, with the social group from which most of my story-tellers are drawn. Thus consumption, by itself, is not an adequate measure of success or the key to a sense of a worthy self. Indeed, the sole pursuit of status and consumption in Alex's narrative is seen as an example of greed and pride coming before a fall. It may be the conflation of these virtues with what it means to be a 'good' manager represents the historical continuity of Weber's protestant work ethic; the virtue of the elect made manifest by their business or career success (Anthony 1977).

What of those parts of the narrator's lives that are not played out at work though? It has been one of my arguments in this book that managerial identities do not take up the entire lives of my narrators. All the stories convey a struggle to contain their managerial selves in order to prevent them taking over their entire lives. Their 'home lives' must be protected from the invasive tendencies of careers, although sometimes their enjoyment must be deferred until retirement. In traditional stories, 'home' is where heroes set out from to perform their deeds and, if they are lucky, return to afterwards. It is a sphere of rest and recovery, rather than where things get done. In the same way, my narrators position their working lives as where they perform as heroes, often idealising home and family as a place of blessed inaction where they can recuperate. The higher ethical claims of home and family give meaning and legitimacy to the pursuit of material and career success as managers, which can be then presented as sacrifice rather than selfishness. For example, Rob's material affluence is valued because it enables him to provide things for his children that his parents could not provide him with. Again, becoming a manager for Mary enables her to be a caring and empathetic boss to her subordinates and to transform less morally acceptable management practice by applying to it the values of the home and parenthood.

If home is idealised as encapsulating the values of love, rest, and an end to competition and striving, the reality can be rather different. Storytellers experience all of the difficulties that result from long working hours and stressful work. In many cases this included the need for both partners to work full-time and bring up children. Managerial work has also required constant job and house moves to sustain career momentum. Women without children agonised over whether and how to have them, men and women expressed regret at not having enough time and energy for their children. Jobs are blamed for the break-up of relationships and so on. As in many traditional stories, home too must be defended and the battles that are expected to take place away from it have a habit of turning up on one's doorstep. Managerial identity proves harder to take off than the business suit at the end of the day.

The desire, only partially possible, to keep two forms of identity separate takes on another dimension for women. Traditionally, it has been the domestic sphere that has been the site of women's existential projects (Rosen 2003). It has been noted elsewhere that the masculine aspects of managerial identities make their adoption particularly problematic for women (Wajcman and Martin 2002). These difficulties are evident from the way that they are utilised by female narrators as further opportunities to present themselves as heroic but often in a different way. There are several references in the women's narratives to being champions for their sex, seeking success for others as well as for themselves. Additionally, Alex, in common with Mary, Janet, and Mona, invokes the role of the 'dutiful daughter', who cares for her parents thus emphasising her moral worth and resolving some of the tensions between the two spheres of work and home. The emphasis on career is partly for the benefit of beloved others. Alex positions herself as an almost stereotypically male manager, the 'imitation man' of some feminist critiques of organisation (Oseen 1997; Kerfoot and Whitehead 1998), when she complains of her female subordinates' irritating obsession with domesticity and motherhood. She is unique in the vehemence with which she expresses her feelings here, but other accounts also suggest an adoption of stereotypical masculine traits, and the suppression of stereotypical feminine sources of identity, when the women talk about their managerial careers.

I think that these insights regarding the way in which managerial work is used to construct a sense of self by and large validate the existentialist version of narrative identity I have developed in this book. Whilst there can be no simple answer to the question 'who is speaking?', I hope that these conclusions at least indicate some new dimensions to the question and suggest possible future pathways for pursuing answers in the future. One obvious response to the question is that the answer is always changing as new possibilities open up and individuals revise their stories in accordance with their 'throwness' into this unknown emerging self.

What, though, are the weaknesses of such an approach? It does, I think, lay itself open to the familiar criticisms of any social theory grounded in interlocution that it is over-cognitive and gives too much emphasis to rationality and individual will and so neglects the effects of social structure, unreflective action, embodiment and emotion. These criticisms apply perhaps more to Heidegger and Sartre than to Ricoeur (1992), who does pay a good deal of specific attention to these very issues. Although such criticisms are useful cautions to an over-simplistic approach to narrative they do not invalidate the overall approach. After all, one is more likely to capture the effects of these neglected elements with narrative approaches than with other forms of text based research where the connections between the story, story teller and the performances of the story are frequently lost. In fact, treating these accounts as stories might be argued to keep the blending of fictional devices with 'fact', emotional identification with characters, shifts in accounts at different performances and the influence of the listener/reader in the foreground. We expect stories to contain these elements and treat them accordingly, unlike more 'objective' seemingly scientific approaches to text.

Finally, before moving on from the question 'who is speaking?', my approach may contribute to our understanding of managerial identities simply because the question requires that one listens to these accounts in a different way; as stories that form a part of continuing and continual attempts to forge identities. In Ricoeur's words 'the situation of interlocution has the value of an event only inasmuch as the authors of the utterance are put on stage by the discourse in act and, with the utterers in flesh and blood, *their* experience of the world, *their* irreplaceable perspective on the world' (1992, 48). To render individuals more fully and empathetically through the medium of stories and narrative interpretations, at its best, can approach the flesh and blood presence of the other. This observation leads me on to my next section. If we now have a better idea of who is speaking, is anyone listening?

Who is Listening?

In Chapter 3 I discussed the ways in which social theory, including organisational theory, conceptualises identity. I have already discussed how managerial identities tend to be prescribed in heroic terms by academics, and consultants. Likewise, for those organisational scholars who see management as essentially an oppressive and politically suspect social institution, implicated in the perpetuation of the worst aspects of free-market capitalism, a management identity may well be considered an insidiously alluring trap into which individuals are hoodwinked into supporting a destructive political and social system. As I have written elsewhere (Reedy 2008), the net result is that in, justifiably, opposing the breathless valorisation of what it means to be a manager, critical scholars tend to reposition managerial identity as being that of a dupe or villain. Whether heroes, villains or fools, none of these characterisations seem to accord with the experiences of the wider lives recounted in this book. It is true to say, however, that such characterisations clearly crop-up as ready-to-hand narrative resources at different points in the stories of the managers in this book. However, the sum of these narratives is vastly more complex than their individual parts.

One might see in these reductionist conceptions of management identity an attempt on the part of commentators such as academics and consultants to construct their own identities on the basis of a managerial 'other'. Such a strategy is not unique to such commentators. The managers represented in this book deploy similar strategies when they attempt to narrate themselves as 'good' managers and successful human beings. They contrast themselves with stupid or deficient subordinates, with less successful childhood peers, with corrupt and incompetent superiors, with hopelessly impractical academics. Perhaps such strategies are inescapable and Nietzsche (Ricoeur 1992) and Sartre (1943/1957) are right, the assertion of oneself involves a form of violence, the objectification of the other. According to this viewpoint listening out for the other without imposing our own selves upon them is an ethical ideal unlikely to be realised.

What lies behind a conception of selfhood as dependant upon the objectification of the other is essentially a form of competitive individualism. Not so much 'one who speaks' as one who shouts in order to drown out the competing voices of others. As long as one is involved in this free market of selfhood then there seems little chance of a genuine conversation with others who speak. The contemporary conception of management as 'the brand called you' (Peters 1997) would seem to reinforce the tendency for one's identity to be achieved at the expense of the other. This is where Ricoeur's ethics of identity provides some hope that such objectification is not inevitable when he insists that the proper answer to the question 'Who is being spoken to?' is 'Another who also speaks'. Heidegger also suggests that we can exist in a form of collective mutually supportive authenticity (Vogel 1994). What might this mean in practice and what implications does it have for an understanding of management identity?

One conclusion I have already drawn is that those of us who write about, and therefore collectively construct, what it means to be a manager need to be more reflexive about our own stake in this construction and to listen more empathetically to the experiences of actual managers as they recount their lives. In doing this we tend only to address an image of our own making. If we recognise the other as one who also speaks we may actually discover that the managerial other is different from who we thought they were. Paradoxically, in having a different viewpoint on the world and on us, they may also tell us more about ourselves than our own projections onto the other can do.

The contribution of this book to a more 'listening' approach, through the stories of managers, has been to show that all my story-tellers have carved out unique selves from the shared, and sometimes unpromising, context of the Crisis Decades (Hobsbawm 1995). As I got to know these managers, over the course of the research, as neither students nor simply research subjects, but as fellow-travellers dealing with a shared set of problems and opportunities, it became impossible to fit them into the stereotypical categorisations of managers I tended to fall back on at other times. They turned out to be different from each other and different from my preconceptions. Conversely, I was amazed to recognise myself in this diversity, in equally unexpected ways. I knew what struggling to find satisfying work with which one could feel 'oneself' meant because I had lived it. I understood how it felt when a parent died because my mother died. I understood the experience of a promising start to a career going horribly wrong. In listening to the other I found myself in ways that made me reflect on my past and on my future afresh. Asking 'who is speaking?' turned out to be a way of asking 'who do you say that I am?'

Clearly, from the above, I believe that research that includes in-depth and extended involvement with the details of managers' lives is of immense value and interest and that this form of listening and reflection could have more widespread benefits. The conversational form which this engagement required meant I was able to listen to what these managers thought of the value of academic study, largely its lack of relevance to their lives and endeavours. In many ways their much more ambivalent attitudes to pursuing their identities through their careers than many academic colleagues (including myself) made me think that, rather than being discursive dupes, they had much to teach academics about maintaining a healthy scepticism towards the significance of their work. To find the real value of one's work in its capacity to provide security and prospects for one's children seems to me to be more defensible than thinking that one is going to bring about social change by writing conference papers or books like this. This does not, of course, preclude the option of more risky and less pleasant modes of opposition available to all of us, academics and managers, as citizens.

It might be objected that this degree of empathy precludes the possibility of being critical about management practice, and particularly of managerialism as an ideology of competitive individualism. After all, my story-tellers will obviously have wanted to present themselves in what they saw as their best light. Why should I assume good intentions or sincerity on their part? My response to this problem is that I do not think that empathy and solidarity with others precludes argument, challenge, critique or even repudiation. There may be those whose values are so removed from our own that no conversation can reasonably take place (Rorty 1989), but my experience with the managers in this research suggests that they may be the exception. For the rest, an attempt to build greater shared understandings of each other can only strengthen the power of our critique. A criticism from someone we believe understands us is more likely to be taken seriously than one whose opinions we hold in contempt. The context in which such conversations between speakers and listeners can take place leads me on to my final concluding thoughts, considered as part of a discussion of 'just institutions'.

Just Institutions

For Ricoeur, drawing upon the work of Levinas, the question of what constitutes just institutions is intimately bound up with the issues of our selves and others discussed above. 'In this way self-appreciation and self-love, without which the good life is no longer *my* life, unite both with friendship, in which I share my life with certain others, and with justice, which is institutionally derived from the point of view of a third' (Waldenfels 1996, 112–13).

I have already intimated that, despite my identification with the accounts of the managers in this book, I consider that the pursuit of managerial identities is politically as well as personally ethically ambivalent. Channelling so many people's existential projects into the pursuit of managerial identities can only act as a support to the current political and economic order which seems to me to be both unjust and unsustainable. If the current irrationality and destructiveness of late Capitalism's technocratic rationality is thus reinforced then any attempt to change direction is compromised by the co-option of ever increasing numbers into the cadres of management. If this is so then, despite the individual successes of the managers in this book, one ought to be more generally 'against management' (Parker 2002) as a political and social institution. It is here that I think that more critical academic accounts of management can make a valuable contribution in seeking to uncover the myriad implications and effects of what, at an individual level, appear to be reasonable and limited compromises. A better understanding of the historically contingent attractions of management identities, as presented in this book, may be seen as a contribution to this project. I would argue that understanding the lives of individual managers in their own terms is not incompatible with this broader critique, rather a better appreciation of how managerialism attracts its supporters is essential to it.

To return to existentialist terminology, being trapped in inauthenticity by the increasing dominance of managerialism, would seem to be a real danger, although it is a fate that my story-tellers did not seem to me to have altogether succumbed to. They were rather more aware of the compromises they were making than such an interpretation implies. However, it may be that the colonisation of their career projects by values that derived from the particular historical context in which they grew up, including the aspirations of their parents for them, have acted as effective sources of resistance, enabling a form of authenticity to be preserved through attachments and commitments to family, place, as well as loved others. Who is to say that equivalent discursive resources will be available to later generations of managers? The continuing march of global capitalism may succeed in obliterating even the limited forms of autonomy that such attachments make available, with the homogenisation of the diverse cultures which in turn act as treasuries for an enormous diversity of stories-of-the-self from which alternative models of identity may be derived.

Conversely, management careers may increasingly be seen as less attractive resources for self-definition as the historical forces that brought together the post-war boom, the expansion of large-scale enterprises, the growth of the public sector, and the increased aspirations and hopes of the upper-working/lower middle-classes are moving inexorably on. The desire for early retirement that is evident in several accounts may reflect an awareness that it would be better to get out of the intensifying Age of Crisis while the going is good. Escape may not be so easy, the collapse of the ability of even wealthy developed nations to provide for their citizens make a prosperous and long retirement less likely than it was for our parent's generation. The credit side of the Faustian bargain of a managerial identity is starting to look distinctly meagre.

The accounts of the managers in this book also indicate that there has been a decline in institutions that provide discursive resources to counter those of managerialism. None of my respondents directly drew upon experiences of political activism, class solidarity, trade union activity, or intellectual radicalism as a way of countering the assumptions of a managerial viewpoint, though faint nostalgic echoes of all of them were apparent in some accounts. This might again be one of the ways in which academic engagement with managers could contribute to the construction of just institutions by keeping alive such counter-discourses, although the modern business school has not proved to be a very conducive environment for such a project. Thus a critique of managerialism could still be a manifestation of being 'for' and 'with' managers themselves, providing that those of us who teach and study management resist the temptation to see managers as straightforwardly representative of managerialism. There is a shared interest in the utopian project of recasting the academy as a 'just institution' in the sense of being a place where a diversity of people can come together and exchange viewpoints. Such a project requires that we continue to ask questions about who is speaking and who is listening and this research has made its own contribution to answering these questions through an examination of managerial identity at the beginning of the twenty-first century.

Finally, though, what of my storytellers, how will their stories turn out? What are the prospects for Janet, Ethan, Mary, Richard, Alex, John, Mona, Elaine, Rob and myself? The answer is, of course, impossible to know, the future continues to provide new possibilities. Already since I first began writing this book my life has taken several major but completely unexpected turnings. As Heidegger (1926/1962) points out, our lives only take on their completed final shape at our deaths, until then all our narratives may be re-written in unpredictable ways either as an act of consciousness or a response to circumstances. As Elaine pointed out, it is this uncertainty that partly makes our lives worth living. Whatever the future, I hope that the longing for prosperity, enjoyable work, contentment, love, happiness and eventually repose that featured in so many of the narratives is realised.

Bibliography

Althusser, L. (2000), 'Ideology interpellates individuals as subjects', in P. du Gay, J. Evans and P. Redman (eds), *Identity: A Reader* (London: Sage), pp. 31–8.

Alvesson, M., Ashcraft, K.L. and Thomas, R. (2008), 'Identity Matters: Reflections on the construction of identity scholarship in organization studies', *Organization* 15:1, 5–28.

Alvesson, M. and Deetz, S. (1999), *Doing Critical Management Research* (London: Sage).

Alvesson, M. and Skoldberg, K. (2000), *Reflexive Methodology* (London: Sage).

Alvesson, M. and Willmott, H. (2002), 'Identity Regulation as Organizational Control: Producing the appropriate individual', *Journal of Management Studies* 39:5, 619–44.

Anthony, P. (1977), *The Ideology of Work* (London: Tavistock).

The Apprentice (2005–2008) BBC television series [created by Mark Burnett].

Armstrong, P. (2001), 'Styles of Illusion', *The Sociological Review* 49:2, 155–73.

Barnes, H. (1957), 'Translator's Introduction', *Being and Nothingness* (London: Methuen & Co), pp. i–xlv.

Barratt, E. (2003), 'Foucault, HRM and the Ethos of the Critical Management Scholar', *Journal of Management Studies* 40:5, 1069–87.

Bauman, Z. (1992), *Mortality, Immortality and Other Life Strategies* (Cambridge: Polity Press).

Benhabib, S. (1992), *Situating the Self* (Cambridge: Polity).

Benson, J. (2003), *Working-class in Britain 1850–1939* (London: I.B. Tauris).

Beynon, H. (1975), *Working for Ford* (Wakefield: EP Publishing).

Blythe, R. (1972), *Akenfield. Portrait of an English Village* (London: Allen Lane for Book Club Associates).

Bochner, A. (2001), 'Narrative's Virtues', *Qualitative Inquiry* 7, 131–57.

Boje, D. (2001), *Narrative Methods for Organizational and Communication Research* (London: Sage).

Branson, R. (2007), *Losing My Virginity: The Autobiography* (London: Virgin Books).

Brook, S. (2001), 'Gender and Working-class Identity in Britain during the 1950s', *Journal of Social History* 34:4, 773–95.

Brower, D. (1988), *The World in the Twentieth Century* (New Jersey: Prentice Hall).

Brown, A. (2001), 'Organization Studies and Identity: Towards a research agenda', *Human Relations* 54:1, 113–21.

Bunyan, J. (1685/1907), *The Pilgrim's Progress* (London: J.M. Dent).
Calvocoressi, P. (2001), 'The Superpowers', in P. Calvocoressi (ed.) *World Politics 1945–2000* (Harlow: Pearson), pp. 3–91.
Carel, H. (2005), *Life and Death in Freud and Heidegger* (Amsterdam & New York: Rodopi).
Carr, A. and Lapp, C. (2006), *Leadership is a Matter of Life and Death* (London: Palgrave Macmillan).
Castells, M. (2004), *The Power of Identity* (Oxford: Blackwell).
Cerulo, K. (1997), 'Identity Construction: New issues, new directions', *Annual Review of Sociology* 23, 385–409.
Chan, A. (2000) 'Redirecting Critique in Postmodern Organization Studies: the perspective of Foucault', *Organization Studies* 21:6, 1059–75.
Chan, A. and Garrick, J. (2002), 'Organization Theory in Turbulent Times: the traces of Foucault's ethics', *Organization* 9:4, 683–701.
Cicirelli, V.G. (2001), 'Personal meanings of death in older adults and young adults in relation to their fears of death', *Death Studies* 25:8, 663–83.
Clark, D. (1993), *The Sociology of Death: Theory, Culture, Practice* (Oxford: Blackwell).
Clark, J. and Newman, J. (1997), *The Managerial State* (London: Sage).
Clifford, J. and Marcus, G. (1986), *Writing Culture: The Poetics and Politics of Ethnography* (London: University of California Press).
Cotterill, P. and Letherby, G. (1993), 'Weaving Stories: Personal Auto/Biographies in Feminist Research', *Sociology* 27:1, 67–79.
Cousins, A. and Hussain, A. (1984), *Michel Foucault* (Basingstoke: Macmillan).
Craib, I. (1976), *Existentialism and Sociology: A Study of Jean-Paul Sartre* (Cambridge: Cambridge University Press).
Craib, I. (1998), *Experiencing Identity* (London: Sage).
Cunliffe, A. (2001), 'Managers as Practical Authors: Reconstructing our understanding of management practice', *Journal of Management Studies* 38:3, 351–71.
Cunliffe, A., Luhman, J. and Boje, D. (2004), 'Narrative Temporality: Implications for organizational research', *Organization Studies* 25:2, 261–86.
Currie, G. and Knights, D. (2003), 'Reflecting on a Critical Pedagogy in Management Education', *Management Learning* 34:1, 27–49.
Czarniawska, B. (1997), *Narrating the Organization: Dramas of Institutional Identity* (Chicago and London: University of Chicago Press).
Czarniawska, B. (1998), *A Narrative Approach in Organizational Studies* (London: Sage).
Davies, A. (2000), 'From Welfare State to Free Market', in A. Sinfield (ed.) *British Culture of the Postwar. An Introduction to Literature and Society, 1945–1979* (London: Routledge).
The Devil's Advocate (1997) Film [Directed by Taylor Hackford].

Denzin, N. and Lincoln, Y. (2000), 'The Discipline and Practice of Qualitative Research', in N. Denzin and Y. Lincoln (eds), *Handbook of Qualitative Research* (London: Sage), pp. 1–28.

Dex, S. (2003), *Families and Work in the Twenty-first Century* (York: Joseph Rowntree Foundation).

Dickens, A. (1967), *The English Reformation* (Glasgow: Fontana).

Dickens, C. (1838/1982), *Oliver Twist* (Oxford: Oxford University Press).

Dickens, C. (1841/1997), *The Old Curiosity Shop* (Oxford: Clarendon Press).

du Gay, P. (1996), *Consumption and Identity at Work* (London: Sage).

du Gay, P., Salaman, G. and Rees, B. (1996), 'The Conduct of Management and the Management of Conduct: Contemporary managerial discourse and the constitution of the "competent manager"', *Journal of Management Studies* 33:3, 263–82.

Dunne, J. (1996), 'Beyond Sovereignty and Deconstruction: the storied self', in R. Kearney (ed), *Paul Ricoeur: The Hermeneutics of Action* (London: Sage), pp. 137–57.

Eco, U. (1987), *Travels in Hyper-Reality* (London: Picador).

Elliot, A. (2001), *Concepts of the Self* (Cambridge: Polity).

Ellis, C. (2007), 'Telling Secrets, Revealing Lives: Relational ethics in research with intimate others', *Qualitative Inquiry* 13:1, 3–29.

Erickson, J. (1996), 'World Security after the Cold War', in B. Brivatt, J. Buxton and A. Seldon (eds), *The Contemporary History Handbook* (Manchester: Manchester University Press), pp. 11–23.

Foucault, M. (1977), *Discipline and Punish: The Birth of the Prison* (London: Allen Lane).

Foucault, M. (1982), *The Archaeology of Knowledge and the Discourse on Language* (New York: Pantheon).

Foucault, M. (1985), *The Use of Pleasure* (Harmondsworth: Penguin).

Frank, T. (2001), *One Market Under God: Extreme Capitalism, Market Populism and the End of Economic Democracy* (London: Secker & Warburg).

Franzosi, R. (1998), 'Narrative analysis – Or why (and how) sociologists should be interested in narrative', *Annual Reviews Social Sciences* 34, 517–54.

Fraser, N. (1989), *Unruly Practices. Power, Discourse and Gender in Contemporary Social Theory* (Cambridge: Polity Press).

Fraser, R. (1969), *Work 2* (Harmondsworth: Penguin).

Freud, S. (1914), *The Psychopathology of Everyday Life* (London: Fisher Unwin).

Freud, S. (1915/2005), 'Timely Reflections on War and Death', *On Murder, Mourning and Melancholia* (London: Penguin), pp. 167–94.

Freud, S. (1917/2005), 'Mourning and Melancholia', *On Murder, Mourning and Melancholia* (London: Penguin), pp. 201–18.

Freud, S. (1920/2003), *Beyond the Pleasure Principle and Other Writings* (London: Penguin).

Gabriel, Y. (2000), *Storytelling: The Poetics of Organizational Life* (Oxford: Oxford University Press).
Garnett, M. (2007), *From Anger to Apathy: The British Experience since 1975* (London: Jonathan Cape).
Giddens, A. (1991), *Modernity and Self Identity* (Cambridge: Polity Press).
Gorz, A. (1982), *Farewell to the Working Class* (London: Pluto Press).
Grey, C. (1994), 'Career as a Project of the Self and Labour Process Discipline', *Sociology* 28:2, 479–97.
Grey, C. (1999), '"We are all managers now"; "We always were": On the development and demise of management', *Journal of Management Studies* 36:5, 561–85.
Griffiths, M. (1995), *Feminisms and the Self: The Web of Identity* (London & New York: Routledge).
Hall, S. (2000), 'Who needs identity?' in P. Du Gay, J. Evans and P. Redman (eds), *Identity: A Reader* (London: Sage), pp. 15–30.
Hallam, E., Hockey, J. and Howarth, G. (1999), *Beyond the Body. Death and Social Identity* (London: Routledge).
Hancock, P. and Tyler, M. (2004), '"MOT Your Life": Critical management studies and the management of everyday life', *Human Relations* 57:5, 619–54.
Hardt, M. and Negri, A. (2000), *Empire* (Cambridge, MA: Harvard University Press).
Hassard, J. and Parker, M. (1993), *Postmodernism and Organizations* (London: Sage).
Heaney, S. (2001) *Beowulf: A New Translation* (New York and London: Vintage International)
Heidegger, M. (1926/1962), *Being and Time* (New York: Harper and Brothers).
Hobsbawm, E. (1995), *Age of Extremes: The Short Twentieth Century 1914–1991* (London: Abacus).
Hobsbawm, E. (2007), *Globalisation, Democracy and Terrorism* (London: Little Brown).
Hodgson, D. (2000), *Discourse, Discipline and the Subject* (Aldershot: Ashgate).
Holmes, L. and Robinson, G. (1999), 'The Making of Black Managers: Unspoken Issues of Identity Formation', paper presented at the 1st International Conference in Critical Management Studies, Manchester.
Holstein, J. and Gubrium, J. (2000), *The Self We Live By: Narrative Identity in the Postmodern World* (New York: Oxford University Press).
Howlett, P. (1994), 'The Golden Age, 1955–1973', in P. Johnson (ed.), *20th Century Britain. Economic, Social and Cultural Change* (London: Longman), pp. 320–39.
Humphreys, M. (2004), 'Getting Personal: Reflexivity and Autoethnographic Vignettes', *Qualitative Inquiry* 11:6, 840–60.
Iacocca, L. (1986), *Iacocca: An Autobiography* (New York: Bantam Books).

Ivory, C., Miskell, P., Shipton, H., White, A., Moeslein, K. and Neely, A. (2006), *UK Business Schools: Historical Contexts and Future Scenarios* (London: Advanced Institute of Management Research).
Joseph Rowntree Foundation (1992), *Household Budgets and Living Standards* (York: Joseph Rowntree Foundation).
Kearney, R. (1994), *Modern Movements in European Philosophy: Phenomenology, Critical Theory, Structuralism* (Manchester & New York: Manchester University Press).
Kearney, R. (1996a), 'Narrative Imagination: Between Ethics and Poetics', in R. Kearney (ed.) *Paul Ricoeur. The Hermeneutics of Action* (London: Sage), pp. 173–88.
Kearney, R. (1996b), *Paul Ricoeur. The Hermeneutics of Action* (London: Sage).
Kerfoot, D. and Whitehead, S. (1998), 'Boy's Own Stuff: Further Education, Managerialism and the Masculine Subject', *Sociological Review* 436–57.
Klein, N. (2000), *No Logo* (London: Flamingo).
Knights, D. (2004), 'Michel Foucault', in S. Linstead (ed.) *Organization Theory and Postmodern Thought* (London: Sage), pp. 14–31.
Knights, D. and Willmott, H. (1999), *Management Lives: Power and Identity in Work Organisations.* (London: Sage).
Kumar, K. (1987), *Utopia and Anti-Utopia in Modern Times* (Oxford: Blackwell).
Lapierre, L. (1989), 'Mourning, Potency and Power in Management', *Human Resource Management* 28:2, 177–89.
Lasch, C. (1980), *The Culture of Narcissism* (London: Sphere).
Lawler, S. (2005), 'Disgusted Subjects: the making of middle-class identities', *The Sociological Review*, 429–46.
Linstead, S. (2004), *Organization Theory and Postmodern Thought* (London: Sage).
Littlewood, J. (1993), 'The denial of death and rites of passage in contemporary societies', in D. Clark (ed.) *The Sociology of Death: Theory, Culture, Practice* (London: Blackwell) pp. 69–84.
MacIntyre, A. (1985), *After Virtue* (London: Duckworth).
McNay, L. (2000), *Gender and Agency* (Cambridge: Polity).
Mellor, P. (1993), 'Death in high modernity: the contemporary presence and absence of death', in D. Clark (ed.) *The Sociology of Death: Theory, Culture, Practice* (London: Blackwell), pp. 11–30.
Michael Clayton (2007) Film [Directed and written by Tony Gilroy]
Miller, R. (2000), *Researching Life Stories and Family Histories* (London: Sage).
Monbiot, G. (2000), *Captive State* (London: Macmillan).
Morris, W. (1894/1980), *The Wood Beyond the World* (Oxford: Oxford University Press).
Mulhall, S. (1996), *Heidegger and Being and Time* (London & New York: Routledge).
Mulkay, M. (1993), 'Social death in Britain', in D. Clark (ed.) *The Sociology of Death: Theory, Culture, Practice*, (London: Blackwell), pp. 31–49.
The Office (2001–2003) Television series [Ricky Gervais and Stephen Merchant].

Olafson, F. (1998), *Heidegger and the Ground of Ethics* (Cambridge: Cambridge University Press).
ONS (2007), *Social Trends* (Basingstoke: Office for National Statistics).
Orwell, G. (1942), 'The Art of Donald McGill', in S. Orwell and I. Angus (eds), *The Collected Essays, Journalism and Letters of George Orwell* (Harmondsworth: Penguin), pp. 183–94.
Oseen, C. (1997), 'Luce Irigaray, Sexual Difference and Theorizing Leaders and Leadership', *Gender, Work and Organization* 4:3, 170–84.
Parker, M. (2002), *Against Management: Organization in the Age of Managerialism*. (Cambridge: Polity Press).
Parker, M. (2004), 'Becoming Manager or The Werewolf looks Anxiously in the Mirror, Checking for Unusual Facial Hair', *Management Learning* 35:1, 45–59.
Peters, T. (1987), *Thriving on Chaos* (USA: Kopf Inc).
Peters, T. (1997), 'The Brand Called You', *Fast Company*:10.
Peters, T. and Waterman, R. (1982), *In Search of Excellence: Lessons from America's best-run companies* (New York: HarperCollins).
Pollitt, C. (1993), *Managerialism and the Public Services* (Oxford: Blackwell).
Polt, R. (1999), *Heidegger. An Introduction* (London: UCL).
Propp, V. (1968), *Morphology of the Folktale* (Austin: University of Texas).
Pucci, E. (1996), 'History and the Question of Identity: Kant, Arendt, Ricoeur', in R. Kearney (ed.) *Paul Ricoeur: The Hermeneutics of Action* (London: Sage), pp. 125–36.
Rabinow, P. (1984), 'Introduction', in P. Rabinow (ed.) *The Foucault Reader* (Harmondsworth: Penguin).
Rainwater, M. (1996), 'Refiguring Ricoeur: narrative force and communicative ethics', in R. Kearney (ed.) *Paul Ricoeur. The Hermeneutics of Action*, (London: Sage), pp. 99–110.
Reedy, P. (2003), 'Together We Stand? An Investigation into the Concept of Solidarity in Management Education', *Management Learning* 34:1, 91–109.
Reedy, P. (2008), 'Mirror, Mirror, On the Wall: Reflections on the ethics and effects of a collective Critical Management Studies identity project', *Management Learning* 39:1, 57–72.
Rees, D. (2001), *Death and Bereavement* (London: Whurr).
Ricoeur, P. (1985), *Time and Narrative* (Chicago: University of Chicago Press).
Ricoeur, P. (1992), *Oneself as Another* (Chicago: University of Chicago Press).
Ricoeur, P. (1996), *The Hermeneutics of Action* (London: Sage).
Rorty, R. (1989), *Contingency, Irony, and Solidarity* (Cambridge: Cambridge University Press).
Rose, N. (1999), *Governing the Soul* (London: Free Association Books).
Rose, N. (2000), 'Identity, Genealogy, History', in P. Du Gay, J. Evans and P. Redman (eds) *Identity: A Reader* (London: Sage), pp. 311–24.
Rosen, A. (2003), *The Transformation of British Life 1950–2000. A Social History* (Manchester & New York: Manchester University Press).

Sandbrook, D. (2005), *'Never Had it So Good.' A History of Britain from Suez to the Beatles* (London: Little, Brown).
Sandbrook, D. (2006), *White Heat: A History of Britain in the Swinging Sixties, 1964–1970* (London: Abacus).
Sartre, J. (1939/1962), *Sketch for a Theory of the Emotions* (London: Methuen).
Sartre, J. (1943/1957), *Being and Nothingness* (London: Methuen & Co).
Sartre, J. (1989), *No Exit and Three Other Plays* (New York: Vintage International).
Sarup, M. (1996), *Identity, Culture and the Postmodern World* (Edinburgh: Edinburgh University Press).
Scase, R. and Goffee, R. (1989), *Reluctant Managers: Their Work and Lifestyles* (London: Unwin Hyman).
Schroeder, W. (1984), *Sartre and his Predecessors* (London: Routledge and Kegan Paul).
Seale, C. (1998), *Constructing Death: the Sociology of Dying and Bereavement* (Cambridge: Cambridge University Press).
Sennett, R. (1998), *The Corrosion of Character* (New York & London: W.W. Norton).
Sievers, B. (1994), *Work, Death and Life Itself* (Berlin & New York: Walter de Gruyter).
Spry, T. (2001), 'Performing Autoethnography: An emobodied methodological praxis', *Qualitative Inquiry* 7:6, 706–32.
Stanley, L. (1992), *The Auto/biographical I* (Manchester: Manchester University Press).
Starkey, K. and Hatchuel, A. (2002), 'The Long Detour: Foucault's history of desire and pleasure', *Organization* 9:4, 641–56.
Terkel, S. (1970), *Working* (New York: The New Press).
Thompson, P. and Warhurst, C. (1998), *Workplaces of the Future* (Basingstoke: Macmillan).
Tolstoy, L. (1869/1979), *War and Peace* (Aylesbury: Penguin).
Vogel, L. (1994), *The Fragile "We." Ethical Implications of Heidegger's Being and Time* (Evanston: Northwestern University Press).
Wajcman, J. and Martin, B. (2002), 'Narratives of Identity in Modern Management: The Corrosion of Gender Difference?', *Sociology* 36:4, 985–1002.
Waldenfels, B. (1996), 'The Other and the Foreign', in R. Kearney (ed.) *Paul Ricoeur. The Hermeneutics of Action* (London: Sage), pp. 111–24.
Ward, J. and Winstanley, D. (2005), 'Coming Out at Work: Performativity and the recognition and renegotiation of identity', *The Sociological Review*, 447–75.
Watson, T. (1994), *In Search of Management: Culture, Chaos and Control in Managerial Work* (London & New York: Routledge).
Watson, T. (2001), 'The Emergent Manager and Processes of Management Pre-learning', *Management Learning* 32:2, 221–35.
Watson, T. and Harris, P. (1999), *The Emergent Manager* (London: Sage).

Weigert, A.J. and Gecas, V. (2003), 'Self', in L.T. Reynolds and N.J. Herman-Kinney (eds), *Handbook of Symbolic Interactionism* (Walnut Creek, CA: Altimira Press), pp. 267–88.
Welch, J. (2000), *Jack* (London: Headline).
Willmott, H. (2000), 'Death. So what? Sociology, sequestration and emancipation', *Sociological Review* 48:4, 649–65.
Wolin, R. (1990), *The Politics of Being: The Political Thought of Martin Heidegger* (New York: Columbia University Press).
Woodin, T. (2005), 'Muddying the Waters: Changes in class and identity in a working-class cultural organization', *Sociology* 39:5, 1001–18.
Zimmerman, M. (1990) *Heidegger's Confrontation with Modernity* (Bloomington & Indianapolis: Indiana University Press).

Index

adventure 147–49, 151, 155, 159, 163
affirmation 12, 43, 112–13, 119, 153, 161–62, 166, 168
affluence 126, 135, 138, 174, 175
age 3, 10, 11, 76, 85, 99, 124, 131, 136–38
agency 87, 88, 91, 93–5, 97, 99, 114, 119, 174
Akenfield 5
anxiety 89, 104, 107–108, 129, 172
Aristotle 115, 116
authenticity 86, 87, 96, 107–108, 110, 141, 153, 162, 178, 180
autobiography 2, 8, 13, 143, 146, 168
autonomy 13, 85, 87, 88, 90, 91, 93–6, 98, 173, 180

Bauman, Zygmunt 96–100, 137, 167
Being and Nothingness 103, 109, 110
Being and Time 105, 107
blessing in disguise 151, 155, 158
Blythe, Ronald 5, 10, 170
Bochner, Arthur 4, 6, 123, 170
business school 1, 2, 7, 168, 181

capitalism 7, 177, 180, 89, 128
character 9, 10, 48, 85, 116, 117, 143, 167, 171
Chicago School 5, 6, 172
choice 87–101, 104–14, 116, 119, 120, 123, 125, 144, 163, 171, 174
class 10, 86, 87, 89, 124, 127, 128, 129–38, 161, 164, 166
    middle-class 87, 120, 125, 127, 128, 129
    working-class 87, 127
cogito 92, 106, 107, 114, 115
coherence 5, 85, 92, 96, 105, 111, 119, 137,
conformity 89, 95
conscience 90, 108

consciousness 97, 90–93, 97, 98, 104, 110–13, 116, 119, 146
constancy 108, 115, 116, 118, 119
consumption 86, 99, 126, 127, 129, 130, 175
Craib, Ian 86, 88, 95, 96, 98, 104, 106
crisis decades 126, 128–29, 130, 136, 138, 161, 162, 166, 178, 180
critical organisational studies 3, 7, 177, 180

death 13, 85, 96–101, 107–109, 113, 119, 146, 163, 172
    fear of 97, 107
    finitude 86, 104, 107, 108, 112, 115, 119
    mortality 96–8, 101, 107, 108
    sequestration 97, 98
Descartes, René 90, 91, 114
    Cartesian 92, 114, 116
determinism 88, 91–6, 101, 103–109, 113, 114, 120

education 124, 125–27, 130, 133–36, 145, 161, 162, 164
empathy 118, 171, 179
Enlightenment 88
ethics and morality 95, 99, 101, 106, 114, 115, 119, 121, 178, 109, 117, 118
    of representation 5, 9, 118, 123
    of the 'good' manager 135, 161, 173–75
ethnicity 11, 88, 117, 127, 130
existentialism 10, 86, 89, 103–105, 114, 168, 172

family 88, 97, 117, 125, 129–35, 137, 161, 164, 171, 180
fate 145–47, 174
    destiny 131, 145, 147, 160
    luck 19, 145, 147–51, 162, 174

folk tales, including fairy stories and traditional stories 86, 141–42, 143, 144–60, 171–76
Foucault, Michel 88, 90, 93–5, 100, 103
freedom 88, 95, 104, 106, 110–13, 123, 172, 173
Freud, Sigmund 86, 91, 97, 162

Gabriel, Yiannis 6, 10, 142, 163, 172
gender 11, 12, 86, 87, 136, 146, 149, 161, 164–65
generations 3, 13, 89, 109, 115, 118, 123–39, 161, 169, 173, 180
Giddens, Anthony 9, 87–9, 92, 96, 97, 99, 100, 161, 172
globalisation 1, 87, 92, 128, 161, 180
Golden Age 126–28, 136, 138–39, 161
Good life 114, 115, 118, 123, 141, 167, 173, 175, 179

Hegel, Frederick 111, 113
Heidegger, Martin 1, 13, 86, 103–109, 112–15, 125, 144, 155, 166, 172, 178
  authenticity 86, 104–10, 112, 141, 144, 153, 162, 171, 172, 178, 180
  being-in-the-world 104, 107
  being-with 106, 113
  Dasein 105–108
  death 86, 107–109, 112, 119, 146, 172
  resoluteness 106–109, 163
  solicitude 106, 107, 114
  temporality 13, 86, 104, 106–108, 111
  the 'they' 104, 107–109, 120, 144, 153, 162, 168, 172
  thrownness 108, 119, 125, 174, 176
hero 91, 105, 106, 114, 130, 141, 143, 146, 149, 151, 161–63, 172–77
history 2, 86, 90, 106–107, 109, 114, 118, 123–36, 142, 166, 173, 180
Holstein, James and Gubrium, Jaber 14, 86, 88, 142, 160, 169
home 128, 130, 132, 148, 162, 164, 175–76
humanism 85, 89, 90–92, 109

identity 'I' 86, 88, 91, 93, 111, 115, 116
  construction 7, 120, 144, 165

crisis of 93
entrepreneurial self 89, 172
idem-identity 115–16, 125, 144, 161, 173
individuality 7, 11, 87, 89–91, 93, 96, 98, 100, 105–106, 108, 120, 127, 173, 178
ipse-identity 115–16, 141, 163, 173
life projects 1, 90, 100, 167, 171
management identity 4, 10, 93, 105, 120, 134, 137, 138, 162, 167, 171, 172, 178
narrative identity 7, 103, 114–19, 141, 176
personal identity 87, 104, 115
reflexive projects 87, 88, 92
selfhood 89, 96, 105, 106, 114, 119, 141, 171
subjectivity 87, 93–5, 100, 113
the soul 90
the sovereign self 91, 103, 119
uniqueness 89–90, 96, 108, 115, 119, 123, 163, 169, 171, 172
immigration 127, 130
individualism 87, 127, 173, 178
inter-generational transmission 89, 130
intersubjectivity 91, 100, 107, 112, 114

Kearney, Richard 86, 103, 106, 110, 111, 114, 118, 119

life stage 136–37
  childhood 85, 130, 136, 143
  maturity 85, 136, 138
  middle age 136, 137
  old age 85, 129, 136
  youth 85, 134, 136, 137, 138, 143
lifestyle 88, 92, 129
love 131, 139, 159, 163, 171, 175, 180
lucky breaks 19, 145, 147

management
  careers 4, 7, 12, 134, 163, 172, 174, 180
  cultural representations of 168
  education 7, 8
  managerialism 2, 131, 162, 179, 180
  managerial work 5, 16

masculinity 148, 151, 165, 176
Mead, George Herbert 91, 115
mimēsis 116
modernity 88, 92, 93, 98, 161, 172

narrative
    accountability 117, 171
    autobiography 2, 143
    autoethnography 6, 123
    biography 6, 85, 100
    character 9, 85, 116–17, 143, 171
    discourse 7, 88, 89, 93–5, 99, 118, 131, 163, 172
    discursive resources 9, 180
    editing 142, 160, 165
    elements 141, 143–44, 163
    epics 172
    fiction 9, 112, 115, 117, 118, 144, 177
    historical 9, 12, 117, 123
    life history 4, 5, 10
    narrative linkage 142, 160, 161
    narrative options 137, 142, 160, 165
    narrative performance 142
    narrative slippage 142, 160, 163, 165
    plot 116–19, 141, 167
    narrative practices 142, 160, 169
    representation 5, 9, 116, 168
    story-telling 6, 142, 163
    testimony 1, 118, 123

organisation studies 177, 2, 5, 6, 86, 89, 95, 121, 142, 177
Other, the 106, 109, 111, 113–15, 119, 137, 170, 177

parenthood 12, 99, 137, 138
    children 136, 161, 163, 175
Parker, Martin 78, 180
phenomenology 103, 104
Pilgrim's Progress 145, 151, 175
place (location) 3, 128, 132, 161
politics 9, 86, 95, 109, 114, 126, 131, 164, 171, 177, 179, 180
    left-wing 127, 135
possibility 91, 101, 104, 107–109, 120, 125, 172, 174
postmodernism 95, 99
poststructuralism 88, 99, 100, 103

profession 86, 124, 128, 133
Propp, Vladimir 14, 141–44, 169
public sector 124, 126, 128, 134

quests 86, 99, 104, 112, 117, 123, 135, 141, 144, 171, 175

reciprocity 113, 115
religion 90, 135, 136,164
    Catholicism 147, 164
    Christianity 89, 90, 92, 96, 135
responsibility 89, 95, 100, 106, 108, 111, 123, 171
Ricoeur, Paul 4, 8, 9, 86, 103, 104, 114–19, 125, 141, 161, 166, 171, 176, 178, 179
    accountability 117, 171
    debt to the dead 118, 129
    friendship 115, 119, 179
    idem-identity 115–16, 125, 144, 161, 173
    interpretation 114, 116, 119
    ipse-identity 115–16, 141, 163, 173
    just institutions 114, 167, 168, 179
    mutuality 115
    narrative time, 115
    narrativity 114, 116, 117–18, 120, 169
    reciprocity 113, 115
    refiguration 116
    testimony 118, 168
    unity 116, 118

Sartre, Jean Paul 94, 103, 104, 106, 109–114, 125, 137, 170, 171, 173, 178
    anguish 110, 111
    emotion 112
    for-itself 109, 111–12
    imagination 110–12
    in-itself 109, 111–12
    nothingness, 103, 109, 110–11
    shame 111, 113
    'sour grapes' 112
social justice 27, 114
social mobility 124, 127, 134, 138, 145, 161
Stanley, Liz 6, 8, 10, 121, 143, 168
symbolic interactionism 87, 91, 100

temporality 86, 104, 106–108, 111, 115
Terkel, Studs 5, 10, 170
Thatcher, Margaret 135

villains 142, 162, 175, 177

virtue 106, 108, 123, 135, 161, 175
vocation 161

women 5, 128, 136, 161, 162, 164, 175, 176